Andrea Janelle Dickens is Assistant Church History at United Theological ....,, ...,, ... written many essays and articles on medieval theology and spirituality, and is also the author of *The I.B.Tauris History of Monasticism: The Western Tradition* (forthcoming).

'Andrea Janelle Dickens appeals to the mystic in every reader with her inviting and informative treatments of a dozen medieval women. She proclaims them "exemplary rather than extraordinary," suggesting, contra their times, that gender is no boundary to holiness. For the widely-known (Teresa of Avila, Julian of Norwich, and Hildegard of Bingen) as well as the less studied (Angela of Foligno, Richeldis of Faverches, and Mechtilde of Hackeborn) matters of love, location, authority, pilgrimage, and anti-clericalism are common themes. This readable introduction is the perfect primer for the religious studies or gender studies classroom and has ample scholarly apparatus to encourage further study.' – *Mary E Hunt, Co-director, Women's Alliance for Theology, Ethics and Ritual (WATER), Silver Spring, Maryland*

'*The Female Mystic* will serve as an excellent introductory textbook to the life, works and thought of 12 leading women mystics, from eleventh-century Richeldis of Faverches to sixteenth-century Teresa of Avila. The discussion throughout is balanced, informed and clear. The author has both an eye for detail and an admirable capacity to sketch an insightful overview of each figure against the background of her own historical period and within her own social contexts. In these pages the mystical texts emerge as distinctively female, though open-endedly so, and as a vital communication of the rich, multi-faceted world of medieval Europe. *The Female Mystic* will open up new horizons for any reader who wishes to come closer to these extraordinary texts and their authors.' – *Oliver Davies, Professor of Christian Doctrine, King's College London*

INTERNATIONAL LIBRARY OF HISTORICAL STUDIES

Series ISBN: 978-1-84885-222-8

47. *Ruskin and Social Reform:
Ethics and Economics in the Victorian Age*
Gill Cockram
978 1 84511 349 0

48. *The Politics of Prayer in Early Modern Britain:
Church and State in Seventeenth-century England*
Richard J Ginn
978 1 84511 412 1

49. *Dean John Colet of St Paul's: Humanism
and Reform in Early Tudor England*
Jonathan Arnold
978 1 84511 436 7

50. *The Ladies of Londonderry:
Women and Political Patronage*
Diane Urquhart
978 1 84511 410 7

51. *Central and Eastern Europe in the
Middle Ages: A Cultural History*
Piotr S. Górecki and Nancy van Deusen
(eds)
978 1 84511 851 8

52. *Feeding the Nation: Nutrition and Health
in Britain before World War One*
Yuriko Akiyama
978 1 84511 682 8

53. *Islam in the Baltic:
Europe's Early Muslim Community*
Harry Norris
978 1 84511 587 6

54. *East India Patronage and the British State:
The Scottish Elite and Politics in the
Eighteenth Century*
George McGilvary
978 1 84511 661 3

55. *Communism in Rural France: French
Agricultural Workers and the Popular Front*
John Bulaitis
978 1 84511 708 5

56. *The Ages of Faith: Popular Religion in
Late Medieval England and Western Europe*
Norman Tanner
978 1 84511 760 3

57. *An Introduction to Medieval Jewish
Philosophy*
Daniel Rynhold
978 1 84511 747 4

58. *Radical Religion in Cromwell's England:
A Concise History from the English Civil
War to the End of the Commonwealth*
Andrew Bradstock
978 1 84511 764 1

59. *Medieval Heresy: The Church's Struggle
for Orthodoxy and Survival*
Louisa Burnham
978 1 84511 573 9

60. *The Female Mystic:
Great Women Thinkers of the Middle Ages*
Andrea Janelle Dickens
978 1 84511 640 8

61. *Holy War, Just War:
Early Modern Christianity, Religious
Ethics and the Rhetoric of Empire*
Patrick Provost-Smith
978 1 84511 675 0

63. *Coleridge and Liberal Religious Thought:
Romanticism, Science and Theological Tradition*
Graham Neville
978 1 84885 089 7

64. *The New Ways of History:
Developments in Historiography*
Gelina Harlaftis, Nikos Karapidakis,
Kostas Sbonias and Vaios Vaipoulos (eds)
978 1 84885 126 9

65. *Naval Shipbuilding in the Age of Sail:
An Industrial History 1100-1800*
Philip MacDougall
978 1 84885 119 1

66. *Spatial Conceptions of the Nation:
Modernizing Geographies in Greece and Turkey*
Nikiforos Diamandouros, Thalia
Dragonas and Çaglar Keyder (eds)
978 1 84885 131 3

67. *Trade and Cultural Exchange in the Early
Modern Mediterranean: Braudel's Maritime Legacy*
Maria Fusaro, Colin Heywood and
Mohamed-Salah Omri (eds)
978 1 84885 163 4

68. *Britain, Portugal and South America in the
Napoleonic Wars: Alliances and Diplomacy in
Economic Maritime Conflict*
Martin Robson
978 1 84885 196 2

The Female Mystic

Great Women Thinkers of the Middle Ages

Andrea Janelle Dickens

I.B. TAURIS

LONDON · NEW YORK

Published in 2009 by I.B.Tauris & Co Ltd
6 Salem Road, London W2 4BU
175 Fifth Avenue, New York NY 10010
www.ibtauris.com

Distributed in the United States and Canada Exclusively by Palgrave Macmillan
175 Fifth Avenue, New York NY 10010

International Library of Historical Studies, Vol 60

ISBN: 978 1 84511 640 8 (HB)
ISBN: 978 1 84511 641 5 (PB)

A full CIP record for this book is available from the British Library
A full CIP record is available from the Library of Congress

Library of Congress Catalog Card Number: available

Designed and Typeset by 4word Ltd, Bristol, UK
Printed and bound by CPI Group (UK) Ltd, Croydon, CR0 4YY

MIX
Paper from
responsible sources
FSC® C013604

Contents

Acknowledgements

I would like to thank a number of people who have helped me immensely in the writing of this work. First and foremost, Carey Newman helped me tremendously by looking over an early copy of this manuscript and offering probing insights about its architecture. A number of colleagues, both near and far-flung, have read parts of the manuscript and offered detailed, thoughtful insights: Dan Joslyn-Siemiatkoski, Horace Six-Means, Melissa Kelley, Tim Hessel-Robinson and David Whitford. I would also like to thank the Board of Trustees at United Theological Seminary for granting me a sabbatical, in which I was able to finish this manuscript. The wonderful staff at the Old Bodleian Library proved immensely helpful during my months of work there. I would like to thank my editor, Alex Wright, for his patience and helpful suggestions and encouragement along the way to the final manuscript. And finally, I would like to thank the Association of Theological Schools for granting me a Lilly Theological Research Grant for a related project; their generous support also aided in my research and completion of this project during my year as fellow.

Introduction

In the high middle ages, women began to take a more prominent role in theological writings, both figuring as the subjects for male confessors' writings and sometimes writing their own works. With this increase in the visibility of women's religious lives come questions about the roles that these women played and their adherence to or defiance of societal norms. Women, and their proclivities to holiness and heresy, served as the subject of much literature. Men said that women were weak and therefore more prone to heresy, and thus needed more guidance, could not teach religious matters and needed men to establish the bounds of orthodoxy for them. On the other hand, the prayers of women were recognized to be more efficacious than those of men, so women were sought out in desperate situations. As one friar requested, 'have women and priests pray for me'.[1] It is in this contradictory complex of conflicting imperatives that these women thinkers lived and wrote.

This book considers the lives and writings of a dozen medieval women thinkers within this medieval matrix. It aims to see women's contributions for what they were and orient the reader new to this subject matter to the contours of modern scholarly discussion. Tied up with the opposing representations were the roles into which the social structures of their days perceived women as able to operate. Since the early 1980s, women's mystical writings of the middle ages have come to be studied more and more seriously. Through this research, scholars have come to identify a women's tradition of writing religious and literary texts. It has been defined on the one hand by the sex of the writer (or subject, in the case of hagiography), and on the other by the lack of scholastic theological training, access to the pulpit or university leadership. From this, a canon of medieval women mystics has emerged. But this renaissance of study of medieval women thinkers has had several pitfalls as well. In particular, many university courses in literature or theology departments now include a course on 'medieval women mystics', suggesting there is something feminine about mysticism. This reinforces the essentialism that ascribes certain types of writing, acting, thinking and behaviours to the sole provinces of either men or women. Such prejudices show that, even today, we are not all that far from having set roles to which we believe we ought to ascribe women's work.

I intend for this book to introduce 12 representative female mystics from the middle ages; in so doing, I will read them as representatives of a wide variety of social, political, religious and literary traditions with which they interacted and which their presence directed. Much has already been written about the women mystics of the middle ages. Such scholarship has often been groundbreaking, introducing new writers, lay spirituality and non-scholastic theology to medieval scholars and students; other scholarship has provided details of a history of women. Some have offered criticism of clericalism and patriarchal 'norms' in church and society, or presented utopian visions of women looking to the New Jerusalem at the end of created time. The 12 women chosen represent many of the major chords of spirituality in the middle ages. The texts by and about these women are available in modern English translations, and this book hopes to find itself useful alongside such translations in the classroom to help introduce the women and explain their milieux.

Perhaps the biggest challenge in studying women from the middle ages is that often the introductions to women's writings and lives present those whom we know about as being different or exceptional, forgetting that any person about whom we know much in the middle ages was exceptional. Another difficulty is that women's writings and lives are often read as somehow presenting a vision of a distinct 'women's spirituality', as if these women's writings have to be separate but equal alongside men's writings. In the course of writing this manuscript, I have come to realize that not only do these women inhabit a number of theological and devotional trends in the middle ages, they also are completely ordinary in the ways in which they operate. They write according to major literary trends open to women: the best examples being the visionary, the devotional, and the courtly love traditions. Much of the writing about women mystics has focused on their peculiarities, seeing them as extraordinary. I shall focus on these women as exemplary rather than extraordinary.

I do not believe that we need to represent the women as participating in some Platonic form of women's spirituality in order to find worth in these women's writings. Nor do I believe that this selection of women (for there are many more medieval women thinkers than merely these 12) creates a canon of women's mysticism. To show that these women are unique both in their femininity and in their non-gender-specific elements, I shall provide a very brief overview in the next few pages of several ways in which historical, theological and literary scholars approach female mystics. As Bernard McGinn notes, the history of mysticism can be sketched according to a model of gradually accumulating layers of tradition, as can the commentary on it.[2]

Women and medieval literature

Medieval women's writings often are classified into the vague description of 'medieval literature', which simply means that they are not seen as technical writings of science, theology, logic or other fields.[3] Within this description of 'literature' there are many genres, ranging from pastoral or spiritual works such as those of Walter Hilton, to dramatic works such as the York mystery plays, poetry and music such as the *Carmina Burana*, to the hymns of Peter Abelard. Even within the 'mystical' we have a wide variety of genres: there is the visionary, in which a person receives special revelations in the form of visual images; prophecy, auditory messages from God or the saints; contemplative devotions; and affective responses to meditations or visions. There is also hagiography, in which a holy person's like is told in the most agreeable terms, either to help her attain canonization as a saint or to offer her life as an example of holy living.[4]

Some scholars read medieval women as 'writers' of set genres, ignoring the intellectual content of the writings. For instance, women such as Julian of Norwich and Margery Kempe wrote in the vernacular language of their time and place. Many of the studies of medieval women writers make the assertion that women were instrumental in popularizing the use of vernacular languages for theological or other writings.[5] Studies of Julian have found that her prose has rhythmic qualities to it that expand the scope of English's aesthetic qualities and have focused on how she expanded the use of literary figures of speech in middle English, much like Chaucer did.[6]

Other studies have shown how Julian and Margery's work coincides with popular English preaching of this time.[7] This approach seeks to set the women mystics within 'literature', basing its work upon the language used, and allowing the difference in language between Latin and vernacular language to be the dividing factor. Since women were not educated in Latin grammar as extensively as the schoolmen, vernacular comes to be associated with the women's writings, and genre distinctions are based at least in part upon these linguistic bases rather than solely on clear genre distinctions. There is a subtle distinction to be made here: in readings such as these, women are seen as literary artists, not as thinkers necessarily. Their writings are most often judged as representative of where a literature has developed or is developing at this time. But the women are not evaluated in this as original thinkers, or theological thinkers, or even as consistent thinkers. Nicholas Watson notes that women were associated with the vernacular because of their humility (having a lower social status than men), and its parallelism with Christ choosing the humble family of a carpenter and Virgin.[8] But there were a fair number of men associated with the vernacular languages, particularly since preaching in the vernacular was an especial aspect of the mendicant orders: Franciscan and Dominican men such as Meister Eckhart, Heinrich Seuse, Johannes Tauler, David of Augsburg, Friedrich Sunder and Bertold of Regensburg, all authored devotional treatises and sermons in the vernacular.

Medieval women and 'popular' religion in the middle ages

Another school of thought posits that women's communities are an intellectual buffer zone of sorts between the institutional and popular, keeping the popular dogmatic and helping to revitalize the institutional. As such, the women represent people with more theological astuteness than average, but they are not properly speaking theologians. In such discussions, there is a clearly drawn line between those who were 'institutional' and had been vested with authority by virtue of training or position and the rest of the people in the church. Women – even nuns – represent the popular as opposed to the institutional or the ruling patriarchy. This view reads the intellectual developments of the medieval era as institutional developments, with institutional history and scholastic theology its two main representatives, and social history describes all else.

Investigations of this social history in this way seek to understand the women and medieval religious practices by reading some of the practices of women as representative acts. Perhaps the primary example of this type of scholarship is the work of Caroline Walker Bynum. Her investigations have run the gamut from popular devotions and scholastic theology to women's fasting practices and bodily integrity in medieval devotions.[9] Certainly topics such as sickness, fasting practices, bodily asceticism, penitential acts or travel receive focus: this dovetails with the preoccupations of modern theology regarding the body, location, geography and liminality.[10]

Second, this type of cultural history allows women's thought to be investigated as a separate trajectory in history. It is a unique women's history or women's theology, 'separate but equal' to men's history and theology.[11] This works off an essentialist understanding of what constitutes 'women's writings' and divides women's texts into the categories of non-traditional (and hence women's writings) or 'mere literature' (writing that is not specifically woman-themed). Furthermore, these investigations associate women's writings with the traditions of affective theology, in which the emotional response to a meditation is the focus of the writing. Yet the best-known proponent or teacher of this type of meditation was Walter Hilton; nor is it clear that women's writings necessarily were more affective than men's. Certainly, this was a genre more open to women than, say, scholastic theology, which required specific training that was only open to men with clerical aspirations. But once again the association of women with affective theology has to be examined carefully along with the assumption that men are all rational and women are all emotional.

Women's writings, power and authority

A third approach is to analyse women's theological and literary writings within a matrix of power, authority and knowledge. According to Foucault, knowledge is power, and it has become increasingly popular for scholars to discern axes of power in both the lives of women and the texts by and about them.[12] For cultural historians, this has meant attempting to discern the place that an individual or community inhabited within the larger social sphere of their time, order and geography. The way in which these individuals have interacted within these spheres, particularly the ways in which they have subverted or transgressed the boundaries established by their own separate spheres, has become a major exploration.

Often this Foucauldian reading emphasizes the unique claims that mystical writings contain: the claim to a divine authority having commissioned the work, which demanded the women speak. In such a setting, obedience becomes power, but God's power trumps human forms of power. The conveyance of power allows mystical commission to trump earthly authority, and thus the weak women have a stronger power (and deeper wisdom or truth from God) than theologians. This reversal is also seen in the Annunciation, when Mary becomes the vessel for the Incarnation in her meekness: 'Women's charismatic, prophetic role was an alternative to, and therefore a critique of and a substitute for, the characteristic male form of religious authority: the authority of office.'[13] A further aspect of power regards who actually declares what is actually valid. For instance, Marguerite Porete's text *The Mirror of Simple Souls* was burned alongside her in Paris, but the work continued to circulate without her name on it.

Holy women and their relations to men

Yet these women are not merely texts – women were people and were subject to interpretations by others. One of the newer aspects of inquiry probes discussions of the relationships between women and their hagiographers. For instance, the work of John Coakley has probed the relationships that holy women had with their confessors and the ways in which the women's and their confessors' perceptions of the women's vocation (prophet, visionary, leader) varied. These perceptions are often passed down through the texts, and thus the authorship of texts matters, and determines to what extent people (men and women) other than the visionary woman herself might have shaped the text's outlook. Every person has an agenda, and, as Coakley points out, sometimes the agendas the men had were substantially different from those of the women.[14] Sometimes the women wanted to be quiet about their extraordinary experiences, or only wanted to communicate their visions to those to whom they were addressed; other texts show women used by men in order to put forth a particular agenda. This is perhaps most clear in the case of Christina of St Trond, where her life becomes a sermon example in the hands of her hagiographer, Thomas de Cantimpré.

What this scholarship has shown is that there are differences in terms of the way the women are perceived, as well as their gifts, their roles (intercessor, penitent) and their usefulness as an example. Another topic that garners scholars' attention is the relationship between women and the men who minister to them, whether sacramentally as confessors and providers of the Holy Meal, or as scribes, collaborators or hagiographers. Elizabeth Petroff notes that the women serve a number of services for the men: they offer a compelling image of lived faith to the priests. The men also find themselves attracted to the women's piety; women served as intercessors to God for men. Men come to women when terrible happenings require divine intervention; the women represent a new kind of teaching in action: spontaneous, compassionate and non-hierarchical. The women have new viewpoints and can respond to situations directly and thus appear to be transgressive in ways that a male ecclesiastic cannot.[15]

Genre and message

If Marshall McLuhan's famous dictum that the 'medium is the message' is correct, then we should find in the various genres of writings that there is an infinite variety in the works we see from these women. Certainly genre affects what we expect we will find in a text and how we respond to what is included in the text. An inherent problem arises when we limit the theological by identifying forms of writing that we consider inherently theological as opposed to literary. I wish to push against this notion, much as Catherine Gardner did in her work *Women Philosophers*, in which she argues that the works of the women she has chosen (including Mechtild of Magdeburg, whom I also consider) are inherently philosophical, despite the differences in genre and the different relationship between reader, author and text that this imposes. At heart, genre problematizes but it also matters. Genre, or the identification at least of writings that are *like* other works in terms of narratorial or authorial stance, helps to identify the ways in which we are to read the claims being made in the text. One reads the immediate descriptions of Julian's visions differently from how one reads her interpretations of these visions. One is full of immediate, sensory imagery, while the other is fully of rumination upon the images, working them like *lectio divina* for years until the crystallization of meaning comes forth.

Our project

As this quick introduction to some of the theories guiding the study of medieval women's lives and texts should show, there has been a plethora of recent study of these women since the late 1970s. And the ways in which they have been studied provide us with a wide range of possible angles from which to consider these women, all of which makes the introduction to these women both easier and harder. It is easier in that only two of the women – Richeldis of Faverches and Mechtilde of Hackeborn – are relatively understudied. On the other hand, the plethora of scholarship can daunt the new student who is seeking an overview of the thought-world of each woman. It is this task that I hope this book shall fulfil.

An aspect of these writings that recommends their being read together is that these women all directed their writings or actions outwards. They did not develop their spiritual lives or their spiritual writings merely for the sake of themselves; they meant to direct the lives of the communities to which they belonged.[16] And yet there is perhaps something disingenuous about the title of this book: all of the people chosen to be studied are in fact women; but the fact that they are women is about all that they have in common. Often, books about 'medieval women' attempt to find some essentialist connection between the women, thus marginalizing the women rather than seeking to find them as writers, theologians, prophets or poets in their own rights. I caution my reader at the start: one of the conveniences about choosing a group of women is that often these visionary and mystical texts are introduced in the university classroom in the guise of a course on 'medieval women' in the literary or religious studies classroom. And for such a purpose, this book is geared, having chosen women whose writings show the vast differences in style, topics, means of reception of writing, and interests. But it is not a book that will show everything that the women have in common. Far from it.

As a final note, it is worth remembering the vast period covered by these 12 women. From Richeldis' vision in 1061 to Teresa's reforms until 1581, a period of over half a millennium stretches. The time period covered from the first to last woman in this book is even greater than the expanse of time removing us today from Teresa's Counter-Reformation Spain. When Richeldis has her vision in 1061, England is still a feudal society, and William the Conquerer's 1066 invasion is still half a decade away. Walsingham is, like most English villages of the time, remote and unconnected. Over the intervening centuries, cities will rise, a new economic class, the bourgeoisie, will be born, and populations will become more mobile. Many new orders will come into existence. Universities will be founded starting in the twelfth century. In the following centuries, the Inquisition will begin, the Reformation will occur, and the Counter-Reformation will follow. By the year Teresa is born, Ferdinand Magellan will be halfway through his circumnavigation of the world, and Spain will be an imperial power, controlling new lands not dreamed of during the lives of most of the other women in this book.

1

Mary's Handmaid:
Richeldis of Faverches

In 1061, only half a decade before the Norman invasion of Britain, a woman named Richeldis of Faverches received a vision from the Virgin Mary instructing her to build a shrine to Mary. Until it was destroyed at the time of Henry VIII's dissolution of the monasteries and stripping of the churches, this model of the house of the Annunciation saw hundreds of thousands of pilgrims who came on spiritual quests, and quests for healing, hope and thanksgiving. The shrine became a popular replacement for travel to the Holy Land when the Crusades made travel abroad too dangerous. The legends about Richeldis focus not on her but on the shrine she founded; in this portrayal, they see Richeldis' behaviour as an example for others: a woman of her time following the example of Mary's *fiat* ('let it be so') in response to the Annunciation. The creation of the Walsingham shrine helped foster the development of Marian devotions and Christ-centred devotions, helping others follow the example of Mary as Richeldis had done.

Richeldis is an emblem of the problem of scanty information that modern readers experience with women's lives and texts in the middle ages. Precisely because of this, she offers a good example with which to start this book. The only written testimony about her comes in a ballad written in 1460, nearly 400 years after her life. Also instructive is the existence of the place of Walsingham and references to it in literature of the middle ages. Whereas the other women in this book have left behind texts, Richeldis left behind a physical shrine for pilgrimage and healing as evidence of her theology of Marian devotion, locational significance and intercessory prayer. The creation of the Walsingham shrine offers an example of a woman's particular abilities to receive divine visions and their importance in establishing and shaping popular devotional practices, and her example also emphasizes women's unique connections to Marian spirituality.

What we do know about the historical Richeldis is that she was named after Saint Richelde, who died in 896 and was canonized 150 years later in 1049.[1] The original Richelde was the wife of Charles the Bald, the great-grandson of Charlemagne. Legends tell how Charles had accused Richelde of adultery, and in her efforts to prove herself innocent she prayed to Mary. After her prayers had been answered and she was no longer found guilty, she publicly pardoned her husband before retiring to the Abbey of Andlau in Alsace. Like her namesake, the later Richeldis of Faverches became associated with the Virgin Mary; but rather than receiving a miracle for herself, the second Richeldis' prayers were answered by the offer of miracles in perpetuity in the place of the Walsingham shrine. In the legends of both women, their intercessor relationship with Mary (identified by her own intercessory relationship) determines their vocation and supports their association with Mary.

The Walsingham vision and foundation

The Pynson ballad, composed about 1460, presents the main account of Richeldis' vision and the shrine's development under Mary's guidance. The ballad addresses itself to those pilgrims travelling to Walsingham and it explains how the miracle of Mary's appearance was followed by a deed of Richeldis in order to secure the grace for all pilgrims.[2] The ballad offers examples of miracles that have occurred to visitors, ending with the promise that Mary will help. The ballad dates Richeldis' vision to 1061. Although a document written 400 years later must be somewhat suspect, Richeldis' vision does bear a number of similarities with the growing spiritualities of the twelfth century, and serves to orient the reader with twelfth-century Incarnational and Marian devotions and pilgrimage in the high middle ages.

Richeldis exemplifies how to imitate Mary, and the gift of the vision for the foundation of the shrine illustrates what the devotee to the Virgin could expect to be offered for his or her devotion. Richeldis shows that the location of Walsingham and the shrine matter in the reception of God's graces. Furthermore, Richeldis' actions show that Mary can also be a model to women in Richeldis' day and that God still grants graces according to this model of obedience. The ballad describes her as a noblewoman and widow, virtuous, and devoted to the Blessed Virgin. These were all virtues extolled in women in Richeldis' time. Richeldis is described in the ballad as:

> A noble wydowe, somtyme lady of this towne,
> Called Rychold, in lyuynge full virtuous,
> Desyred of Oure Lady a petycyowne
> Hir to honoure with some werke bountyous.[3]

This is a selfless petition in which Richeldis only asks Mary to provide some means for Richeldis to offer homage to Mary.

The poem continues by describing the conditions of the shrine's foundation:

> Bylded the yere of Crystes incarnacyon,
> A thousande complete syxty and one,
> The tyme of sent Edward kyng of this region.[4]

By instigating the vision in response to her request to Mary, Richeldis exemplifies how Mary responds to the requests of people who ask her. By showing the initiative to ask, Richeldis also exemplifies the habit and optimism of prayer. Mary appeared to Richeldis and instructed her to construct a copy of the little house in which the Annunciation took place. In the original house of the Annunciation, the angel Gabriel came to Mary and told her that she was to bear God's son.[5] Mary's act of obedience in her response, 'Let it be', meant that she would accept the role to be the Mother of God. This role granted Mary a particularly efficacious intercessory power with God because of her proximity to Jesus. Being the sinless, blessed mother of Jesus, and having been bodily assumed into heaven at her death, she is considered the second most effective intercessor, second only to her Son.

For the construction of the house in Walsingham, Mary provided Richeldis with a spiritual blueprint for the house; these plans then required Richeldis to keep artisans of various sorts on retainer. The ballad describes this as a 'miracle' that is followed through by the 'deed' of Richeldis' actual establishment of the shrine. The human becomes the agent through which God's miracles can be accomplished. Mary repeated the vision to Richeldis three times in order for Richeldis to remember the measurements precisely.[6] Mary promised to assist and intercede for all who came there for her aid. In the vision, Richeldis was spiritually transported to the Holy Land in order to see the original house to help her know what she was building:

> In spyryte Our Lady to Nazareth hir led
> And shewed hir the place where Gabryel her grette:
> 'Lo doughter, consyder' to hir Oure Lady sayde,
> Of thys place take thou suerly the mette,
> Another lyke thys at Walsyngham thou sette
> Unto my laude and synguler honoure;
> All that me seche there shall fynde socoure.[7]

Mary identifies the spiritual effect this house will have on those who visit; the spiritual transportation also suggests the difficulty in getting to the house in Nazareth. At the time, the Holy Land was under Saracen control, which made travel dangerous or impossible for pilgrims. The vision also emphasizes Mary's own association with visions, apparitions, angels and miracles. Mary herself received a visitation by the angel Gabriel and became associated with the host of heaven making visitations to people. Richeldis' reaction is abundant joy; then, immediately, Richeldis calls her artificers to follow Mary's instructions and build the requested house:

> This forsayd hous in haste she thought to spede,
> Called to hir artyfycers full wyse,
> This chapell to forge as Our Lady dyd deuyse.[8]

Soon after the vision, Richeldis set to work with skilled woodworkers to build a wooden-framed house to the exact specifications that she had seen in the vision. In short order, they had built the house frame and were ready to erect it. But for Richeldis and the workers to know exactly where to place the house, another miracle needed to occur. Like the story of Gideon's fleece from Scripture, an area of dewless ground the next morning was to mark the spot where the house would stand.[9] But Richeldis found two spots of practically equal size without dew:

> All this, a medewe wete with dropes celestyall
> And with syluer dewe sent from hye adowne
> Excepte tho tweyne places chosen aboue all
> Where neyther moyster ne dewe myght be fowne,
> This was the fyrste pronostycacyowne
> Howe this our newe Nazareth here shold stande,
> Bylded lyke the fyrste in the Holy Lande.[10]

Everything went wrong when the workers tried to erect the house on the spot. She sent her artisans home, and spent the night in prayer.[11] The next morning, Richeldis discovered that Mary had come during the night and used the materials of the artisans to erect the house on the other location with the help of some ministering angels. Mary was Walsingham's 'chief artificer'.[12] Mary commanded the teams of ministering angels who constructed the house, suggesting her power to command the hosts of heaven to grant intercessions as well. Following this miraculous construction, the shrine, along with other buildings on the same property and nearby, became a place of pilgrimage. In Mary's miraculous completion of the building, it becomes clear that Mary's concern was not that Richeldis successfully complete the building; rather, Richeldis merely had to show that she would submit to the request of Mary and try to accomplish it obediently. In the shrine that grew up around this original building, other buildings would come to be incorporated in the Walsingham pilgrimage location, such as the Slipper chapel, dedicated to Saint Catherine of Alexandria, a mile and a half down the road from the Walsingham shrine. It was at this location that pilgrims would remove their shoes for the last portion of the pilgrimage, and receive the sacrament of Penance.

The story of the house's building points to a combination of miraculous plans and emphasizes the power of Richeldis' prayer to bring the project to completion, Mary's willingness to listen to prayers at Walsingham, and Mary's ability to effect miracles. The ballad lists the sorts of miracles one could expect at the shrine. It says that: 'many seke ben here cured by Our Ladyes myghte', as well as the 'dede agayne reuyued'. The ballad's catalogue continues, enumerating Biblical-sounding miracles: the 'Lame made hole and blynde restored to syghte', as well as lepers and 'Defe, wounded and lunatyke that hyder haue sought'. The shrine also helped cure those who were possessed by fiends, wicked spirits or any other form of tribulation. And since the shrine was in East Anglia, sailors also had recourse to the Virgin: 'Maryners vexed with tempest safe to porte brought.' The list of those who have found help at the shrine concludes with the promise that, 'to all that be seke, bodily or goostly, / Callynge to Oure Lady deuoutly', the Virgin of Walsingham will have a special ear to listen. All the aspects of the legend point to the purpose and theological understanding of a medieval pilgrimage shrine: the earthly and temporal working in concert to bring people to the heavenly. Human prayers meet with divine response and saintly intercession to alleviate the physical and spiritual troubles of the people of God. This intercession occurs because the likeness of the shrine to the house of the Annunciation affects what happens at the shrine: at the shrine, people daily remember the joy of the Annunciation, and by remembering the joy of the Annunciation, remember the joy that brought salvation into the world. It is this joy that undergirds the miracles that take place at the shrine.[13]

The very structure of Richeldis' vision exemplifies the Marian devotion that the shrine embodies. Richeldis first petitions Mary, asking permission to do something to commemorate her. Richeldis receives a spiritual vision of Mary, which includes a spiritual pilgrimage. Then, after the vision is granted, Mary's help is needed in order to construct the house, but this help is required not because of Richeldis' fault or due to the poor work of the builders – rather, Mary's intervention shows that divine grace is needed for humans to fully respond to supernatural visions granted by God. Mary's building intervention is also a physical intervention of a different nature from the earlier spiritual transport to Nazareth; in the second intervention, Mary's grace affects the physical world of Richeldis. Yet even this is not the end of the Marian significance of the shrine. Such a shrine has a two-fold purpose: first, to give evidence of the claim that England is 'Our Lady's dowry'; and, second, to establish a place of pilgrimage and healing. Once again, it manifests Mary's gifts both in a supernatural title and in physical words and deeds among the living.

Eleventh- and twelfth-century Marian devotions

The Marian character of Richeldis' vision is typical of devotional trends from the late Carolingian period in the Latin church. A number of Marian devotions took root first in the monasteries, especially among Carolingian Benedictine reformers and later among the Cluniacs and the Cistercians in the high middle ages. Marian devotion often incorporated intercessory prayer with healing. The Pynson ballad describes Mary through her virtues, as crystallized in her greatest deed, the *fiat*: she thus is a saint by virtue of her acceptance of being mother to Christ, and this motherhood occurs through her virtue of humility and her state of sinlessness. During this time, the use of the 'Ave, Maria' ('Hail, Mary, full of grace ...') as a prayer that emphasizes Mary's roles as blessed by God through the Annunciation and her roles as intercessor on behalf of all humans began to spread.[14]

Devotion to Mary as the Mother of the Incarnate Christ emphasized her role bringing humans to God, thus undergirding Christ's role as mediator. As the mother of Christ, Mary had a special role in Christianity; with Christ's physical gestation and birth, Mary was the vessel through which God became incarnate. Through an act of her will, the *fiat*, she allowed God to act through and with her. Throughout Christian history, theologians found various significance for her 'yes'; Ambrose and Augustine stated in the fourth century that Mary was the origin of the church, which was that group of people who echoed Mary's 'yes'. Furthermore, just as Christ was the salvation through which humans were reconciled to God, Mary was the 'gate of salvation' through which salvation could be offered to humans and through which humans enter into God's offer of the salvation of Christ. Gottschalk of Limburg wrote in a hymn on the Assumption of Mary: 'As God did not come to man without you [Mary], so also men can never come to God without you.'[15] Far from insisting that Mary was passive, Marian devotion in the middle ages presented a strong female figure alongside Christ, integral to the saving work of the Incarnation.

The Middle Ages sought to venerate the human Mary as the mother of the human Jesus in conjunction with a growing Christological devotion that emphasized Christ's human nature more fully. The early and high middles ages were a time when theologians explored the human nature of Christ more frequently and fully in the theology of both the schools and monasteries. From the time of the Carolingian Renaissance (ninth century) onwards, the Latin church developed a defined Mariology that emphasized three unique roles of Mary. The first was Mary as intercessor alongside the role of Christ as judge of souls. This role was based on the events of the Nativity and Mary's role as the one who nurtured Christ; she was the first to serve Christ and keep Him safe from Herod's dangers. This role emphasized Mary's ability to nurture, protect and care for others. As an extension of being Christ's mother, Mary became mother to all humans. In the second role ascribed to her by various Marian devotions, Mary was known as a miracle-worker. Mary became associated with miracles because of her request for Christ's miracle of the multiplication of wine at the wedding feast of Cana: Mary encouraged Christ to continue providing gifts in abundance for humans, as He first did at her insistence at the wedding feast at Cana. Mary's third role was as one who brought heavenly visions or apparitions to humans, based upon her Assumption into heaven. These apparitions, which are perhaps the best-known of Mary's vestiges, were usually associated with the physical places where they occurred, since shrines of devotion to the Blessed Virgin sprang up at these locations. In Richeldis' story, we see aspects of all three Marian roles. Mary appeared to Richeldis and a shrine grew up at the location of the vision, confirming Mary's third type of role. In fact, she appeared in two visions: the initial visitation and the second nighttime build of the house. Confirming the second role, Mary also provided miracles for Richeldis and for those people who visited the shrine. Finally, Mary promised to be an intercessor on behalf of those Walsingham pilgrims who called upon her, like the first role.

By Richeldis' time in the eleventh century, Marian devotion was firmly a part of the successive waves of monastic reform, beginning with the Cluniac monks (founded 910). Odo of Cluny received a vision of Mary in which the name *Mater Misericordiae* (Mother of Mercy) was revealed to him as a special name for Mary that the Cluniac monks were to use. Many Marian visions and devotions based themselves upon revelations of special titles for Mary which emphasized her various gifts.[16] Another Cluniac monk, Odilo of Cluny, was healed of childhood paralysis when he touched the altarcloth at a church dedicated to Mary. After this miraculous cure, Odilo dedicated himself to Mary. Later he became the Abbot of Cluny for over half a century and helped to spread Marian devotion, and its associated healing ministries, throughout western Europe. Cluny, a Benedictine monastery that grew to be the most powerful monastery in the high middle ages, was a centre of monastic reform and responsible for founding many monasteries that were established as pilgrimage sites by Marian visions.[17]

In Richeldis' generation, hymns, prayers and devotions to Mary increased. Anselm of Canterbury (Benedictine monk and Archbishop of Canterbury between 1093 and 1109) penned several Marian hymns and prayers, as well as treatises about aspects of Mariology. In Anselm's writings, Marian devotion meets the nascent Scholastic theology and provides further theological and philosophical weight to the devotional practices of the monastery and popular religion. A generation later, Anselm of St Saba, the Abbot of Bury St Edmunds from 1121 to 1148, produced perhaps the earliest Marian miracle collection.[18] The Mariology of the Pynson ballad accords with other special devotions England had to the Annunciation in the middle ages. The curfew (cover fire) would be rung at sunset, which comes to be known as the Gabriel bell. At the ringing of this bell, people would say three Hail Marys to honour the Incarnation.

Pilgrimage shrines

Even in the earliest days of Christianity, devotees venerated the shrines of the martyrs as places where intercessory prayers to various saints would be especially well heard and efficacious.[19] Pilgrimage experienced a rebirth in the high middle ages due to its focus on the human nature of Christ. Pilgrimage sites associated with saints, martyrs and holy places arouse; some of the most well-known shrines included Rome, Jerusalem, Santiago de Compostela and Canterbury as well as local shrines important to regional populations. The growth of medieval pilgrimage shrines was also indebted to medieval devotional focuses on Christ's relationship to material creation, the body of Christ's presence in the Eucharist, and relics of saints as well as geographical places associated with Christ and various saints. Pilgrims found many motivations; they sometimes went as a part of a penance, often to a particular shrine.[20]

Pilgrimage was not always easy. Especially during the Muslim occupation of the Holy Land, medieval English pilgrims from Richeldis' time to the time of Pynson's writing suffered much insecurity in the Holy Land. Jerusalem, alongside Rome and Santiago de Compostela, was a place of pilgrimage for those with the means and desires to travel, as well as for those forced on pilgrimage to atone for sins, and those off in search of relics. Jerusalem of course offered the pilgrim the opportunity to follow the footsteps of Christ through the land in which he had preached and died. Santiago offered the bones of the apostle James. In Richeldis' time, Jerusalem was under Saracen control and the Moors were threatening to cut off access to Santiago in northern Spain. During this time, the closer shrines of Canterbury and Walsingham served as popular substitutes and their popularity continued even after the Holy Land became accessible again.[21]

A person might go on pilgrimage for any number of reasons. In the middle ages, the Holy Land was a place of pilgrimage, but it also was a place that people went to out of a sense of biblical tourism![22] Other pilgrims went to specific shrines for healing and curing ailments, because they had made a promise to a saint to fulfil a promise for favours granted, out of devotion, or finally to escape familial, business or ecclesiastical duties. Sometimes pilgrims even went on pilgrimage just 'to deny their parish priest his monopoly over their spiritual welfare' by travelling beyond where their local priest had authority.[23] A pilgrim was to travel without any weapons, and was not to take any unnecessary money or clothes. He or she should only take what would be necessary for the journey. People often travelled in groups. If they travelled alone, they would often join up with groups they met in pilgrims' hostels or at various shrines. As some of the writings of the middle ages about pilgrimage – such as the *Canterbury Tales* – tell us, the people on pilgrimage were average folks, not saints, and represented a wide spectrum of people from all classes.

Although pilgrimage was a process that began the moment one walked out of the door, about a mile from the Holy House at Walsingham the pilgrim's progress would have become more focused on the final arrival at the shrine. At about a mile from the shrine, a small chapel dedicated to St Catherine, known as the slipper chapel, was the first stop for all pilgrims. Here, they would remove their shoes and walk the last remaining distance to the Holy House barefoot. After walking sometimes hundreds of miles to reach the shrine, this last act would be difficult on their feet; the additional pain was meant to be penitential, and the act of removing their shoes was in deference of walking to holy ground. The shrine itself was a small, one-room house, about 20 by 30 feet. Inside, there was an altar on which a wooden statue of Mary holding the infant Jesus stood. Pilgrims would stop in front of the altar and offer prayers. Medieval descriptions of the shrine indicate that it was a common practice for pilgrims to bring mementoes and presents to the shrine and leave them on the altar. These would be left as a token to show the person's devotion to Mary when they were asking for her intercessions. Pilgrims would often light candles in the shrine, and the smoke from the candles eventually darkened the wood of the statue of Mary, making it a lustrous black colour.

But if pilgrimage aided the souls of so many pilgrims, it also helped the organization, ecclesiastic outreach and economics of the land. The urge for pilgrimage led monasteries and the local parishes to develop a whole network of roads or 'pilgrim's ways' that connected various towns with pilgrimage centres. Along these roads, pilgrims needed hostels, places to eat, and remedies for medical problems such as blistered feet that might occur along the way. Local churches and religious orders also established roadside shrines, which accepted the offerings of pilgrims who wanted the added intercessions that the shrine's saints could offer. These pilgrimage routes became trade routes as well, and market days were often associated with places of pilgrimage (for pilgrims brought extra trade and needed supplies); the rights of Walsingham's Friday marketplace were granted to the Walsingham priory in 1226 by King Henry III while he was on pilgrimage there.

Walsingham itself was granted substantial royal pilgrimage over many successive generations. Many generations of Royals up to Henry VIII came to Walsingham on pilgrimage: Richard I the Lionhearted was one such reported pilgrim. King John went in the last year of his reign. His son, Henry III, in 1255 confirmed substantial donations from eight donors. He also undertook at least two pilgrimages, one on 24 March 1241 and one in 1248. Edward I made two visits as well, and on one he reported that a miracle had occurred where he had narrowly missed being crushed by a falling stone when he suddenly got up and left a game of chess.[24] Edward II visited, in October 1315, and he even gave protection to Robert Bruce to travel there, with an escort of knights that Edward provided, to seek a cure from leprosy. Queen Isabella of France travelled to Walsingham in 1332, and Richard II, Henry VI and Edward IV all made pilgrimages. Royal patronage helped to establish the economic security of the shrine and promote it as a place of religious significance. All this would pay off, as Walsingham became the pre-eminent Marian site in England for pilgrimage.

Pilgrims in medieval England had three reasons for travelling to the shrine of Walsingham: first, it was the English Nazareth, a Marian shrine that pointed to the mystery of the Incarnation. English pilgrims to Walsingham even became known as 'palmers', the traditional title for Holy Land pilgrims. Second, Walsingham was founded at the request of Mary herself, and was thought therefore to be an especially favoured place. Mary's favour in giving Richeldis a vision was universalized to include 'all that the deuoutly visyte in this place'.[25] Third, Walsingham had a healing spring that the sick visited for relief and healing.[26] Unlike the larger pilgrimage sites of Rome, Jerusalem and Canterbury, Walsingham was a smaller shrine with a different claim: it held no ecclesiastic power, but Walsingham offered the Holy Land's proximity of purpose.[27] As such, it was the 'Everyman's shrine' rather than a mere outreach of ecclesial power.[28]

Walsingham and Loreto

Reduplication was a common theme among shrines erected during the turbulence of the middle ages. Other shrines that claimed to be reduplications or which housed translated artefacts from the Holy Land included Our Lady of the Pillar in Zaragoza, the shrine of Santiago de Compostela (which miraculously received James' bones) and Our Lady of Montserrat, which miraculously received a statue of the Black Madonna that was based upon one carved in the early days of the church in Jerusalem. Walsingham claimed to be a copy of the house of the Annunciation, which was still located in Nazareth in 1061 when Richeldis had her vision, and the Loreto house in Italy claimed to be the actual house in which the Annuncuation occurred, miraculously transposed to Italy.[29] Both houses, similar in shape, size and layout, point to the widespread character of the growing Marian devotion. The legend of the Loreto house states that the house left Nazareth and arrived for a stay of three and a half years in Tersatto, Dalmatia (modern-day Croatia). There, the house was discovered by a shepherd. The house was made of materials native to Nazareth, not Dalmatia: limestone, mortar and cedar. It contained an old stone altar, a Greek cross and a statue of Mary.[30] The local priest and other ecclesiastic and civil authorities, believing that it was the true House of the Annunciation, sought confirmation from eyewitnesses in Nazareth that the House of the Annunciation was no longer in Nazareth, which they received; the dimensions of the Tersatto house were identical to the house foundation that remained in Nazareth. But after settling in Tersatto for three and a half years, the house re-settled in an Italian forest called Lauretum, which was across the Adriatic from its first stop. Here, near the town of Loreto (whose name derived from the nearby Lauretum woods), the house remained until the two brothers who owned the land feuded. Then, the house moved a short distance to the Rancanati Road, still in the environs of Loreto. A plaque on the wall tells its history of divine translations.[31] This last move was in 1294, and by the Jubilee year of 1300 the town had received notice as a growing centre of Marian pilgrimage.

The peripatetic nature of the Loreto house shows that, like the Walsingham house, the new location was important to the permanence of the Loreto structure; the house would not remain in places where feuding occurred. The Walsingham shrine shows that Mary's grace is attached to place: to the architecture of the house. And place can be somewhat relative: the exact placement in Walsingham mattered, but the fact that the house would be in England rather than the Holy Land did not matter. An imitation would do, when the original was not physically accessible. But the imitation's actual structure was closely regulated by Mary herself, and was meant to look like the original house; Mary's shrine in Walsingham was not meant to look like an English cottage or anything other than the original. The Loreto house places importance, like a relic, on the actual physical remnant of the original Annunciation story, translated for safety (like the bodies of some apostles and martyrs and saints). Both sites show that there was a great deal of importance placed on the physical structure as well as the physical location of Mary's shrine; reduplication, though, does not seem to limit its efficaciousness.

Conclusions

The charter of Geoffrey of Faverches mentions the shrine in Walsingham (here called a chapel) as he goes off to the Second Crusade (1145–49):

> Granting to God and St Mary and to Edwin, his chaplain, in perpetuity the chapel which my mother has founded in Walsingham in honour of Mary ever Virgin, together with possession of the church of All Saints of the same village, and all its appurtenances in lands, tithes, and rents, to come in to the possession of Edwyn on the day on which I leave for Jerusalem.[32]

'Mother' means Richeldis was a female ancestor, not necessarily his birth-mother; if nothing else, this charter tells us a date by which we know the shrine was operational, less than a century after the foundation date offered by the Pynson ballad.

Pilgrimage is a theme that reoccurs throughout this book: Margery Kempe goes on pilgrimage to Canterbury, Jerusalem, Rome and many other places. Angela of Foligno had her big conversion experience while on a pilgrimage to Assisi, the home of Saint Francis. Other women such as Hildegard of Bingen, Catherine of Siena and Teresa of Avila travelled extensively in carrying out their work. Movement, place and Incarnational devotions are all key aspects of medieval theology. Here in the petition of Richeldis we have one of the patterns of women's involvement in the middle ages: Richeldis is almost anonymous. She did not leave her own stories; she became the subject of another's tale about her and those stories that we have come to at a distance of four centuries after her life.

Richeldis lived at a time when England was undergoing a number of changes in its social structure, following the Norman invasion of 1066; yet, despite all this, the structure of pilgrimage gave voice to medieval religious aspirations through pilgrimage and devotion to saints' shrines. Richeldis offers an example of a medieval woman conforming to the Marian model and acting in imitation of her willingness to do God's will. This imitation could take many forms, but what we see in Richeldis is a life patterned on the Annunciation. As a result, she received a supernatural visitation, from Mary, just like Mary received one from the Holy Spirit. It is this role of the woman as willing handmaid of divine wishes that Richeldis fulfilled. Unlike many of the women after her, Richeldis is not important for having deep or unique theological thoughts, nor for the beauty of her poetic expression, nor the number of mystical visions. Rather, she is important for simply saying yes and following through on Mary's request for a shrine.

In this vision, Mary returns as the one who sends the message, rather than as the receiver. In so doing, she asks another woman to say yes to helping bring Christ into the world, not as an Incarnation, but as a shrine that will help build up the faith of the pilgrims who visit. Mary's help by the angels reinforces the relationship this vision bears to the Annunciation, as does the establishment of a house that is a replica of the Annunciation house. The existence of the material shrine then becomes a several-centuries-long Incarnation of Christ and so outdoes the first Incarnation of Christ in its ability to endure over time.

2

Sybil of the Rhine: Hildegard of Bingen

I saw a great mountain the color of iron, and enthroned
on it One of such great glory that it blinded my sight.
On each side of him there extended a soft shadow, like
a wing of wondrous breadth and length. Before him, at
the foot of the mountain, stood an image full of eyes on
all sides, in which, because of those eyes, I could discern
no human form. In front of this image stood another, a
child wearing a tunic of subdued color but white shoes,
upon whose head such glory descended from the One
enthroned upon that mountain that I could not look at
its face.[1]

With these words, Hildegard describes her first vision of God enthroned
before her. This visionary life became the basis for her writing the *Scivias*
and for her claims to prophecy; it served as her authority, allowing her to
preach, and gave her credibility for many other projects, including the
relocation of her own monastic community, while also allowing her to
claim the roles of sage and prophet. In her visionary world, God's might
flows forth from God to all creatures in all circumstances, as a result of
creation, and it does not merely flow out to visionaries. Such plenitude is
also found in the ways Hildegard lived out her life. During her time,
women had open to them very few vocational options. The two main
options were being either a nun or mother. While choosing the first
option, Hildegard found ways to widen the scope of this vocational

option; God's plenitude expressed itself in her seemingly endless variety of projects and writings.

Likewise, throughout her writings Hildegard provides a rich repertoire of spiritual visions, philosophical and medical training, and literary and musical knowledge. All of her work was aimed at the reform of her community and the church, and her reforming agenda parallels that of various schoolmen of her time. She achieved a level of learning and expression enjoyed by few in her day, male or female, and her writings show both breadth and originality not found in many others. Hildegard's life and writings crystallize the twelfth-century renaissance in a single person: she was a nun and a *magistra* (leader) in charge of a convent, conducted preaching tours, wrote songs, wrote medical treatises, had visions that she recorded and illustrated, and fought for the rights of her monastery's independence from the protecting male monastery. She wrote compassionate letters to those seeking advice and scathing letters to those who were seeking political gain out of the papacy, and wrote letters humbly asking for ecclesiastic recognition of her visions. And, above all, she was ruled and guided by the Benedictine tradition into which she entered and upon whose *Rule* she wrote a commentary.

Hildegard also stands out among medieval women simply by the fact that we know so much about her life, unlike most of the other women in this book. We know about her career from her biography, *Vita (Life)* by Theodoric of Echternach,[2] Hildegard's letters, autobiographical passages in her works, and the *Protocollum canonisationis*, which was a thirteenth-century investigation of her life and miracles gathered together for her canonization process. The purpose of the *Vita* was to document miracles attributed to her for a popular and religious audience. These miracles were then officially presented in the administrative documents of the canonization protocols.

Around the year 1098, this startling little girl Hildegard was born into a family of upper nobility in Bermersheim near Alzey (in the western part of modern-day Germany, along the Rhine). Some time before the age of five, she began receiving visions that allowed her to see hidden things in the world around her and predict the future: for example, she was able to describe the markings of a calf still in a cow's womb.[3] At age seven or eight, she was sent to live with a recluse aunt named Jutta, who had taken on a life of secluded prayer apart from other humans. Jutta's isolated dwelling would become the basis for a Benedictine convent. By age 14, Hildegard had professed her vows to become a member of this community. In her youth, Hildegard was often sickly, and this would continue throughout her life as she would experience debilitating illness before each of the big decisions of her life: 'to begin writing, to found her own monastery, to obtain financial independence for it, to undertake her first preaching tour.'⁴ Her life thus moved within the traditional roles of anchoress and convent, under the careful guidance of the charismatic Jutta.

In 1136, Jutta, the recluse-aunt-turned-mentor of Hildegard, died. In her place, Hildegard was elected to the position of *magistra* (leader) of the young community, which was associated with the monastery of Disibod. Five years later, in 1141, a voice from heaven instructed her to 'tell and write' the visions she had been receiving since her childhood. It was only at this point, at age 43, that she told anyone in her community about the visions she had been having for the last 38 years. These visions were joined by a voice from heaven that would communicate with her in Latin and dictate her books and letters. The voice also helped her interpret the visions during the process of writing them down. It is through this two-fold process of vision and interpretation that Hildegard's *Scivias* unfolds: first the vision is described, then each detail, figure or colour is explained in terms of its allegorical significance.

During this busy time, the Synod of Trier, which met between 1147 and 1148, marked a major turning point in Hildegard's life within the larger church. The previous year, Hildegard had written to the Cistercian monk Bernard of Clairvaux, asking him to affirm her visions and gift of prophecy. Although the response he wrote was somewhat perfunctory, Bernard contacted his friend and fellow Cistercian Eugene III, who was the current pope. Eugene gave papal approval to the visions of *Scivias* (which was half-written) at the Synod. A wide range of people began asking Hildegard for her counsel – from Frederick Barbarossa to the Paris Master of Theology Odo of Soissons – and Hildegard functioned much as a 'Dear Abby' of her age.⁵ Her correspondence includes letters to a number of popes, archbishops, priors, abbots and abbesses. In this same year another turning-point occurred in the life of her community: Hildegard told Kuno, the Abbot of Disibodenberg, the monastery that oversaw her convent, that it was God's will that Hildegard and her community establish their own convent on the slopes of the Rupertsberg on the Rhine, near the hamlet of Bingen. Kuno and his community did not want to see Hildegard's community separate from them, and fought to keep them in their current location. In response to Kuno's disagreement, God inflicted upon Hildegard a wasting disease with strange effects: even as she wasted away, her body grew so heavy that Kuno could not even raise Hildegard's head from her pillow. As soon as Kuno desisted from his opposition, Hildegard's strange symptoms disappeared. The abbot only reluctantly gave his approval, but by 1150 Hildegard's community had received land-holdings and arranged to begin construction. The new convent was organized to be independent from the monks' administration, but would receive a provost to oversee their spiritual welfare. It was also state-of-the-art in its day, with running water in the workrooms and *scriptorium*.

Over the next three decades, Hildegard played a more and more public role in the church politics and spiritual renewal of her time. Twice she attempted to intervene in Barbarosa's schism, in 1160 and 1177, after he had nominated four different contenders to the pope.[6] Also during this time, Hildegard went on four preaching tours. Even with her public work, the convent was not immune to the ecclesiastic rules and procedures of the day. In 1178, the prelates of Mainz placed the Rupertsberg under interdict because of burial within the convent's cemetery of a man possibly not reconciled to the church before his death.[7] Interdict was the most serious ecclesiastic sanction that could be enacted against a group. It forbade chanting, which was a central part of the liturgy in a Benedictine monastery. Even more seriously, interdict forbade the celebration of the sacraments.[8] The sisters could not receive the sacraments of penance or Eucharist, and any member of the community that died during this time would die without the rights of the church (and hence would die in sin, and be damned to hell). It was not until March 1179 that the nuns were restored to rights. Six months later, on 17 September 1179, Hildegard died, and in a show that was fit for the visionary of Bingen. Records of her death tell that the cosmos acknowledged her passing: two arcs illuminated the night with a glowing red cross and cross-studded circles.

An all–encompassing quill: Hildegard's writings

The sheer volume of Hildegard's writings and their wide variety of forms and styles give us our clearest glimpse of Hildegard and her passions. Hers was a grand vision that attempted to document, explain and integrate supernatural visions of God and the host of heaven as well as mundane matters on the earth, such as the human body and cures for sickness. When Hildegard mediated the divine, though, she insisted that she tried to be transparent. The words are God's, not hers, and even the interpretations come from God. She was merely an instrument and tried to leave no lasting trace on the message she mediated. She even warned Guibert not to alter the meaning of any of her visions.[9]

In her most central work, the *Scivias*, Hildegard recorded elaborate visions with potent allegorical details: these were then rigorously interpreted according to how a divine voice explained their significance to her. Hildegard offered a view of the universe and salvation history that was set among a frenzied prophetic sense of the peril of the church. God addressed through Hildegard a church whose leaders had not proven sufficient in their leadership. This was a call to reform that rooted itself in the infused knowledge that God gave her to preach. She used these visions to show that God continued to care about the state of the church, and she used God's intervention in the form of her visions to provide evidence that the church officials who have lapsed in their duties must find ways to reform themselves and their flocks. Another crucial work in her corpus is the *Book of Life's Rewards* (completed in 1163), which is an allegory of vices answered by corresponding virtues. This work reads as a work of theological anthropology in which the virtues and vices battle over the possession of the soul, and this book also incorporates a theology of penance alongside its visions of the afterlife. Next she wrote the *Book of Divine Works* (written between 1163 and 1173), a speculative theological tract written in the same vein of theological speculation as found in other twelfth-century innovators such as Bernardus Silvestris, and the apocalypticism of contemporaries such as Rupert of Deutz and Anselm of Havelberg. Here, Hildegard's work revolves around commentaries on two pieces of Scripture: the prologue to the Gospel of John, and the first chapter of Genesis. Through commentary on these texts, she develops a theology of God and of the Son that is a vision of love and unity.

The most creative work of Hildegard is undoubtedly her collection of liturgical hymns and sequences known as the *Symphonia*. In this work, she presents a collection that in size and scope is comparable to the medieval hymnist Notker's *Liber Hymnorum* (*Book of Hymns*).[10] Peter Dronke, who has studied Hildegard extensively, writes that 'these songs contain some of the most unusual, subtle, and exciting poetry of the twelfth century'.[11] Another genre in which Hildegard showed herself to be an innovator was the liturgical drama; her *Ordo virtutem* (*Order of Virtues*) is a highly allegorical drama that combines elements of psychomachy (a contest between the devil and virtues), as well as being the first liturgical drama. This text is a morality play that expands beyond this genre into mystical realms through its use of interwoven images, ideas and language. But her innovation did not end with theological or spiritual works. She also produced a medical treatise composed of two parts, the *Physics* and the *Causes and Cures*; two works that employ pieces of a language that she invented, the *Lingua ignota* and *Litterae ignotae*.[12] And Hildegard tried her hand at some more 'typical' forms of theological writings, including gospel explications, two saints' lives, a commentary on the *Rule of Benedict*, and letters.[13]

Throughout her life, Hildegard worked with several collaborators who helped transcribe her visionary life on paper. The monk Volmer was her scribe for almost two and a half decades, from 1150 until his death in 1173. For the next few years a succession of others would help. When she was 77, Hildegard began to correspond with a monk named Guibert of Gembloux, who would be her last scribe. Their communication began when Guibert wrote expressing admiration and asking for specific details of how Hildegard received her visions. When Hildegard replied, Guibert then responded with more admiration, and he attached a list of questions that the Cistercian monks of Villers addressed to the nun. Guibert eventually came to live at Hildegard's convent until a few months after her death. During this time of living with the sisters, Guibert began writing a *Vita* to document her life which he never completed, although he tried to continue working on it at least once after her death.

Hildegard's methods of composition also required other types of collaborators, for Hildegard's *Scivias* included illuminations. She had significant control over the creation of the illustrations to her works that were produced at the Rupertsberg, particularly over the *Scivias* illustrations of the visions, to the point where 'Hildegard supplied drawings with colour notations for her *Scivias*, and oversaw the execution of finished illustrations'.[14] Thus these illustrations can be read as further texts of Hildegard's.[15] Linking text and image in this way makes Hildegard's *Scivias* a unique type of object when it is compared to other writings from her generation; her movement beyond just the textual into the text and image makes it hard to find true peers with whom to compare her.[16]

Her writings are also notable because they address a number of audiences that overlap with and extend her other activities. Thus, she did not write only for the group of women in her convent. She was an advisor to many of the powerful clergy in her time, and her writings reflect her work as a counsellor to both the notable people as well as religious of her time. She wrote letters to the clergy in Cologne and Mainz to warn them about the threat of Cathar heresy.[17] She also addressed clergy in many of her preaching tours in Franconia, Lorraine, Schwaben and Werden/Trier (Pentecost 1160) and Cologne (1163).

Reading Hildegard

Within the wide variety of her works, we see a number of recurrent interactions Hildegard had with the theological, philosophical and literary currents of her time. First, she writes in allegory. Allegory becomes part of the process of encoding (and decoding) her mystical visions for a wider audience. Her writings use allegory to provide characterization of the virtues and vices, thus heightening the drama in which her narrative explored the soul's choice to develop virtues and forsake vices. Second, she saw the human as a microcosm of the larger universe. Microcosmic speculation was in philosophical vogue in her times, best represented by the *Cosmographia* of Bernardus Silvestris. In his work, Bernardus described the human as a smaller image of the cosmos, which reflects God's ordering and providential care and structure. Hildegard's wide range of writings show both her place in the 'twelfth-century renaissance' and her uniqueness among twelfth-century writers. Hildegard 'reflects, in her rationalizing Platonism, the brief and brilliant period of transition from the symbolic cosmology of the prescholastic era to the orderly coherence of Aristotelian and Ptolemaic astronomy'.[18] Of Hildegard's writing, Peter Dronke notes that 'It is the language not of a polished twelfth-century humanist but of someone whose unique powers of poetic vision confronted her more than once with the limits of poetic expression'.[19]

Additionally, the twelfth century – particularly twelfth-century monasticism – saw a remarkable flourishing of Marian devotion, which is evident in several of Hildegard's antiphons. She offers beautiful images to describe God's use of Mary, and her verse echoes the *Song of Songs*, mentioning the bridal chamber and the dawn. The image of the Incarnation as a portal, and the cloister/portal word play are typical of Hildegard's fascination with liturgical language.

> Priceless integrity!
> Her virgin gate
> opened to none. But the Holy One
> flooded her with warmth

> until a flower sprang in her womb
> and the Son of God came forth
> from her secret chamber like the dawn.
> Sweet as the buds of spring, her
> son opened paradise
> from the cloister of her womb.
> And the Son of God came forth
> from her secret chamber like the dawn.[20]

Hildegard uses many of the Biblical images associated with Mary, but her use forefronts the erotic imagery in order to stress the fruitfulness of the Incarnation, made possible through Mary. Christ is a flower from Mary's womb, which is brought forth from this garden by the flood that occurs through her 'virgin gate', stressing Mary's chaste fertility.

In the monastery, Hildegard and her sisters' lives were structured around the singing of the Divine Offices or Liturgy of the Hours seven times per day. These offices, which stretch from pre-dawn to evening, were laid out in the book that regulated Disibod and the Rupertsburg's liturgical life, the *Rule of Benedict*. Each consisted of psalms and scripture lessons, and each is set off with scriptural canticles, antiphons and responsories. Additionally, the liturgical calendar required a variety of hymnody: feast days of the liturgical calendar, Saints' celebrations and the memorials of Saints of special importance to the monastery meant that the readings, antiphons and responsories would change to reflect the festival.

Symphonia offers many antiphons that were sung or read before and after a Psalm, and free or votive antiphons, which conclude major hours after the canticles. These longer, more elaborate antiphons account for 14 of the 43 antiphons in the collection.[21] About 18 of Hildegard's compositions in the *Symphonia* are responsories, or freely composed pieces that alternate a cantor or leader and a choir. These occur primarily at Matins, following the readings of Scripture. Singing, with its combination of words and melody, was a token of the original unity of Adam, and the unity of Christ exemplifies and tries to re-establish: 'The word designates the body, but music manifests the spirit. For the harmony of heaven proclaims the divinity of God's son, and the word makes known his humanity.'[22]

Hildegard the visionary, prophetic and apocalyptic thinker

Hildegard's writing intertwines three genres: the visionary, the apocalyptic and the prophetic. The visionary refers to the visions she received, whereas the prophetic refers to those messages to be fulfilled, and the apocalyptic refers to those aspects of her writing that relate to the end times. The only aspect of her writing that remained most influential during her time and for centuries afterwards was her apocalyptic preaching. Hildegard's prophecy was both public (apocalyptic preaching) and private (monastic reform and letters to answer individual questions).[23] Hildegard was not alone among twelfth-century women who claimed to have been given the gift of prophecy. Her colleague Elizabeth of Schonau (1129–64) also claimed this gift, and in fact they asserted that prophecy was a part of the role of all members of the Mystical Body of Christ.[24] That role was defined as being the speaking of God's visions and warnings to the church with personal submission to the transmission on the divine message.[25] But even more so were the apocalyptic writers of the twelfth century such as Rupert of Deutz.[26]

'Write what you see and hear' God tells Hildegard. And so she begins recording these visions in the *Scivias* at age 42. The book describes and interprets visions that she received starting at the age of five, and which had reached a feverish pitch in 1141, causing her to finally break her silence. Her visions, as we have them, are didactic and allegorical; she did not write in states of ecstasy, for, as Hildegard notes, she perceived her visions initially according to the spiritual senses, the Augustinian faculty of the 'inner man'.[27] Hildegard had a dislike for the 'ecstatic' state in which one would be overwhelmed by the visions, and spoke out against ecstasy.[28] After Hildegard perceived her visions through the spiritual senses she encoded the visions into images and symbols.

'Vision', to Hildegard, meant three things: first, it is the faculty or capacity to see hidden things in the world or of God; second, it refers to Hildegard's experience of seeing such things; and, third, it is the actual content of these visions.[29] Her visions engaged multiple senses, and evoked various aspects of medieval Christianity: 'The visions are a composite of geometric, symbolic and narrative elements that seem to combine essentially countless patterns with meaningful material from the memory and consciousness.'[30] Hildegard exploited this multiplicity of senses and details when she analysed the details in order to plumb them for theological significance. Most importantly, the visionary is what gave Hildegard her authority. Without it, she would be a merely presumptuous female; with it, she found she had power precisely because that power came from God and not from her.[31]

Her visionary *Scivias* has a tripartite structure of three books, which moves from the creation to the end of time and finally to the heavenly Jerusalem. The visionary images build up to view the world full of motion and flux. The first book includes six visions that reflect how God interacts with creation and how the world evolves through salvation history. The imagery of this first set of visions is intense and dynamic, full of motion and drama. The second book of the *Scivias* includes seven visions that describe the process of redemption. This book describes the coming of a saviour, the battle of the church and sacraments against the onslaughts of the devil, and incorporates apocalyptic imagery. Book three provides an overall description of human salvation. After the apocalyptic view of the second book, this provides a calmer one that focuses on the vision of edifice with all sorts of virtues: faith, humility, patience, charity. The *Scivias* concludes with a revelation of the final days, including sights of the damned and saved and the universe purified of all mean and perishable things.

The *Book of Divine Works'* view contrasts with that of the *Scivias*: it shows an ordered disposition of relations in which cosmic structure accounts for divisions of past and future history rather than the dynamic and apocalyptic upheaval of the *Scivias*.[32] The *Book of Divine Works* begins with a vision detailing the life force moving through all things. This creative power is shown to be the mediator between God and the world, which is a wheel: the rays or spokes show the connected nature of everything in her cosmic vision. At the centre of the wheel, we find the human person, who is a microcosm of the entire world. In this image, Hildegard reinforces the idea that human bodily operations depend on and parallel the activities in the larger system. In this microcosmic approach, Hildegard paralleled the microcosmic speculation in western theology that was based on Plato's *Timaeus* in curricula, especially in School of Chartres after about 1150.[33] The other visions emphasize the human's place in the cosmos, the human and the reintegration of the created world with the divine realm. The *Book* focuses much more on the human and its nature than the *Scivias*, which allows her to de-emphasize the end-times apocalypticism of the *Scivias*.

Hildegard and twelfth-century cosmology

Although the twelfth century also saw many men – such as Alan of Lille, Hugh of St Victor and Bernardus Silvestris – construct vast symbolic theological systems, Hildegard's writings have a much stronger voice and prophetic dynamism than any of her contemporaries. Her cosmographical view also formed the basis for her allegorical visions of the world, in which successive layers of meaning would be found opening up the various layers of symbolism of her visions (much like opening up Russian nesting dolls). This approach serves to stress the interrelated, repetitive nature of the various aspects of God and creation through order and imitation. Hildegard's voice is a visionary voice rather than a reactionary voice. She claims mystical inspiration, and looking carefully we can see influences of scriptures, natural sciences, classical Latin literature and Neo-Platonic philosophers such as Eriugena and Denys, as well as classical authors such as Lucan and Cicero.[34] And it is her cosmological view born out in her prophetic works that undergirds how she organizes these successive layers of tradition which have been bequeathed her.[35]

Hildegard displays a fundamentally optimistic theology in which her vision always concludes in God's final victory and reintegration of cosmos in the divine sphere.[36] She viewed the world as one organism, in which each creature was both a symbol of God's overflowing plenitude and at the same time could be an instrument through which God worked. Her vision starts with the being of God, primordial, which is what creatures return to in their being.[37] She asks, 'how could God be known to be life, except through the living things which glorify him, since the things that praise his glory have proceeded from him?'[38] Hildegard believed that all creation lived in God.[39] Underlying this is the idea that Hildegard viewed history as a search to recover the unity of paradise.[40]

Hildegard lived in an age that would not last for long, but one whose theological and literary contributions were a bridge to the high middle ages and scholasticism. Before this time, writers were not yet amassing such large symbolic visions nor were they developing such scientific works. After her time, scholasticism swayed the theological focus away from the symbolic cosmologies of her own age towards vast systematizing compositions. Hildegard and her contemporaries flourished in a brief time in the twelfth century in which science and theology came together in creative ways: 'And for the historian of science and the historian of ideas, she reflects, in her rationalizing Platonism, the brief and brilliant period of transition from the symbolic cosmology of the prescholastic era to the orderly coherence of Aristotelian and Ptolemaic astronomy.'[41]

Hildegard as sapiential thinker

In an attempt to set Hildegard within a larger, historically derived context, Barbara Newman has provided key insights into the relationship between Hildegard and the sapiential tradition, which has been the main historical milieu for giving the divine a female face. Newman traces threads that show how traditionally female representations of the divine in the biblical forms of Sophia (Wisdom), as well as late classical representations of Lady Philosophy in the medieval allegorical tradition, such as Boethius' *Consolation of Philosophy*, all have their analogues in Hildegard. Other more contemporary accounts include Queen Sapientia in Prudentius' *Psychomachia*, and the learned bride in Martianus Capella's allegory 'The Marriage of Philology and Mercury'. Historically, wisdom has had the theological 'roles' of being the Bride of Christ, the creatrix, the *anima mundi* (soul of the world), and wisdom has been the visible glory/clothing of God in the world. Furthermore, Caritas (Charity) is a female figure. In Hildegard's day there were other traditionally feminine theological ideas: for instance, the Cistercians feminized the language for God by replacing 'God' with 'God is love', and, because love (*caritas*) was a feminine noun, God could be denoted as 'she'.[42] In Hildegard, the feminine is expressly a symbol of the divine counsel.[43] Hildegard's use of feminine imagery arguably is at its best in her writings about the figures of Eve and Mary and the ways in which she moulds them within God's provident care for creation and plans for redemption. Mary was

> the capstone of the arch formed by the celestial fore-shadowing of Wisdom on the one side and the embodied fertility of Eve on the other. It is Mary who brings the sapiential visions to their fulfillment; she reveals the eternal counsel, predestined by Love before the world began, because through her the Incarnation is accomplished and God becomes man.[44]

Mary united the heavenly and earthly, the divine and human.

Hildegard as woman: self-awareness and feminine construction

Just as her cosmology was a product of her age, so were Hildegard's views about women. Although she sometimes worked outside of traditional female roles, her views on women were formed by the age in which she lived. Her view of her weakness as a woman was something she inherited from her times, but it was also something that she said marked her out for special gifts from God. Hildegard falls back on theological assumptions about the humility and humble nature of the Virgin Mary, arguing that God chose the lowly female because men and priests were not listening. Her being female is meant to shame churchmen who are negligent in their duties, rather than shame Hildegard. Very few of her works contain references to scholastic thinkers, even though many of the ideas are ones that she probably encountered in books she had read. This reticence to cite others may well have been a conscious choice on her part. When she asked Bernard of Clairvaux for help authenticating her visions, the Cistercian monk was already on the warpath against Peter Abelard, and central to Bernard's concerns were Abelard's uses of secular materials in his writings. Thus she knew well to distance herself from secular learning, but she also knew to distance herself from scholarly sources so she would not appear too learned or presumptuous a woman. Had she admitted that she was as influenced by contemporary thinkers of her time as she was, she would have been subject to censure, and most certainly Bernard of Clairvaux would have had a more similar reaction to her as he had to Peter Abelard, in which Bernard denigrated Peter's integration of various writers into his theology.[45]

Hildegard's liturgical writings emphasize Eve's transgression in order to magnify Mary's decision. In her scientific writings Hildegard's style is much more naturalistic, almost clinical, and not moralist. In Hildegard's writings, we also find a variety of personal reactions to her situation, including doubt about her missions, doubt about her acceptance as well as a strong conviction she has a prophetic gift. What also stands out is her awareness of her separateness from others through the gifts she has been given. Guibert of Gembloux depicts Hildegard in light of her monastic calling, and this centrality of the monastic vocation means that he finds in her a colleague with whom he is connected. When Hildegard describes herself, her uniqueness and her calling to be a prophet separate her from the others around her. Similarly, Hildegard notes her illiteracy and her lowly status as a woman in order to draw attention to the divine origin of her inspiration (setting her apart from other writers who write by their own abilities); the fact that she writes visions of God when she can barely write Latin points to the divine aspects of what she receives.

Conclusions

Hildegard's acceptance as a wise woman and her official 'approval' from ecclesiastic authorities granted her a particular role open to few women of her day: that of the sage or wise woman. The authenticity granted to her visions and the way that she was allowed to use her gifts outside the convent meant Hildegard could live out this role. The fact that she was a *magistra* of a Benedictine community – a well-established order with a recognized Rule and expected set of ideals and behaviours – helped to reinforce her in these new duties and works precisely because her initial location was also one that was recognized by the church. Hildegard's place at the beginning of such a work describing the contributions of women thinkers sets up a rigorous standard of women's contributions that we shall not see in all of the writers.

That Hildegard can be placed within the social settings of women and also within the literary traditions of men of her times speaks to a particular breadth of learning that would have been quite unusual. That some of her roles included work 'improper' to women in the middle ages, such as preaching, speaks to a further breadth in her skills, but it also speaks to the freedom that official support could offer. Hildegard was not a woman who made her own fate; rather, she was a woman who allowed those with authority to grant her privileges which she then exercised based upon the Spirit of the Lord that she spoke. It is this Spirit that Hildegard describes:

> Wisdom contemplated her own work, which she had arranged in proper order in the reflection of the living water, when she revealed through that aforementioned unlearned figure of a woman, certain natural virtues of various things and certain writings about the life of merits, and certain other deep mysteries which that same woman saw in a true vision and which exhausted her.[46]

3

Penitential Demoniac: Christina of St Trond/ Christina Mirabilis

Christina of St Trond (also known as Christina Mirabilis – Christina the Astonishing) followed the various penitential shapes of the Christian tradition bequeathed to her. In the *Life* written by her biographer, Thomas de Cantimpré, Christina's spiritual life is recorded through the examples of her atrociously odd behaviours, and thus she appears alternately possessed, hysterical, holy, penitential and Christ-like. But even more, Christina's story shows how she is able to blend the life of the demoniac ultimately to this vision of the penitential life. The very limits of female sanctity come into question in de Cantimpré's text. Christina's demoniac behaviours place her further outside the realm of traditional forms of female sanctity than the other 'untraditional' forms such as beguines. Yet, at the same time, Christina's *Life* presents a very traditional picture of female sanctity – or at least traditional in male terms – for she becomes a sermon *exemplum* of the mediatorial roles of sacramental grace in de Cantimpré's writing. Though the words we have about her are those that a man used to describe her rather than self-description, her *Life* challenges the traditional ways of understanding women in cloister and home, but it is a challenge that ultimately roots itself in other traditions.

Christina's life

Christina was born in the Low Countries in the town of Brustem around the year 1150 and died in 1224 in St Trond. The Dominican

confessor Thomas de Cantimpré wrote about her life 8 years later as part
of his collection, which included the lives of other holy women in the
Low Countries, a collection such as the lives of Margaret of Ypres, Lutgard
of Aywières and Marie d'Oignies.[1] Another hagiographer of the holy
women in the Low Countries, Jacques de Vitry, also attested to the
historical truth of the *Life*'s story in the prologue to the life of another
holy woman of this era, adding that he was an eyewitness to Christina's
mission.[2]

De Cantimpré's *Life* says Christina was the youngest of three sisters,
who after being orphaned worked to eke out an existence; Christina's task
was to take the herds to pasture. There, her visionary life began.[3] As her
visionary life continued, she became exhausted and underwent a mystical
death. While dead, Christina visited purgatory and heaven, and Christ
came up to her in this afterworldly vision, offering her a choice: she could
remain with Christ in heaven or return to life and have a public ministry
of intercessory prayer on behalf of the living and the dead. Christina
explains her choice to go back to the living:

> At once the Lord answered my desire and said,
> 'Certainly, my dearest, you will be with me, but now I
> offer you two choices, either to remain with me now or
> to return to the body and suffer there the sufferings of
> an immortal soul in a mortal body without damage to
> it, and by these your sufferings to deliver all those souls
> on whom you had compassion in that place of purga-
> tory, and by the example of your suffering and your way
> of life to convert living men to me and to turn aside
> from their sins'.[4]

Christina's role becomes one in which she offers public prayers, sufferings
and examples on behalf of other souls to free them from the sufferings of
purgatory. With her decision, Christina casts herself into a life that is
above understanding and which even her hagiographer describes as consisting of such things that 'have not been seen among mortals'.[5] Upon her
return to earth, Christina exhibits astonishing behaviour modelled after
the miracles that Christ and the disciples and saints had performed in the
past. Many people, including her sisters, thought she was possessed by a
demon. Not professing to any religious order or group, Christina lived her
life as a laywoman before she entered the convent of St Catherine at the

very end of her life.[6] This is significant because it freed Thomas de Cantimpré from having to portray Christina as an example of a particular religious order's tradition; her lay status opens up the scope with which he can probe the theological significance of her apostolate free of making her conform to a particular order's model of spirituality.

Thomas has a two-fold purpose in writing Christina's *Life*: first and foremost, the story of her life as he writes it is hagiography, meant to portray Christina as a woman whose whole ministry was miraculous and which produced further miracles.[7] The *Life* starts with her descent into purgatory, hell and paradise and her choice to return to life to help Christ win souls. The story ends with the miraculous healing of a woman upon visiting Christina's bones; the story of Christina's supernatural effects lasts after her earthly life. But de Cantimpré also explains that the purpose of his book is to encourage those people who hear about her to repent of their sins and do penance.[8]

Christina's efficacy lies both in the prayers she offers for the sins of others and in Thomas' hope that her example will encourage others to do likewise by reading about her life. In the *Life* we see three forms of modelling: first, the male writer uses Christina's example to bring errant male clergy back into right praxis. He asserts that if a woman – the weaker and more prone to error of the two sexes (following after Eve) – can be an *exemplum* of holiness, then men should be especially ashamed of their inability to live up to the ideals of their clerical office. Second, de Cantimpré focuses on Christina's asceticism. This is not an aspect of spiritual practice that women of Christina's time emphasized in their own texts, but it is stressed much more frequently by men writing about women. Christina's suffering served to identify a particular role into which the confessor, a member of the clergy, found it appropriate for women to be moulded.[9] Finally, the *Life* offered a model for women: it is, after all, a woman who in this story transcended the roles imposed on her of wife, mother and virgin, and finds a role that allowed new ways of responding to God.

Despite the attestation of de Vitry and de Cantimpré, the reception of Christina's life and works has not always been enthusiastic. Before the last century, Christina's *Life* was accepted as a genuine piece of hagiography and even a historical document.[10] But in modern times the scholarly opinion has generally held that the work is an 'embarrassing example of credulous mediaeval superstition'.[11] Modern scholars such as Simone Roisin and Herbert Thurston have aligned themselves with the textual characters of Christina's sisters in their assessment of the diabolical nature of Christina's outrageous behaviour.[12] They accept the existence of Christina, but deny the historical trustworthiness of the testimony to her life and works. Much of the reason for scholarly reticence to take this work seriously rests, undoubtedly, with the difficulty of finding other *exempla* to help explain the excesses and strange behaviours of Christina. Based on the competing categories of these traditional theological and spiritual works, the shape and purpose of the *Life* is hard to capture.

The structure of the *Vita*

The *Life* provides an exceptionally rich selection of spiritual gifts in the person of Christina, and although these gifts look incredibly disparate at first, their relationship becomes clearer after we discern the structure of the work. The structure of Christina's *Life* relies upon two narrative bookends in the text: her temporary death and decision to return to life (1.5–1.7) and her death at the end of the story (5.52–5.53). She crosses a boundary in her first death and resurrection, and through her resurrection and return to life at the beginning of the story she undertakes a new form of religious life. The old life of the three sisters was structured according to prayer, housework and farm labour, with Christina, the youngest sister, acting as farmhand.[13] Her resurrection from her first death marks the end of that form of life for Christina; thereforward, she will live a different type of life in the service of souls. The telling of her life ends with a second resurrection: Christina 'wakes up' from a second death long enough to tell a nun that it is time to let her go. This resurrection is one that only serves to confirm her passing and thus is not a resurrection into earthly life again. These two resurrections bookend the telling of this tale, where the first represents her birth into a particular vocation, and the second initiates her into the community of God in the afterlife, allowing her to complete this role of intercession more perfectly. Her choice to return from death and serve as a penitent on behalf of others places her in a larger context of people who undertake supernatural voyages to purgatory, heaven or hell.[14]

Within this larger structure, the narrative of the *Life* of Christina follows the three stages of Cistercian educative practice: *nutruit, educavit* and *gesta*. The three-fold divisions of the text follow a natural pattern, where a miracle separates each section of the text and practice from the others.[15]

King bases this structure upon the three-levels of spiritual development found in the twelfth-century Cistercian abbot William of St-Thierry.[16] King's suggestions of this structure imply that the *Life*, like the *Dialogus Miracoli* of Caesarius of Heisterbach, is meant to be an *exemplum* of some larger point that Thomas de Cantimpré is trying to make. The *Dialogus Miracoli* provides *exempla* which are all short enough to be stories in sermons, whereas the *Life* is too long to be used as such and must have been intended for free-standing, non-liturgical usage. As such, the moral-catechetical purposes of Caesarius' work seems clearer than that of Christina's life if only because it is presented in smaller pieces that teach in small units.

Desert spirituality and the stylites

One of the most noticeable aspects of this strange story is Christina's frequent and violent vacillation between life among society and people, and her flights to the 'desert' or other secluded places. There are no fewer than half a dozen sustained references to her penchant for remote places. As the *Life* describes, 'then Christina fled the presence of men with wondrous horror into deserts, or to trees, or to the tops of castles or churches or any lofty structure'.[17] She often escaped from people whose sins assaulted her senses, such as her sense of smell. She also fled in order to find rest from those who persecuted her for her odd behaviour or who tried to make her perform various prayers for them. 'Desert' referred to some form of secluded place, and rather than referring to sandy topography it referred both to geography and to a ministerial model. The traditions of the desert mothers and fathers and of the stylites had been brought to the Low Countries by Irish missionaries.[18] The desert also appeared in beguine *Life*, such as the *Life of Marie d'Oignies* by Jacques de Vitry.[19] The lives of desert fathers and mothers use many of the same markers of holiness that we find in Christina's life: demon attacks, lives of penance, and extreme ascetical lifestyles lived in the service of others. Underlying the image of the desert are two Christian archetypes. First is the life of Christ, who went out to the desert before his public ministry began and occasionally during his public ministry to avoid the crowds of followers.[20] Christina's forays into the desert and treetops follow the pacing of Christ's life – she went there before her public ministry began.[21] The *Life* also notes that she went to these secluded spots sometimes because she claimed that she could not stand the stench of humans (presumably their sins).[22] That the moral corruption of others could affect her body in this way shows a remarkable integration of the physical and spiritual in Christina, testifying to the spiritual provocation of her physical works, or her advanced spiritual development. At another time, Christina's flight from others was based upon her self-consciousness about the wonders she performed. As the *Life* recalls, 'Then, terrified that this highest wonder of miracles might exceed human senses and that the carnal minds of men might see in these divine operations an occasion for evil, she fled the presence of men and ascended into lofty places like a bird and lingered long in the waters like a fish.'[23] Here, her flight was one of humility, lest she appear vain for continuing to seek attention because of the special gifts God had given her. This humility is key: she did not perform these acts because she wanted to be like Christ or claim divine authority. She returned to the desert in order to have the room to do what Christ wanted.

The second Christian archetype for her flights into the desert were the stylites and dendrites of the early Christian traditions. The stylites lived in the desert and sat atop poles, and the dendrites lived in trees. Their life was one of penance in which their physical seclusion helped to define their vocation and their limited range of motion helped define their penitential practices. Christina 'would stand erect on fence palings and in that position would chant all the Psalms for it was very painful indeed for her to touch the ground while she was praying'.[24] In this explicit reference to standing on a pole while she chanted the Psalms – surely a long undertaking! – high places such as treetops, fence posts and castle crenellations physically represent elevation, physically parallel the language of 'spiritual ascent' to God.

Crossing boundaries, penance and the afterlife

During Christina's lifetime, women's religious life underwent a number of changes due to a severe underlying problem: too many women felt called to religious life, and the established orders and convents could not respond to the demand. Although some orders had made concessions to allow women to religious life, not all had, and even those which had could not meet the demands of the sheer number of women who wanted to join religious orders. As a result, extra-religious groups began to form. The beguines, which had started as urban groups of women loosely connected through handiwork and shared liturgical prayer, slowly came to be cloistered together. Additionally, some women who were attracted to the religious life found homes with any of a number of heretical sects that were also popular at the times such as the Waldensians or Cathars.

Christina's life does not fit any of these models. She was a laywoman, and a former poor shepherdess. Mendicancy was the unintentional model of Christina's life, and it 'was the mendicancy not of a St Francis, but of the ordinary poor, subject at whim to the pity, charity, or scornful abuse of the fortunate'.[25] Christina and her two sisters, who largely remain silent at the edges of the story, were teenaged orphans, whose major challenge was how to make a living in the wake of their parents' death. This bereavement placed them outside the social realm of being able to marry, and each sister had to perform menial tasks in order for the group of sisters to survive, with Christina, the youngest, performing the most menial and liminal, living as a shepherdess outside the city tending to their small flocks. Yet the 'family' of Christina serves as a strong force against her in the story; the notion of Christina and her sisters representing the disenfranchized poor does not fit with the physical, spiritual and social force that her family exerts against her. They act as a force that represents the city society at large when they censure her strange behaviours; they serve to show her continued isolation from the society around her.

This liminal position runs throughout the work; Christina was a psychopomp whose role was one of ferrying souls across the boundaries of life and death. Throughout the *Life* we see physical symbols of these boundaries she crosses to remind us of the otherworldly nature of her life's work. The text presented her both within a family, and outside the society of the town, for she is a shepherdess. At her funeral, she is differentiated by having crossed the boundary from death back to life; she becomes someone who can transcend the earth's gravitational pull, and fly into the rafters. Throughout her second life, Christina persists in this inclination towards the hard-to-reach places by living on roofs and in treetops. These hard to reach places serve as a physical reinforcement of the liminality of her purgatorial-helper role. When she attempts to cast out her demon, she goes to the Meuse River and stands in it in penance, where once again a physical boundary reinforces that she plays a liminal role. Rivers and water run throughout the *Life* to serve as reinforcement of the liminality of Christina's actions. The liminality of Christina's ministry of penance also appears in her psychology. Deep tensions exist between the otherworldly vision and living in this world for Christina:

she cannot stand humans and constantly flees from the stench of sin, yet she feels compelled to live a life that brings her into constant reminder of it.

The *Life* restructures her life for the conversion (*'et vitae tuae converti ad me'*)[26] of others and for the correction of others (*'et ad correctionem hominem redonata sum vitae'*).[27] This term – correction – is a technical term attached to preaching in the writings and preaching of Thomas de Cantimpré.[28] His use of this word witnesses that Thomas saw Christina's life as a preaching apostolate, for in his 15 years as a Victorine (whose house he left during the writing of Christina's *Life*), he learned *docere verbo et exemplo* – to teach by word and example. Christina would not have been allowed to teach, as this was restricted to men, but Thomas thought her example was an appropriate form of sermon. Thomas says:

> What else did Christina cry out during her entire life except that we do penance and be men who are ready at every hour? By the example of her life and with many words, with tears, lamentations and boundless cries she taught more and shouted louder than anyone we have known either before of since through writings or by report about the praise and glory of Christ who, with the Father and the Holy Spirit is God living and reigning forever and ever. Amen.[29]

In about one-quarter of the *Life*, de Cantimpré shows how Christina received other skills related to preaching – all miraculously conferred – such as exposing the *themata* of Scriptures.[30] Interestingly, as the church's clericalism increased the significance of the priests and canons as sacramental mediators, so too the role of these *mulieres sanctae* also grew in importance because of the religious and quasi-sacramental aspects of their lives.

Christina's body as spiritual force

At the centre of Christina's enigmatic life is her body. The *Life* repeatedly references her body and the unusual events it undergoes in order to stress that it is not merely by an act of the human will that Christina becomes *mirabilis*; her physical body's torments and feats identify the ways in which she becomes an *exemplum mirabilis* for all Christians. Examples of her body's miracles fill the *Life*, including the way she 'escapes' death the first time and the unusual physical manifestations that are attendant on this (such as flying around the church rafters), her body's ability to endure physically challenging situations such as immersion in the icy cold Meuse River, and the miraculous lactation and oil producing of her breasts.

After her descent into the dead, Christina's body is still very much physical, but it works with the physical and spiritual worlds in very different ways from how it had before; her body's miracles showed spiritual favour and gifts from God to Christina and others for whom she offered her sacrifices. Her body levitated and could live among the treetops. It was also incorruptible – it could survive many physical assaults in order to undergo purgation without any physical effect upon her. For instance, 'she crept into fiery ovens where bread was baking and was tormented by fires – just like any of us mortals – so that her howls were terrible to hear. Nevertheless when she emerged, no mutilation of any sort appeared in her body.'[31] This lack of bodily mutilation in the face of all the sufferings and tortures she underwent is a common trope in this story, and it underlines the fact that the very physical body Christina now had was in fact a physical but resurrected body which would always show forth completeness and perfection rather than death, decay or damage. Her body offered a secret knowledge that those who have not yet undergone death will not be able to decode in the story. This combination of the body being sensitive to pain but incorruptible underscores her ministry: to suffer for the sake of others. Her bodily incorruptibility adds to her ability to continually undertake this suffering.

At other times, Christina jumped into boiling cauldrons of water or the icy water of the Meuse River for a week at a time. She would also, 'in the winter … stand upright in a water wheel throughout its entire revolution and the waters [would run] over her head and limbs'.[32] The *Life* tells how she endured the rack and gallows. In these tortures and physical pains, her physical body becomes the conduit for her apostolate of atoning for the sins of others. Her body underwent physical representations of the spiritual pain of purgatory. In doing so, this penance paid for the sins of others by undergoing their purgations for them. The emphasis on Christina's body highlights how it works in non-natural ways, showing this work to be similar to Christ's miracle-working. Thus, her body did not show an ambivalence towards women but the wonder at the human body the incarnate Christ wore.[33] In this sense, her apostolate is one of atonement for other sinners, much like Christ's.[34] But whereas Christ died for atonement, Christina's body must fall short of her saviour's sacrifice; hence, she continues to live through these physical changes. But her body does underscore the same thing that Christ's does: the harmony of body and soul.

Christina's body also provides food miraculously as another way of showing that it could provide for herself and others. Early on, Christina gave up food because she had nothing else to give up for Christ.[35] The *Life* also tells how Christina begged in order to have food to give away. Her desire to have food to feed others shows one way in which she patterned her life upon providing for others. In these situations, she tried to provide for their material existence. In other situations, she provided for their spiritual existence, through miraculous feedings and penitential prayer. This pattern of giving up food was a common element in many women's stories as we will see in later chapters, such as the chapter on Catherine of Siena.[36]

But Christina did not merely forsake food in order to undergo sacrifice; while de Cantimpré emphasized her lack of eating, he also emphasized that her body had became the locus of miraculous feedings for both herself and others. Shortly after her initial resurrection, her sisters and friends bound her in chains because they were afraid of her outlandish behaviour. She escaped, but Thomas explained that because her body was still a normal, natural body, she felt hunger and she prayed for Christ's mercy. Christ then made her own breasts drip 'sweet milk', which sustained her for nine weeks.[37] Elsewhere, the *Life* says that Christina's frustrated sisters placed her in a large wooden yoke that caused festering wounds in her neck and shoulders, which made her so wasted by pain that she did not want to eat the dry bread and water they gave her. In a moment of pity, Christ grants Christina a miracle that helped cure her by means of her body's own fluids:

> Her virginal breasts began to flow with a liquid of the clearest oil and she took that liquid and used it as a flavouring for her bread and she ate it as food and smeared it on the wounds of her festering limbs as an ointment. When her sisters and friends saw this, they began to weep and they struggled no more against the miracles of the divine will in Christina and they released her from her chains and knelt down begging for mercy for their injuries to her and let her go.[38]

The oil that her body exuded helped to heal her in order to allow her to continue to persevere against her family, who tried to prevent her ministry. Curing fluids are a motif in Thomas de Cantimpré and here they take on a sacramental element;[39] in these examples we see Eucharistic moments – her body providing sustaining food through which God's grace is present to help her persevere against her enemies. Normally these would be the functions that the Eucharistic host would provide. In this second instance we read healing and anointing, in a parallel to the sacrament of the healing of the sick. If de Cantimpré's *Life* of Christina was meant to lift her up as an example to the errant clergy of his time, then these sacramental images show God working through a woman (!) to manifest sacramental grace, as opposed to in the sacraments themselves. Below, I will talk more about Christina's relationship with the sacraments of baptism and Eucharist as she encountered them in the institutional church.

The sacraments

Christina lived in a time of growing clericalism, where the priest was given increased significance for his role as the person who could mediate God through sacramental means; this correlated with an increased significance in the priest's role as the only person who could consecrate the Eucharist, and in increased regulation surrounding the states in which a lay person could receive the Eucharist.[40] Christina's life follows a similar role, and her role as one who helps souls through *viaticum* is noticeable throughout the text. Christina's apostolate has aspects that situate it particularly with the dying or dead. As the *Life* says: 'She assisted the dying most willingly and gladly and exhorted them to a confession of their sins, to the fruit of penance, to a hope of everlasting joy, and to a fear of the destroying fire.'[41] A particularly clear example of this apostolate to the dying is seen in her interactions with Count Louis:

> When Count Louis was near death ... the Count pulled himself up with all the strength he could summon and lay fully prostrate before the feet of Christina and, with great lamentation, recited to her all his sins from his eleventh year right up to that very day. He did this not for absolution which she had no power to give but rather that she be moved by this atonement to pray for him.[42]

Christina's role meant she helped shepherd people to the afterlife, and deposit them in purgatory (thus guaranteeing them salvation). In this pericope, her intercessions were on a par with the sacrament of *viaticum*, for they shepherd the count into purgatory. Christina's life centred upon her ability to provide quasi-sacramental moments for her devotees; her reception of the Eucharist coincided with times in which she felt the need for Christ's help and strength, such as when she feared that she was possessed by a demon. For Christina, the Eucharist also highlighted the close connection between the physical and spiritual; at times her intense penitential and fasting practices blended with the fasting required as preparation for receiving the Eucharist.[43]

Christina the demoniac

Christina is alternately described as holy and demoniacally possessed, precisely in order to challenge the notions of traditional forms of feminine holiness: 'Demoniacs, no less than the saints who healed them, offered supernatural confirmation of the church's doctrines, especially those most crucial to the pastoral agenda of Fourth Lateran: the urgency of sacramental confession and the sanctity of the Eucharist.'[44] The authors of medieval texts often played saints and demons off of one another in order to reinforce moral and doctrinal teachings in the religious literature and saints' lives of these times. Saints were obsessed by demons because they tried the saints' sanctity and ultimately proved it; texts depicted demoniacs as sometimes mimicking the powers of saints. The crux of her argument is that Christina *must* be possessed in order for the reader to make sense of her life and behaviour.

Yet the story of Christina provides a different model from the stories of demoniacs even a generation before her. In the early middle ages, demoniacs would be in saints' lives for the purpose of being driven out by the saint and thus show saints' holy powers. Or they would provide spiritual (though not holy) witness to the Godly power of the saint. They served as foils that pointed to the divine power, and would sometimes affirm it in their own declarations; but they did not hold any divinely granted power of their own. In the case of Christina, though, Newman asserts that the difference is that the demoniac is the saint.

Evidence for de Cantimpré depicting Christina as demonically possessed includes her being under the power of constraint by the sacrament and the priest's request.[45] Next, most of her bizarre behaviours such as throwing herself into fires and standing for days in the icy cold Meuse seem to be unique to her: they do not follow patterns of saintly purgative behaviour. There are also two attempts to exorcize Christina in this story. The first occurs early in the narrative, when Christina receives communion and immediately flees the city; she takes off into the wilderness (like the Holy Fools).[46] Second, she takes refuge in a church in Wellen and immerses herself in the baptismal font. Of this, it is said that after she does this, 'she behaved more calmly and was more able to endure the smell of men and to live among them'.[47] In other passages, it is not Christina herself who says she is a demoniac, but it is the people of the community. For instance, the *Life* notes that, 'thinking her to be possessed by demons, the people finally managed to capture her with great effort and to bind her with iron chains and although she endured much suffering and privation, yet [she suffered] even more from the stench of men'.[48]

Yet there still arises the question of whether the category of demoniac is meant to be the overarching explanation for her life, or if it is merely one element that helps to explain some of her more outlandish behaviours. If the main emphasis of Christina's apostolate is her being a demoniac, one would expect the narrative to come to a head at the point of her exorcism, or for the exorcism attempts to form some sort of structuring function. One could also expect that the clerical figures could serve as counterpoints of right practice, whether initially or as converts from the demoniac's own obsessive and excessive mistakes. What we see is a deeper ambiguity with respect to her demonic possession. There is no clear end to the behaviours that might be classified as demoniac. Further, too many of her gifts (such as healing and purgation prayers) are not at all related to her being a demoniac. Like all parts of Christina's life, the cultural background of demoniacs gives us only partial guidance in how to interpret aspects of her behaviour.

Conclusions

Unlike many of the other women we read about in this book, Christina does not give us a self-presentation in the *Life*. Instead of telling us about her own self-perception, the *Life* shows the reader how the thirteenth century viewed a particular woman's apostolate. The fact that it draws a woman's witness that does not follow the conventions of conventual life, or even of beguine life, tells us that it was possible (though probably rare) for women to live outside of traditional moulds of women's roles in church and society (wife, nun, beguine). What undergirds her ability to do this is Thomas' ability to see a theological tradition pointing to her particular expressions of spirituality.

I began this chapter noting that I hoped to base it around the question of the overarching structure, theological emphasis and patterns of Christina's life. In the light of this question, Christina's silence about how she viewed her own work is especially poignant, for what we see is how much Thomas' telling relates her to a few of the devotional practices associated with women such as fasting, bodily miracles involving lactation and feeding, and penitential prayers for the dead. Yet a large part of what undergirds Thomas' telling of the story is also a rather traditional theology – *docere verbo et exemplo* – in which Christina's actions come to indict the men who did not carry out their clerical duties as required, and hence the realm in which she acts sometimes blurs the lines of medieval 'prescribed' practices for women. In addition, the combination of demoniac and saint in the person of Christina blurs the boundaries of the holy and the diabolical.

Adding further to the complexity of this tale is the fact that Thomas does not explicitly relate the architecture of spiritual traditions that he wishes to draw upon. But perhaps the overarching point of the telling of her life seems summed up in a passage about Christ, whose life Christina tries to follow the example of: 'Today Christ has produced something worthy from what had been an insult to himself, for the land has been delivered into shame although it had been consecrated by his Passion.'[49] From the perspective of her hagiographer, the overwhelming hermeneutic of telling Christina's life is that shameful events (such as all her weird behaviours, which Thomas de Cantimpré warns the reader about in the first section) are the opportunity for salvation. In particular, these outrageous acts are necessary where the clergy themselves have fallen from their duties. It is not enough merely that the negligent clergy be chastised by having a woman have to pick up the slack; that she is an outrageous, demoniac woman is one of the ways Thomas means to shame the clergy. The fact that she is not reducible to merely representing one tradition nor reducible to only following the trends of her time (for the desert models were over 800 years before) suggests that Thomas means to offer his writing's subject as a particularly complex offering. Yet Christina is not merely a chastisement to her era's church and society. For the ministry that de Cantimpré portrays in all its complexity is ultimately a life that conforms to a number of different forms of rites of penance: thus, it is a life lived in the service of others for whom it seeks out not division but ultimate reconciliation.

4

Jouster for Love:
Hadewijch of Brabant

Perhaps some of the best-known works of medieval literature are the stories of knights battling for the hearts of fair ladies, tales in which castles keep their inhabitants separate from the world, providing safety for the fair, delicate and defenceless female who is the object of her lover's imagination. These are the stories in which the knights must prove their worth by successfully carrying out quests, battling on the jousting pitch, and slaying beasts. It is into this world that we enter when we read the poetry of the early thirteenth-century woman Hadewijch of Brabant. But instead of her kings and queens being Troilus and Criseyde or Arthur and Guenever, her characters are the three Persons of the Trinity and the human soul. Hadewijch translates the courtly love tradition to the drama of the soul's ascent to God, and in so doing makes courtly poems theologically significant while also vivifying religious literature's use of language to describe the human return to God. At the core of her work are the twinned human and divine desires for each other. Hadewijch's language makes her writings appear quite different from everything else we have seen, but underneath them all is a theological vision that focuses all its attention on human union with God.

Life and writings

Like Richeldis, Hadewijch of Brabant's life remains obscure. Attempts to discover biographical information about her have uncovered 111 religious women named Hadewijch living in the Low Countries in the early thirteenth century. Most likely born in Flanders in the late twelfth century, Hadewijch's writing career flourished between 1220 and 1240.[1] She either founded or joined a group of beguines and became its spiritual mistress. This community was a small group of women leading a life similar to conventual life, except they lived in private houses and held no official status. In this community, we know the names of several of those she found dear, even after she left the community: Hadewijch mentions Emma, Sara and Margriet in one of her letters.[2] At some point while supervising the spiritual development of young beguines, Hadewijch seems to have run into trouble. Both members of her group and outsiders in the larger city community called her authority into question and she left. We have no record of how or when her life ended, although presumably she died in exile from her city and community.[3] While other beguines such as Marie d'Oignies Lutgard of Aywières and Margaret Ypres had *vitae* written by male confessors, unfortunately there is none for Hadewijch that would fill in the missing information about her life.

The beguine communities deserve some explanation, since we will see this term connected with three of the women in this book: Hadewijch, Mechtild of Magdeburg and Marguerite Porete. The term 'beguine' refers not to a recognized order but to a sort of living arrangement with a common purpose. Because of the diffuse nature of this type of devotional life, and because of institutional constrictions placed on the beguines, the movement undertook a number of different types of living arrangements depending on place and time period. There was no real codification of the practices – liturgical, economic or devotional – and there were no central leaders or founders, as there were with the religious orders. The group was mainly a movement in the Low Countries and northern Germany, although one beguine community existed in Norwich, England. The movement began some time in the twelfth century, and lasted until the French Revolution. Because of the diffuse and changing nature of the beguine 'movement', it is useful to identify various stages in it. When the beguine communities began, individual ecstatic women lived scattered about cities such as Liège. These communities began at a time when cities were beginning to be formed, and the new bourgeoisie class began to exert civic power and organize itself in ways that challenged the feudal hierarchy of the early middle ages. As such, these new social forces created space where women found they could gather into economically independent communities that worked in the world, but did not live behind convent walls. The beginnings of beguine living were spontaneous movements with no leaders. These individual women were known as *mulieres sanctae*, holy women – to the people around them.

In the second stage, which probably began some time in the early thirteenth century, these individual women began to organize themselves into congregations based on their spiritual discipline and common tasks. These groups would then submit to a grand mistress in charge of each group that found its economic and devotional patterns in sync. As this began to happen in Europe, the church intervened, insisting that if women were going to build communities they needed to be under the direction of an order. The institutional concern was for these communities going 'astray' and becoming heretics if they were not guided by one of the officially trained keepers of orthodoxy, namely friars. Because these self-employed women came without substantial economic means, and were seen to be a drain on the finances of an order that were to 'adopt' them, no order wanted to take charge of them. Jacques de Vitry became the spokesman for these new foundations, and he helped the beguines receive papal consent to become self-regulated communities.

Yet the story did not end there, for self-regulated communities still presented problems, as the civil and religious authorities wanted these groups to be under the control of the bishops or orders, for these women wielded substantial spiritual power based on their popular reputations of holiness, they held economic power for the work that they did and the goods and services they exchanged, and they provided a number of services within the developing urban communities, including providing health care to the sick and infirm and taking care of the dying. In the last stage, the beguine communities gradually became enclosed, as communities became limited to certain trades, usually around health care. Spiritual guidance was provided by mendicant friars, particularly the Dominicans, and some Cistercian houses in the Low Countries also helped provide spiritual direction to beguinages.

It is within this context that Hadewijch's writings address some unknown group of followers, either beguines or lay folk. Her writings, known through three complete manuscripts and a fourth incomplete one, include 31 letters, 45 poems in stanzas, 412 visions and 16 poems in couplets. Two of the manuscripts include an additional 13 poems in couplets.[4] Her letters are of varying lengths, but in almost all of them she takes an advisory tone that suggests she is responding to people she knows and who respect her advice. Although it is not clear to whom she addressed these letters and advice, in these letters we can see the clearest evidence of her spiritual theology laid out. The longer epistles read like treatises on religious and spiritual problems. Her shorter letters are her most intimate communications and offer practical advice about the occasions that prompted the communications.

Her *Visions* are perhaps the greatest achievement in Dutch artistic prose,[5] but they present several challenges: first, her visionary imagery is far from unique. Most of the images are stock apocalyptic images from Scripture and include images from *Ezekiel* such as the chariot, lambs and eagles, and the New Jerusalem from *Revelation*. Second, we do not know precisely when the *Visions* were written. Scholars tend to date them early in her writing career because of their lack of creative integration of the tradition. This dating is based on the assumption that the longer Hadewijch wrote, the more creative she became in her use of imagery. Yet despite the lack of creative development, the imagery and theological insights of the visions integrate well into the visionary world of her poems.[6] The *Visions* show Hadewijch's theological vision and contain strong religious insights, which tells us that creative development is not the only mark of her writing's development.

It is upon the quality of the style, language and uniqueness of her poems that Hadewijch's reputation is most solidly based. The *Poems in Stanzas* offer reflections on the experience of seeking and obtaining God's love and are written using the imagery and emphases of the courtly love tradition.[7] The *Poems in Couplets* also focus on this theme of the love of God. Their strongly erotic content completely meshes with the divine focus of the narrator. This poetry is among the only Dutch poetry from the late twelfth and early thirteenth centuries to survive the later bourgeoisie purging of courtly love poetry in the Low Countries.[8] Hadewijch's writings were known for several centuries after her life, and were in the libraries of the Canons Regular of Windesheim and the Carthusians of the Dienst house, as well as in the Abbey of Groenendaal, Brussels, founded by the well-known mystic and theologian Jan van Ruusbroek. Her writings influenced the fourteenth-century Dominican theologian Meister Eckhart, before passing into obscurity to be rediscovered in 1838.[9]

Hadewijch and the traditions of love

Hadewijch's central emphasis is love, and she develops conceptions of love in her works that derive from the Christian tradition and from the courtly love tradition. She refers to Augustine, giving the fifth-century theologian the role of a guide who helps mediate the divine message to her. She recognizes that Augustine's theology describes the love God has for the world and the influence God's love has upon the human's love-response to God, yet at the same time she uses the tropes of the courtly love tradition to express the human's longing for return to God. Because love is such a central part of her thought, scholars have read Hadewijch within each of three major traditions of mysticism, all of which identify love as central to the mystical journey. These three traditions are *Wesenmystik* (essence mysticism), *Brautmystik* (bridal mysticism) and *Minnemystik* (love mysticism).

Wesenmystik is a form of mysticism rooted in the negative theology noetic tradition. It catalogues an ascent to God based on apophatic theology; the soul comes to know more and more what it is that it does not and cannot understand about God. Stripping away categories and intellectual assumptions about God is what allows the soul to progress towards God. In this type of mysticism, intellectual or metaphysical constructs serve to direct the soul's progress. As the soul ascends to God, certain categories are stripped away (one such example is the surpassing of the use of images in contemplation). This form of mysticism found expression through thinkers such as Maximus Confessor (sixth century) and Denys (late fifth, early sixth centuries), and the Neo-Platonic theology of John Scotus Eriugena (ninth century), then further developed it and helped make it accessible in the high middle ages to theologians such as William of St-Thierry and Meister Eckhart.

Brautmystik, or nuptial mysticism, makes the soul's mystical marriage to Christ the shaping metaphor of the religious experience. The *Song of Songs* provides a scriptural warrant for these emphases. Just as a marriage is the closest form of relationship between two people, so mystical marriage symbolizes the closest relationship between a person (or the church as a corporate entity) and God in this life. It is often possible to identify the Beloved with God or Christ in Hadewijch's writings; if her writing were only bridal mysticism, though, nuptials would be implied any time Christ appears as the person of the Beloved. But Hadewijch does not mention the specific name of Christ often, nor does she explicitly use bridal themes often.[10] Finding bridal themes in her work often requires extensive re-interpretation of her courtly imagery. *Minne* sounds quite abstract when you read her work; it is certainly not the clearly personified character of the husband-Christ that one sees in the traditional Bridal mystics.

The third type of mysticism, *Minnemystik*, or Love Mysticism, originates in Bernard of Clairvaux, who wrote a series of 86 sermons covering the first half of the *Song of Songs* that sought to explain the role of Love in orienting the human to God. Other Cistercians after him, including John of Ford and Gilbert of Hoyland, further developed Bernard's thought after his death. This type of love mysticism expresses *Minne* as primarily an experience and then moves to personification.[11] The beguines, who were often influenced by the spirituality of the Cistercians, imbibed much of the Cistercian influence on divine love for humans and human loving responses to God. Hadewijch's *Minne* includes elements of this sense of love as an experiencing of God.

Although Hadewijch has some elements in common to each of these types of mysticism, it is the *Minnemystik* to which she most fully belongs. In order to see how she represents this form of mysticism it is important to discern how to read through her widely variable works in order to understand her key themes; the key to Hadewijch's writings is that her letters form a doctrinal core, from which we can understand the themes of the rest of her writings, especially her poetry. Just beyond these core *Letters* are her *Visions*, which overlay her quite orthodox theology with a rich level of Christian symbolism and help show the depth of her understandings of Christology, sacramental theology, sin and forgiveness and the beatific vision, and which convey her overarching sense of love as directing the human return to God and the inner relations of the Trinity. Her poems all presuppose this spiritual and theological core and add onto it the layer of the courtly love themes as a means by which to describe her relationship with God.

Minne *(love) in Hadewijch*

Hadewijch's use of the word *Minne* is unusually complex, and does not assume only one meaning of *Minne*. It refers to God or Christ personified to be the ultimate object of human desire; Hadewijch's use of *Minne* compares with the usage of the monastic scholars of her time, such as Bernard of Clairvaux, who portrayed God as the beloved object of human affections and will.[12] Hadewijch also uses *Minne* to refer to her 'experience'.[13] In still other places, love refers to a bond between the Persons of the Trinity and humans, for 'Hadewijch uses the term *Minne* to indicate the emotion "love" and the actions that follow from it, as well as to plumb the paradoxical and dynamic inner nature of God the Trinity and the identically paradoxical and dynamic nature of the bond between God and human beings.'[14] Norbert de Paepe distinguishes three basic moments in Hadewijch's *Minne*: first, an awareness of distance between *Minne* and herself; second, complete surrender to *Minne*; and, finally, restored balance. Here he has captured one of the main aspects of her love: it is accompanied by both unrest and tumultuousness.

Hadewijch navigates between two well-established sets of metaphors in her use of *Minne*. First is the Augustinian concept of love as the binding force of the Trinity and the forming and binding force between God and creation. Second is the courtly love tradition in which the narrator tells of questing after and winning the beloved. In the first tradition, the quest is spiritualized to describe states of the soul, and love is a force showing mutual binding. In the second, the quest is one of domination and love becomes a tool of winning through its forceful and treacherous ways. The word *Minne* can and does refer to both divine love and human love, for after all these two are ultimately connected, since human love is derived from divine love.[15] Hadewijch intends for *Minne* to be an expansive concept, and she uses it to refer to the beloved as goal, and the means to the beloved, and she also uses love to refer to the relationship a human person has with the divine beloved in its many, varied forms.

The Augustinian tradition of love

Augustine's understanding of love is most clearly summarized in Book VIII of *The Trinity*, in which he summarizes that the Trinity of Father, Son and Holy Spirit can be seen as the Lover, Beloved and the Bond of Love between the Father and Son. Inasmuch as the human desires God and wants to gaze on God in the beatific vision, the human enters into this Trinity of love in heaven. This triune picture of love appears frequently in Hadewijch, not only to talk about the Trinity but to talk about the human response to God. She utters words such as, 'If we loved with love all that Love loves',[16] or 'Nobody who has loved Love with love'.[17] All these express love as tripartite, consisting of the subject, object and bond of love, just as Augustine conceptualizes the divine love in the Trinity. And these are just a few from many similar utterances she makes. Further, all of these quotations hint at Love as a transformative force. Love is something into which the human is initiated, and this initiation is into something both divine and communal.

Augustine appears in Hadewijch's visions to teach her about love. She understands that Augustine's theology is highly erotic in focus and that he sees love as a key attribute of God and humans. In one vision she sees a phoenix swallow a young grey eagle 'with some old feathers' and an old yellow eagle who sports some young feathers. The old yellow eagle is Augustine, and the young grey one is Hadewijch. The phoenix who swallows both of them is the Unity of God. Augustine is like a parent bird who helps nurture Hadewijch, his offspring. She explains the mixed plumage of the two birds: she bears some of Augustine's old feathers as a sign of his influence on her, and 'the young feathers of the old eagle were the renewed splendor he received from me in the new heavenly glory of my love, with which I loved him and so greatly desired with him to pour forth one single love in the trinity, where he himself was burning so totally with an unquenchable love'.[18] That Augustine is the person she united with in the centre of such a vision – and that she goes on to explain how this vision depicts both human union with the Trinity and the social aspects of union between the Persons of the Trinity – is evidence that she understood the central theology of the central book of *The Trinity*, Book VIII: 'The youth that the old feathers that were yellow had signified also the renewal of Love, which continually grows in heaven and on earth.[19] The phoenix that swallowed the eagles was the Unity in which the Trinity dwells, wherein both of us are lost.'[20] She places the older bird in a position of guiding her, but also stresses her own influence upon Augustine, identifying him with some young feathers in her vision, suggesting that as part of the Mystical Body of Christ, he benefited from her own spiritual teachings.

Hadewijch explains that she is united not only with the Trinity but with Augustine, saying 'I was not contented with what my dearly Beloved had just permitted, in spite of my consent and emotional attraction; it weighed on me now that this union with Saint Augustine had made me so perfectly happy, whereas previously I had possessed union from saints and men, with God alone.'[21] Hadewijch passes through this vision to communion with Augustine and continues onward towards God, and this movement allows her to deepen her knowledge of love itself. Community with other humans – even theologically brilliant ones such as Augustine –

is not the end the human ought to seek, but rather community with God is. And if the Augustinian tradition provides her with a theological grounding for her understanding of love, the courtly love tradition provides her with the means both literary and figurative in which to express both love and her quest for God. This literary tradition, with its emphases on the lady being the unobtainable distant woman and the narrator being the knight errant, allowed Hadewijch access to a whole realm of gendered language about God that would ultimately make her discussions of *Minne* more accessible to the female beguines she addressed, precisely because of the role reversals involved in her own use of these tropes.

Courtly love traditions

Her letters as well as her poems in stanzas and couplets make it clear that she was familiar with the rhythms, vocabulary and imagery of the courtly love tradition and chivalry. Scholars debate whether her images of courtly life are based on her having been from the nobility or whether she simply learned them from other writings in the love tradition, but it is clear that her use of the tropes of courtly love shows that she knew of the courtly love traditions regardless of what status she was born into.[22] She writes for women who would have known these traditions, and because she writes about love of God we can tell that she writes for women who are principally interested in religious life and the development of the soul as God's lover. Since her audience would have been one interested in the pursuit of God, she could use the metaphors of the schools in her 'school of love' poems.[23] Scholastic theologians themselves would not have been particularly interested in the courtly love tradition, since it was primarily a secular tradition of poetry and songs, but religious women such as the beguines found nurture in this tradition as much as from the established theological traditions known to lay people.[24]

The courtly love tradition is still being investigated, and it is a tradition whose canonical texts and the tropes of its writing are very much debated by modern literary scholars even today. Gaston Paris coined the term 'courtly love' in 1881 to describe several traditions of secular love poetry. There are three traditions the term encompasses: the troubadour poets who flourished from 1150 to 1210 in the Occitan region of Southern France; the trouvère poets who flourished for a bit longer, 1150–1300, in the northern regions of France; and the trobairitz tradition of women troubadours in the Occitan region. In general, courtly love sang of inaccessible love which demanded an unreserved pledge of love that governed the moral life of the lover.[25] This pledge of love then dictated what types of behaviour were to be expected of the questing lover as well as the beloved, best known through the 'chivalric code'. Common tropes within the imagery of courtly love included: the unattainable lover – usually a woman of high rank (a Lady or Queen) that a knight sought to serve – and the knight's submissive service to love. Courtly love poems frequently included the knight's complaints about the trial and tribulations of love and service, and because of these trials the knight often experienced alternating hope and despair of love. Courtly love poems exude a sense of the all-pervading power of love, even to the point of its being the organizational scheme for the life and strife of the knight. Hadewijch's poetry emphasizes many of the specific virtues upheld by the courtly love tradition, such as fidelity and faithfulness, and service to the lady that one seeks.[26] Service is the virtue of a lover that has been transformed by the love that he has for his lady, and Hadewijch believes that this service is the whole point of being involved with God. A result of this service is good works performed for the beloved.[27] Yet a further aspect of this love is the mutuality and the demanding nature of love. Hadewijch also employs the traditional courtly love themes of the hardships caused by striving for love, heightened by the presence of enemies who want to destroy love.

It is not merely Hadewijch's themes or images that show her familiarity with the courtly love tradition; her poems use both the rhyme schemes, set clichés and set phrases found in the courtly love tradition. Furthermore, her stanzaic forms involve the same complicated rhyme structures as are found in the tradition. Similar to the courtly poetic structures, each poem contains two or three stanzas or parts with enclosed rhymes in each stanza and a final last stanza to sum up the movement of the entire poem.[28] She also employs wordplay between words that sound similar in parallel passages to provide playfulness and strife to her poems, helping them to echo the emotions and actions described therein.

In the courtly love tradition, the unattainability of the beloved is a literary convention; hence the knights perform endless quests to prove their love to a distant beloved they only see in glimpses. However, in Hadewijch the unattainability of God is based on the ontological divide between the all-powerful eternal God and the small, limited creature; God cannot be fully known or experienced by the human during mortal life. The strength of this ontological divide encourages Hadewijch's use of courtly tropes and allows her to emphasize the suffering that she-as-knight-errant undergoes away from her beloved, while also helping her to stress the distance that she must travel – in terms of time and physical separation – before she can (re)unite with her beloved. We see here how the two motifs reinforce one another: the Augustinian motif identifies the goal and the ideal community of the Trinity towards which the human strives. The courtly love tradition provides a means of imagistically expressing it. Yet the courtly love imagery can tend towards an objectification of God, making it seem as if God is available to be conquered, just an object for the human to somehow possess;[29] the courtly love motifs work here precisely because the presence of these Augustinian elements protects Hadewijch from making God a mere creature among God's creatures.

Her relations to contemporary theologians

There were a large number of other contemporary thinkers who influenced Hadewijch's thoughts on love and on the nature of God as beloved. Some of the thinkers her writings refer to include Bernard of Clairvaux, William of St-Thierry, Origen, Augustine, Hugh and Richard of St Victor, and Hildebert of Lavarandin. In some cases, we can trace clear textual references: for instance, Letter 18 incorporates a piece from William of St-Thierry's treatise *On the Nature and Dignity of Love*, in which he expounds upon the two eyes of love (the *via affirmativa*) and reason (the *via negativa*). The eyes of reason can only see what God is not – because discursive reason is limited and cannot comprehend the infinite God. Love does not try to know or define its object and thus can probe further than reason. Her use of William's definitions of the work of love and reason help us to see whose notions of love from contemporary writings influenced her own; her incorporation of a piece of his text indicates that Hadewijch had access to at least some theological writings and could make use of them.

Perhaps Hadewijch's strongest theological contribution is her avoidance of the dichotomies and hierarchies that were so often prevalent in medieval theology, and which grew out of the Augustinian traditions that denigrated matter and opposed it to spiritual or intellectual. The medieval feudal model organized everything – including people – in a hierarchy that assigned each a special place. For humans, the medieval world divided them into three estates or social classes. Among men, the first estate consisted of clergy, the second consisted of nobles, and third was peasants and all others. Women were similarly classified according to the estates of virgin, widow and wife. In a like manner, the Neo-Platonic tradition taught that the human was composed of a hierarchy as well: the human body was not as noble as the soul, and the soul was governed by its own rational faculty. This philosophical hierarchy dictated that even the human body was something to be transcended. Hadewijch's writings, however, find the physical helpful in the human's love of God.

Another dichotomy that Hadewijch inherited involved the distinction between affective experience and contemplative experience, as well as the further gendering of these two types of prayer. The affective experience was one in which the emotional response of the recipient was most important; the contemplative experience favoured the human's absorption into the divine presence. The affective was an outer experience, and being outer it was therefore a 'lower' experience, and therefore womanly, as compared to the contemplative, which – being intellectual, inner and higher – was therefore masculine.[30] Hadewijch's own writings keep the affective and contemplative in tension, giving neither a dominance over the other. All these dichotomies come together in Hadewijch's unifying view, which allows her to see all of them passing away through the unifying power of divine love.

Suffering

Suffering was a common trope in courtly love, because the one who loves suffers when he cannot be present with the beloved he seeks. Hadewijch uses the idea of suffering to emphasize the already/not yet character of love for God; love will be fulfilled only when she gazes forever on her Beloved in the beatific vision.[31] Until then, God is (at least partially) absent and this causes her to suffer.[32] Her exploitation of the notions of presence and absence contrasts with the understanding of love that monks such as Bernard of Clairvaux emphasized in their nuptial theology: in his theology, fulfilment is imminent. In the case of Hadewijch, she suffers because she does not have a promise of imminent fulfilment. Lady Love causes Hadewijch to suffer by her distance, by her tempestuous nature, which is demanding, sometimes even abusive (it buffets her with blows,) and suggests that love can always be taken away.[33]

This unstable nature of love causes constant buffets of longing and suffering for the one seeking her. Hadewijch's ideas here parallel Richard of St Victor's *Four Degrees of Violent Charity*.[34] Love is a conquering force, even within the Trinity where the Persons of the Trinity attempt to conquer one another; the internal economy of God is the reciprocal demand made by love that love be given in return.[35] Outside the Trinity, this same love forces itself upon Hadewijch, and is the cause both of great joy and also suffering, as she is literally forced to do its bidding, making her an alien to other humans. Hadewijch explains that the one bound to love has to choose an allegiance to love over-and-against other humans: 'If you wish to follow Love, at the urging of your noble nature, which makes you desire me in totality, it will become so alien to you to live among persons, and you will be so despised and so unhappy, that you will not know where to lodge for a single night, and all persons will fall away from you and forsake you.'[36] Elsewhere, she explains that the human who comes to perfection exhibits a growing likeness to God that causes suffering.[37] In the poems of the courtly love tradition, all the players must ultimately submit to the power of love, but this submission leads to empowerment; submission allows the knight in turn to conquer and subdue love ultimately.[38] For Hadewijch, submission allows the human to love rightly and more fully, and it ensures her beloved will receive her into heaven after death. Yet as the lover grows more like God, she grows less like other human beings, and so her sufferings from other humans increase precisely as she grows in her love relationship with God. Human suffering is like a see-saw: as the sufferings caused by God grow less, the sufferings caused by humans grow greater. Yet Hadewijch believes that all types of suffering will pass away in the society of heaven. Until that time, Hadewijch envisions a world divided into those who seek love and those who do not.

Hadewijch's spirituality has its deep roots in the pain and suffering of the human for the beloved. Suffering is a key moment in which the human becomes transformed because it tests the reserve of the human in her determination to seek God. Throughout Hadewijch's works, we find passages such as 'Suffer gladly, in all its extent, the pain God sends you; thus you will hear his mysterious counsel, as Job says of him: *You have spoken to me a hidden word.*'[39] Elsewhere, Hadewijch writes that she both suffers for others and suffers in order to ascend to love:

> And if you wish to turn with me to Love,
> See in what suffering I have borne
> What you were unready to suffer.[40]

But Hadewijch is not the only one who suffers; in the Incarnation, Christ also experienced suffering. Hadewijch unites the trope of suffering she had inherited from literature with the theological idea of the imitation of Christ, thus giving theological content to suffering. Christ was an alien among other humans with no place to lay his head; those who would follow him must aspire to be like this. God causes suffering for the human who seeks God, but it is part of the shape of the life God took on in the Incarnation and thus is part of the shape of the life that the human must also take to follow Christ's example. Rather than identify with the weakness of Christ through illness, Hadewijch identified with his weakness through the tropes of persecution and loneliness.[41] For Hadewijch, as well, suffering lifts her to likeness and also gives her (she thinks) the prerogative to ask God to release condemned souls.[42] Her ideas parallel the Augustinian notion of the two cities and their citizens; while Hadewijch lives on earth, she is a stranger from her heavenly home. Thus, she will never find true rest, peace or happiness until the final union with her beloved. Only then will her longings and her sufferings be over.

Gender and its uses

Hadewijch's courtly love imagery must bring us to consider how Hadewijch as a writer uses gender in her writings. In the *Poems in Couplets*, her narratorial voice is decidedly female, as it is in the visions and letters. The narrator describes being inexperienced in love and therefore not a great authority. These humility formulae are not connected to her female gender, unlike Hildegard's use of humility formulae; Hadewijch believes only someone in spirit with God truly has authority to speak of God. But Hadewijch's use of gender also stands out in several unique manners: she never refers to herself as a 'poor female'. In fact, she identifies herself with Mary Magdalene, the '*apostola apostolorum*' (apostle to the apostles).[43] This medieval title for Mary Magdelene refers to her receiving instructions from Christ at his tomb to go forth and tell the apostles that he was risen; the Magdelene was the first evangelist of the Resurrection. Hadewijch draws upon the theological tradition in which women such as Mary Magdelene had unique evangelical vocations to the service of Christ.

Furthermore, in the poems in stanzas, where the courtly love theme is the guiding metaphor, Hadewijch uses a male narratorial voice. In most courtly poetry, the object of love is female and the one who is questing is male, although in the *trobairitz* tradition, the genders were often reversed, with the object being male and pursued by a female. Hadewijch also uses male pronouns to refer to the narratorial voice. The significance of this is that it means the guiding trope of her writings – the courtly love tradition – affects her sense of self-description and her sense of how to describe the divine. But when Hadewijch does use female pronouns to refer to the questing narrator, she uses masculine pronouns to refer to 'Lady Love'.[44]

The gender reversal in which Hadewijch describes herself as a male suggests that she was writing for an intended female audience. Many male writers, such as Bernard of Clairvaux, used gender reversal in their writings or sermons, identifying themselves as female and using this as a way to talk about them uniting with (the male) Christ in union. This gender reversal had two main aspects to it: first, by calling the male voice female, it was symbolically stripping it of the inherent power medieval society associated with maleness. Second, by taking a female persona, these writers were de-familiarizing their discussion of love of the divine, keeping the monks being preached to from relying solely on their paradigms of previous love experiences. In Hadewijch and others, the reversal of gender works differently. If she were merely to claim a male voice, she would in fact be claiming power, so her gender reversal here must work in a more oblique manner. If she is to use a male narratorial voice, she must use it in a situation in which a male has little or no power. Here the courtly love tradition fits well, for the male is the one seeking but being withheld from union by physical separation from the female. Additionally, the world of the questing male emphasizes the absurd and otherworldly nature of the human relations with God.[45]

Conclusions

> I wish to write something
> By which we may learn to recognize
> Great marks of spiritual love,
> And also find a great example
> In what union she [the seeker] gave herself to Love.[46]

This is the primary goal of Hadewijch: to give an example that will serve as a guide for how God loves humans, and therefore how humans should reciprocate. This example comes from the courtly tradition as much as it comes from Christianity: 'It is in her representation of the lived experience of *Minne* that Hadewijch explodes the boundaries of the troubadour tradition. *Minne*, for Hadewijch, is a Being, Lady Love, not the personification of an abstract idea and not the forbidden wife of the vassal's lord.'[47] Her vision of love is also beyond the limits of Christian representations up to her time.

There are many aspects of Hadewijch that still deserve more discussion here and elsewhere. Among these is Hadewijch's use of the tropes of hungering and devouring repeatedly in her poems and letters as images of love for God and her search for God.[48] Hadewijch's God is one that the human relentlessly ought to pursue, a God who is worth all the energies of the human. In the pursuit of God, Hadewijch explains that the human will only glimpse God as the absent beloved for most of the courtship. The few moments the questor basks in his beloved's presence fill him with illimitable joy that then turns to sorrow, anguish and acute suffering when the lovers are once again parted. Only a union that is indissoluble will ever fully satisfy this anguished lover, and it is for such a union that he seeks. This union only God the beloved can grant; and God fully wants to grant such visions in the afterlife, and promises this to those who continue faithfully to quest for God. Hadewijch says that the greatest danger is to try to avoid pain, and indeed this informs her view of the cosmos as well as the ways in which she sees God working to bring the human to unity.[49] Ultimately, Hadewijch's view is one of optimism and joy, even in the face of being treated ill by love, for, after all, it is love that is treating her that way and she knows the project of God will be victorious, and that the creature's joy will always be the outcome.[50]

5

Divine Lover:
Mechtild of Magdeburg

The *Flowing Light of the Godhead* represents in concrete form Mechtild of Magdeburg's (1207–82) training as a beguine: be in the world, but not of it. Her book expounds this idea both through its words and through the ways it blends the inherited literary forms and conventions of the courtly love tradition with the theology of union of the monastic Christian traditions. Mechtild of Magdeburg's *Flowing Light of the Godhead* synthesizes the courtly love traditions with theological insights in much the same way as Hadewijch of Brabant, but with different emphases: Mechtild forefronts the religious dimensions of her work, using its borrowings from courtly literature as decoration. Thus, the tropes of courtly love do not run as deep in her work, and courtly images of love for God are mixed with more traditional Biblical and theological images for love. Mechtild's work mirrors how the book of nature teaches humans about their end in God, God's role in the guiding of the universe, and God's sheer superabundance itself.[1]

Her life

Originally born to a family of minor nobility, Mechtild first received a call to religious life at age 12, although she did not acknowledge it until about age 22. Her call came in the form of daily visions of God, which continued from age 12 to 43.[2] These would later become the fodder for the *Flowing Light of the Godhead*. In 1230, when she was about 23, Mechtild left home and moved to Magdeburg, Lower Saxony, to become a beguine. She does not tell us why Magdeburg was her new home; all she says is that she knew only one person there, whom she assiduously avoided. Magdeburg most likely offered her isolation from family and friends so she could pursue her ascetical and religious devotions without interference.

Around 1270, Mechtild left the beguines of Magdeburg and entered the Cistercian convent of Helfta, Eisleben, Saxony. The situation surrounding her move is unclear, but it seems that Mechtild left Magdeburg because of divisions among the beguines in Magdeburg; moving to a convent for her final years would have made sense from a health perspective as well, for she could receive convalescent care more easily in a community than while living alone. At the convent of Helfta, Mechtild of Magdeburg became friends with the Cistercian chantress, mystic and writer Mechtild of Hackeborn (see chapter 7), who was around 30 years old when Mechtild of Magdeburg joined the community, and the mystic, writer and theologian Gertrud of Helfta, who was yet a teenager. It was after Mechtild of Magdeburg's arrival at the monastery that the Helfta community became known as a place of writing;[3] she collaborated with these other two women in a number of writing projects.

Her book

Mechtild of Magdeburg's book presents nearly as many challenges as does the paucity of information about her, because the *Flowing Light of the Godhead* offers very little sense of structural unity. Mechtild wrote *The Flowing Light of the Godhead* in pieces, on individual pages; it includes writings in many different genres, including mystical visions, letters, allegories, parables, reflections, prayers, criticism and advice. Although Mechtild refers to it as a 'book', there is little to connect the various parts of her composition.[4] One cannot find unity in terms of chronological exposition of her visions, nor is there unity of genre, nor is there a clear 'plot' of spiritual ascent. Although some of the books appear to circle around particular themes, such as Book VI's discussions of afterworldly punishments, it isn't the only theme in that book, nor is that the only book in which Mechtild plumbs the topic. Often, Mechtild's literary styles mix, even in the middle of passages: a passage may begin in poetry and end in prose, or move between monologue and dialogue.

Mechtild says that she composed the *Flowing Light of the Godhead* in response to a request from God that she record her visions. Her comments suggest that what follows finds a unity in God's request, if not in imagery, time, place or anything else. It is thus in the unity that is God that the unity of this text is grounded. Mechtild describes this divine command that set her to writing:

> I was warned against writing this book.
> People said:
> If one did not watch out,
> It could be burned.
> So I did as I used to do as a child.
> When I was sad, I always had to pray.
> I bowed to my Lover and said: 'Alas, Lord,
> Now I am saddened all because of your honor.
> If I am going to receive no comfort from you now,
> Then you led me astray,
> Because you are the one who told me to write it'.[5]

Mechtild realized the divine command to write engendered the very real danger of death as a heretic. The passage states that Mechtild did in fact receive criticism when she began to write. Because of this divine imperative, Mechtild explains that the array of images in her book are not mere wordcraft (as it would be in the case of courtly literature without a divine focus or orientation). Rather, her writing is an expression of both physical and spiritual truths that she has received from God: 'I do not know how to write, nor can I, unless I see with the eyes of my soul and hear with the ears of my eternal spirit and feel in all the parts of my body the power of the Holy Spirit'.[6] Mechtild explains that it is the things of the spirit – those things she senses not by her physical senses, but by her spiritual senses – that are what God intends for her to write. Thus, the absence of extensive autobiographical passages is in keeping with her insistence that God has commanded precisely what she write. The book is about God, and the visions God has granted; it is not about the historical Mechtild.

But Mechtild has two acts of obedience: she obeys both God's command to write and her own confessor's command to write. When Mechtild's confessor Heinrich of Halle ordered her to write, she spent the next 15 years writing on loose sheets in her native low German and then handed these loose sheets to Heinrich to compile into book form. She had written the first four parts of the *Flowing Light of the Godhead* by 1250 (when the visions ceased). Books 5 and 6 took the next 19 years to write. When Mechtild retired to Helfta at age 63, the first six books were circulating; she wrote Book 7 while in the convent of Helfta. Mechtild's confessor Heinrich edited the first six books very little. Although she wrote in Low German, shortly after her death a Latin translation was made (1290), as well as a High German translation made by Henry of Nordingen in the fourteenth century. All of this tells us that the text we have is a mediated version of Mechtild's own work, although one that is probably close to what she wrote.

Mechtild was not a systematic writer. To try to read her as one is to miss much of what makes her language so poetic and startling. One such problem that arises is the voice of the narrator, for sometimes the voice appears to be Mechtild's and at other times it sounds like a divine voice. Thus, figuring out who is speaking in some places (God, Mechtild, an allegorical character, or some other person such as a saint) can be difficult. We must separate the narratorial voice from the historical personage of Mechtild, for it is not clear that any (or all) of the book is necessarily autobiographical. Furthermore, Mechtild repeatedly defers to God as the principle (and only) author of the book.[7] Thus, the narratorial voice presents multiple opportunities to trip up a reader who looks for a unified voice; key among these is the fact that the voice of Mechtild herself contains none of the markers of authority we would normally hear in the voice of the author of a text. Because Mechtild was female, she had none of the traditional markers of authority, such as being male or having clerical status. Even among women, she was not in an order nor did she have a title such as Abbess that would give her some power.[8]

For this reason, some modern scholars have suggested that the contemporary philosopher Mikhail Bahktin helps provide a theoretical framework for understanding Mechtild's book. In the absence of a clear form to her book, and one narratorial voice, Bahktin's notion of heteroglossia can help to at least make sense of the variety of forms within the *Flowing Light of the Godhead*, allowing the reader to see it as one work.[9] In his idea of heteroglossia, Bahktin claims that there can be a variety of different forms within a larger work; for example, a 'novel' allows a variety of sub-forms within it, such as diary entries, poems, letters and pictures.[10] Thus, one can understand Mechtild's larger 'work' to comprise many different sub-forms. This sidesteps the question of how the work fits together by just accepting that it does, allowing discussion to move forward.

Yet even once we can view the collection of writings in the *Flowing Light of the Godhead* as one work, the question still remains concerning what overarching genre the work most clearly represents or resembles. Multiple scholars have tried to posit genres into which to fit the work. The book has alternately been read as a diary, a book of spiritual ascent, the 'poetry of meditation' or even a *confession*, such as Augustine's *Confessions*, in addition to other forms. The *Flowing Light* may well have had its origins in writings of some sort of diary: the force of her writing comes from the way her writings repeatedly circle around a number of themes, probing each topic slightly differently with each pass. And within each pass over a topic, Mechtild appears to gain new insights, and the different forms her writing takes appear to help with that. This unsystematic discussion may well result from diary-like musings on various topics and theological ideas, such as the love affair between the soul and God, paying homage to God and the saints, visions of God, the virtues and vices, and the afterworld.

Ruh and Haas recommend reading the *Flowing Light* as a *confession* in the Augustinian sense (confessing sin and offering an act of faith and praise of God, while centred around the development of an 'I' in the text). Rather than her conversion being one of becoming baptized, as was the case with Augustine, it initiates her into a life fully devoted to God.[11] The text that unfolds is then an exploration of the inner life that follows such a dedication. Another scholar, Elizabeth Andersen, takes a different approach and thinks that the book's unity lies in the narratorial voice rather than in its literary form.[12] She notes that the narratorial voice assumes a number of different roles, such as prophet, visionary, teacher, critic, lover, counsellor and mediator. This unity of narratorial voice is found by Andersen to be rooted in a distinct author with a unity of authorial intent rather than in a unity of form. In order to read a uniformity of authorial voice, she has to read the allegorizations of the *Flowing Light* as all referring back to the historical person of Mechtild. In so doing, she ignores Mechtild's words that God is the author and Mechtild is, at best, a channel. To re-read the book as Andersen does is to downplay the divine origin of the work – which is precisely what Mechtild needed to emphasize in order to establish authority – and reframe the point of reference from the inner divine life of the Trinity to human experiences of God. A better proposal for how to read this comes from Catherine Gardner, who notes that the idea of shared authorial responsibility for this work makes sense. Gardner points to the ontological connection between the Divine origin (for God is love) and its identity with the love that flows outward as the message to all Christians. Mechtild would have shared in this divine love, both as the person to whom it was revealed and as the messenger of the book.[13] Searching for a unity in voice or form, then, has to include a recognition that this unity must encompass the multiplicity of the human and divine, for they work in concert here.

When considering the genre and voice of this book, scholars have uniformly overlooked the most basic work of comparison: the Bible. Composed through a variety of 'narrators' (and accordingly read either as divinely inspired or as God's exact words), with utterances of poetry, prose, prophecy, even the (secular) love *Song of Songs*, prayers, canticles (such as Miriam's and Anna's), praise and lament, the Bible shows how a unified book can contain a whole variety of literary forms and styles within one work. We must also recognize that the Bible was the main text with which Mechtild was familiar. This comparison helps us make sense of her claims that God was the sole author, and that the *Flowing Light* is a physical extension of God.[14] Her language echoes the theology of Aquinas, that the Scriptures were a second type of Incarnation of Christ.[15] This is a rather bold claim, but also a rather topical one, for the claim that direct inspiration for special revelations makes is that it has a divine origin (just like the Bible).

Courtly love in Mechtild

Mechtild is the link between Hildegard and the *Minnemystik* of women such as Hadewijch. Her link to Hildegard is through her overarching sense of a cosmic and symbolic vision of the universe, which presents an epic describing salvation.[16] Mechtild envisions the Trinity's *Jubilus* as God's response to God's own superabundance, and it catches up the human soul into its joy by using the moment of *Jubilus* to be the moment of God's creation of the soul. The human is the direct product of God's love and joy, and Mechtild reports that the human continues to act within the sphere of God's superabundant love. Mechtild's link to individuals such as Hadewijch is through her use of the courtly love tropes, which appear extensively in the *Flowing Light of the Godhead*. She uses the language of courtly culture, its life and customs, to create metaphors of the human experience. The soul's journey to God is a journey into a prince's court, and her mystical experiences of being in the presence of God are expressed in the language and imagery of courtly love. Mechtild offers images of herself as the lover of God, whom she imagines as emperor, king, knight and lord. Most often, God is the king of the high court of heaven. But these images are precisely that: they are merely descriptive vehicles for describing God and the human; unlike Hadewijch, who integrates the imagery of courtly love into the soul's journey, Mechtild does not.

Underlying her descriptions of God and the eros of the soul is not only the courtly love tradition, but also the language of the Augustinian tradition and the monastic traditions of *Song of Songs* commentaries.[17] Mechtild uses highly erotic language to describe the relationships between the Persons of the Trinity as well as the relationship between God and the human soul. Some of her images come directly from Scripture, such as the inebriation of the soul from the *Song of Songs*, which describes the pinnacle of mystical union.[18] Her visions also include a number of other forms of memorable sensory descriptions of heaven, hell and purgatory, where Mechtild interacts with the souls in each place. In one vision of purgatory, for instance, Mechtild described the atmosphere, saying that it was 'as grim a place as ever was seen by human eye – a horrifying bath, a mixture of fire and pitch, of much, smoke, and stench. A thick fog was drawn over it like a black hat. The souls were lying in it like toads in filth. Their form was like that of humans, and yet they were spirits and had about them a similarity to the devil.'[19] But after Mechtild provides this description of purgatory, Christ reminds her of the blessed souls destined for 'a mountain covered with flowers. There they shall find more happiness than I know how to express.'[20]

Mechtild also structures her visions according to her own numerology (or gematria) allowing numbers with Christian significance to provide literary conceits for short pericopes. There is a long tradition dating to the earliest days of Christianity in which numbers with especial Christian significance figure prominently in Christian theology. Augustine uses numbers such as one (signifying the unity of God), two (the dual natures of Christ) and three (the Trinity), when he expounds upon music, harmony and revelation in his treatise *On Music*. Mechtild uses each chosen number to direct a series of parallel phrases, sentences or lines of poetry within a section. The result is an intensification of her ideas and feelings through repetition. For example, Mechtild says to God:

> You are my softest pillow,
> My most lovely bed,
> My most intimate repose,
> My deepest longing,
> My most sublime glory.
> You are an allurement to my Godhead,
> A thirst for my humanity,
> A stream for my burning.[21]

In this example, each of the descriptions is the human's experience of God providing something good, restful or joyful for her; they serve not as a logical argument but achieve their strength through their cadences and parallelism. There are hundreds of examples of these lists throughout the *Flowing Light*. Some other examples include the 20 powers of God's love,[22] the eight virtues,[23] 16 kinds of love,[24] seven kinds of perfection,[25] and the five praises God gives to the soul.[26] These are not stages, nor are they true organizing principles. Rather, her use of significant numbers in these schemes aims to show God's ordering and repetitive patterns in creation. In conjunction with the wide variety of her images, these numbering structures speak to Mechtild's sense of the sheer plenitude of God's providential care for the individual soul.

Alongside these other literary devices, we also see several courtly themes. In her vision of Christ's crown, Mechtild sees all people from lowly peasants up to nobility.[27] The imagery that she uses to describe the world she envisions is the language of courtly love, to which she adds theological content. She also uses imagery that is based upon the clothing of court.[28] She describes the wooing of the bride by the bridegroom.[29] She uses the imagery of the hunt.[30]

Because Mechtild envisions God as her suitor, she uses sexual imagery to describe her closeness to God. As far back as the Bible, sexual imagery served to express the intimacy of humans with God himself. In one such dialogue between Mechtild and her spouse, Christ tells his bride:

> 'Stay, Lady Soul.'
> 'What do you bid me, Lord?'
> 'Take off your clothes.'
> 'Lord, what will happen to me then?'
> 'Lady Soul, you are so utterly formed to my nature
> That not the slightest thing can be between you and me.'[31]

Anything that creates distance between the creature and God (here, this distance is symbolized by 'clothes') needs to be removed. This intimacy that God offers Mechtild is the intimacy of naked lovers lying together in bed. She places the desire for intimacy in Christ's mouth, not hers, suggesting that the human, made in the image of God, is already very intimate with God. Mechtild believes the relationship between God and the soul is best described as that of a bride and bridegroom, and this influences the way she talks of relations between the Persons of the Trinity and the human soul. Thus she reports, 'then the Holy Spirit spoke to the Father: "Yes, dear Father, I shall deliver the bride to your bed".[32] Such erotic imagery is not for the sake of mere pleasure (as the courtly love tradition was). Rather, its purpose is to entice or seduce the human soul into a relationship with Christ. Here also, the language of the courtly love tradition is not easily distinguishable from Christian language (from the Bible and authors such as Augustine and the monk Bernard of Clairvaux) that used love and erotics to describe the relationship of the human soul to God. Unlike the other two women associated with the beguines that I discuss (Hadewijch and Marguerite), Mechtild used nuptial imagery. In her writings, we sense a warm, marital relationship between Mechtild and God that is both free of the vexation that Hadewijch points to and is much more personalized than the elusive and abstract allegory of Marguerite.

Mechtild's constructions of gender offer a glimpse into how she theologically manipulates societal constructions of weakness and strength. Many passages in the *Flowing Light of the Godhead* show Mechtild constructing herself as a 'mere wretched woman'.[33] These passages turn her female identification not into an apology but into a recognition of her role of prophet. Biblical prophets were usually people who stood just outside society, and who came to correct it. They were not kings or people in power. She identifies with the lack of power associated with the prophet, and thereby accepts her own role of prophet. She sees herself sent to correct those who should have power but are misusing it; her being female is a sign of her humility despite the elevation of her prophetic mission.

Human relationship to God

Looming over all her writing is Mechtild's strong theological focus. The whole purpose of Mechtild's dalliances with God here is to lead to an eternal dalliance with God in the afterlife. In support of this, Mechtild's writings echo the Neo-Platonism of Denys, which imply a particular metaphysics: the human originates from God, goes forth and must return to God. This cosmology is summed up in her vision where heavenly beings orbit their creator (who is their gravitational midpoint), facing inwards towards that centre.[34] Mechtild says of the human:

> God has created all creatures to live according to their nature.
> How, then, am I to resist my nature?
> I must go from all things to God,
> Who is my Father by nature,
> My Brother by his humanity,
> My Bridegroom by love,
> And I his bride from all eternity.[35]

Human nature thus 'hard-wires' people to return to their creator, God. Mechtild's description of God as the bridegroom evidences how this theological–cosmological structure becomes secondarily overladen with the courtly love image of a bride and bridegroom to explain Mechtild's focus upon return to God by the power of the Christian mystical union. The result is that Mechtild uses the courtly imagery to emphasize the eros of the final union; in so doing, she shows the courtly language can describe the advancing states of the soul.

The soul's progress (with or without the body)

Mechtild's narrative begins as a dialogue that fragments the human: the body stays behind while the soul attempts to commune with God. Only as the body is left behind does the soul discourse with God and pass beyond the vision of the Trinity into the secret place where the soul can play with God. Union with God increasingly requires a division within the human to the point of the annihilation of all bodily desires. Also distancing the body and soul is the lopsided way in which the soul and body are transformed at different rates.[36] Mechtild records that the soul transforms first into something beautiful, bold, daring, powerful, lovely, generous, holy, content and satisfied, while the body still waits to be transformed.[37]

The transformation of the soul takes place through the imitation of Christ, which Mechtild explains as spiritual poverty and humility. As these two virtues suggest, Mechtild's idea of how to imitate Christ involves just the soul and its virtues, not the whole human being of body, soul and spirit. Her dichotomy of body and soul grows into a full dialectic theology in which she views the body as cursed and a hindrance to the soul's spiritual progress towards God. This spiritual progress occurs through a virtue in the soul of spiritual poverty, in which humility draws the soul up again into the abyss.[38] Imitation of Christ's humility (and hence humanity) is the way to Christ's divinity (and hence glory).[39] It is through the paradoxes of humility that she associates herself with the humanity of Christ or with her own humility (as we saw above in the humility formulae surrounding being a poor female).[40] Once this occurs, the soul surpasses the humanity of both Mechtild and Christ in favour of all things spiritual.

This paradoxical praxis also announces itself in other ways: Mechtild's mysticism is one of ascension and descension, absence and presence.[41] The works of love move the divine downward towards humans and they move the human upward towards God so that both the human and the divine are moved towards each other by love. In her discussion of ascent, the dichotomy of body and soul grows into a full dialectic theology in which Mechtild curses the body as a hindrance to the soul's spiritual progress towards God.[42] In her estimation, the human soul becomes identified with the historical, embodied Jesus through the sufferings that happen to it. Here suffering is not because the body is in pain; rather, suffering occurs because she still has a body. She explains: 'The way of pain is necessary because of the embodiment of humans, which can not sustain the eternal embrace of God without suffering and death, and because of their sinfulness, which must be purified in love and suffering.'[43]

Anticlericalism

One last theme that resounds clearly in Mechtild's writings are her strong words of condemnation regarding various practices of the church. Anticlericalism was a common enough phenomenon that it was not necessarily seen as a mark of heresy in Mechtild's time. There were definitely groups that were antisacerdotalists (people who denied the efficacy of the sacraments), and heretics who were anticlerical. Some of the clergy were ill-educated; others lived lavish lives at the expense of their parishioners. Others flaunted rules regarding clerical celibacy, while still others were unable to preach with authority. Other social factors also accounted for anticlericalism: the tensions due to rapid social change and central-ization of the church's authority also contributed to genuine calls for reform that took on anticlerical tones. Rapid social change meant that towns were being built up by new money under the commercial revolu-tion; as these towns were constructed, the episcopal authorities for the local area would create new taxes to support the building of churches and cathedrals. But during Mechtild's time, the church was centralizing its authority in new ways; more money from the collection of tithes was sent back to Rome or given to those levels of the church hierarchy such as bishops, cardinals and the Pope that the bourgeoisie associated with the aristocracy. The bourgeoisie also saw the church's demands for money as demands for power that competed with their own attempts at authority. Complaints about clergy often had much to do with power and class; a common call among reformers of this time (including Saint Dominic and Saint Francis) was a call to a return of evangelical poverty among the clergy at all levels. The concern was that a clergy that lived 'high on the hog' would be too far removed from the average person to whom they ministered. Along with money came power: the church was consolidat-ing power over the local clergy by introducing a system of canon law that regulated clerical behaviour and by formulating more clearly doctrine in such a way as to identify 'dissent' from orthodoxy. One way in which this was expressed was the development of universities and a systematizing of theology. This new intellectualism of the clergy meant that it became more removed from the simple messages preached to the people as the discussions among the theologians in the universities became increas-ingly specialized. As a result, the changes in the church structure began to mimic the class divisions in society, increasing the concerns of some that certain parts of church hierarchy saw themselves as entitled. Conversely, at this time, the friars were very popular preachers for their ability to preach the Gospel with authority and their apostolic poverty.

Mechtild is not alone in her attacks on clergy; Hildegard also saw herself as called because those in charge of the church were not leading it adequately and had fallen by the wayside. Mechtild of Magdeburg held a similar self-perception to Hildegard. She saw those who led the church as stagnant and intellectual rather than loving. In one passage she commented that God does not bestow special gifts or revelations on the scholastic theologians; rather, God grants special revelations to humble people:

Daughter, many a wise man, because of negligence
On a big highway, has lost his precious gold
With which he was hoping to go to a famous school.
Someone is going to find it.
By nature I have acted accordingly many a day.
Wherever I bestowed special favors,
I always sought out the lowest, most insignificant, and most
    unknown place for them.
The highest mountains on earth cannot receive the revelations
    of my favors
Because the course of my Holy Spirit flows by nature downhill.
One finds many a professor learned in scripture who actually is
    a fool in my eyes.
And I'll tell you something else:
It is a great honor for me with regard to them, and it very
    much strengthens Holy Christianity
That the unlearned mouth, aided by my Holy Spirit, teaches the
    learned tongue.[44]

In this way, she makes the claim that she is much wiser than the foolish scholastic; her authority comes directly from God, whereas the scholastic's authority is limited, derivative and partial. It is the Holy Spirit's 'run off' from humble mystics such as her that is granted to the theologians. Other groups within the institutional church that come under Mechtild's attack include traditional cloistered monastics.[45] Mechtild also criticizes the church in her time, saying that those who serve the church lack good works and zeal, and put their own interests before the interests of God.[46]

Purgatory

Perhaps some of her strongest theological imagery came in the form of her descriptions of purgatory. Purgatory was first defined officially at the Council of Lyons in 1274 as a place where those who were promised salvation would go to be purged of their sins before being able to enter the company of heaven. Hell would result in eternal damnation, but those in purgatory were destined to be saved after release from their sins. This same council was also the start of when the beguines began to be subject to censure, as the document *Collectio de scandalis ecclesiae* records. We have seen earlier women such as Christina of St Trond work as intercessors for those in purgatory, and Mechtild also makes it a special function of her work. The central place that the expiation of sins carries in her work is evident from the fact that Mechtild writes about more than a dozen visions of purgatory.[47]

Much of the *Flowing Light of the Godhead* focuses on the afterlife and emphasizes the porosity of the veil between the living and the dead. Mechtild describes how demons and humans in hell help to rightly order the actions of those still living. And the intercessions of Mechtild helped free the souls of those in purgatory. The tradition of visions of heaven and hell was a well-established theological genre, as the chapter on Christina of St Trond has already shown.[48] But Mechtild takes prayers for the departed a step further than even Christina had taken them, for she repeatedly prays for souls in hell.[49] Mechtild, like Julian after her, held some form of unease with the notion of a loving deity who would condemn sinners to hell. By praying for the damned, Mechtild hopes to still win the release of their souls, presuming that the charity and mercy of God can trump God's justice.[50]

Conclusions

Mechtild has been described as a second apex in charismatic theology in the middle ages, the first peak being Hildegard and the third being Meister Eckhart.[51] This adulation and praise is due in part to her known influence on Meister Eckhart.[52] Hildegard, as we saw in chapter 3, was a prophet, visionary and cosmological thinker. Eckhart was a mystic who wrote about the soul's ability to know and love God, and he was a popular Dominican preacher who preached both in the vernacular and in Latin, to lay and religious audiences. To compare her to Hildegard highlights the wide variety of types of writing that Mechtild offers in the *Flowing Light of the Godhead*, and it shows the charisma that is quite in evidence in both women; in part, this comparison is also due to the strongly imaginative character of both women's work. To read her according to her images shows her charisma. To compare her to Eckhart is to emphasize the philosophical systems that supported her writing. It particularly highlights her continuing within Neo-Platonic tradition, helping bring new life to Neo-Platonic mysticism of emanation and return, and shows that these ideas had taken hold outside of theological schools as well.

Yet the charisma with which Mechtild wrote is another aspect of her writing, and it is to this legacy that I have devoted much of the discussion in this chapter. Mechtild incorporated theological ideas within a writing that also used many tropes from the literary and devotional writings of her time, allowing her to accomplish many things within her own writings. She could explicate her own experiences while encouraging others along in their spiritual development; she vivified theological and philosophical ideas; she presented a jubilant vision of the soul who seeks and serves God.

6

Community Visionary: Mechtilde of Hackeborn

Mechtilde's writings document a cornucopia of visionary experience rooted in the community's liturgical experiences and provided for the community, which are expressed according to the spirituality of the Cistercians. Mechtilde of Hackeborn (1240–98) represents the flourishing of the Convent of Helfta at a time when it housed several visionary writers among the sisters. In *Mechtilde's Book of Ghostly Grace* we find profound theological vision expressed through her recorded visionary experiences and used to teach and direct the community. Like her older mystical sister Gertrude of Helfta, Mechtilde's writings show the flourishing of this community and the ways in which the community's identity was determined by the work of its members.

Mechtilde's visions provide a glimpse into different literary and visionary traditions from those we have seen in other writers so far. Decoding any of her visions relies upon a knowledge of the significance that colours, objects and people had in the medieval world, a knowledge that can be quite daunting to the student new to medieval work or even to the seasoned hand. In her visions, she relies upon the details to help buttress her main points. Thus, details such as clothing, gems, saints and their associated stories, liturgical music, hymns and antiphons, feast days, plants and animals, among others, all help to establish the meanings of her visions.

Writings and visions

Mechtilde, like many of the other women receiving visions that we have discussed, did not reveal these for over a decade, and it was only after she had fallen gravely ill that she only admitted to her sister the abbess Gertrude of Hackeborn that she had received visions.[1] The *Book of Ghostly Grace* was written down in Latin and it was translated into a number of vernacular languages including middle High German and middle English, and circulated widely both alone and as part of anthologies of spiritual writings.[2] The world that these visions tells is the life within the walls of the convent of Helfta; the visions are steeped in the shared liturgical life of the sisters, and their prayers and intercessions for themselves, their patrons and those who posed a threat to the community. The visions offer guidance on those issues that were at the forefront of Mechtilde's worries and those of the other sisters: the presence of Christ in the community, the sacraments, and the states of their souls and of those who had departed. The imagery of the visions also suggest the worldly and cultural knowledge that the women brought into the community, such as Mechtilde's remarks concerning dress and fashion, and courtly expectations of behaviour.

The convent of Helfta was both exceptional and the norm for women's communities in the twelfth and thirteenth century. The convent itself represents the liminal position that even established women's communities in the middle ages felt. The community was under the patronage and protection of its two founders, Elisabeth of Schwartzenberg and Burchard, count of Mansfield, her husband. The community continued to receive the patronage of the Mansfield counts, as well as other noble families, and had close ties with the archbishop of Mansfield and religious communities in Halle and Magdeburg. The convent community would move four times in all during the high middle ages, when under various threats, including financial, military and lack of water. Life behind walls, even for such a pre-eminent community as Helfta, was not secure in either a financial or economic sense.

During the middle ages, the community was pulled in different directions. In 1251, it elected Gertrude of Hackeborn as abbess. Her leadership would usher in a golden age of the convent, in which the community saw several members become prominent spiritual writers and during which time the community received many spiritual gifts in the form of mystics and their visions. It was a time in which we know the library contained works of both theology and popular 'romances' or novels of the time, as

Gertrude the Great relates in her *Herald of Divine Love*. The convent of
Helfta flourished in the middle ages as a centre of learning for women.
Under Gertrude of Hackeborn, the girls in the convent learned the seven
subjects of classical medieval education – the *trivium* (grammar, rhetoric
and logic) and the *quadrivium* (mathematics, geometry, astronomy and
music) – as well as rudimentary theology including the works of such
people as Augustine and Bernard of Clairvaux.[3] The *trivium* was the basis
in medieval educational theory for the liberal arts; the *quadrivium* completed the liberal arts in the curricula of the medieval cathedral schools
and the universities that began to form in the twelfth century. These were
preparatory for the study of philosophy and theology. The women of
Helfta received a robust education that was rather parallel to the level of
education men at religious houses could receive, and it shows the scholarly tenor of the community. The continued life of the mind, whether in
the form of courtly literature or in the form of theology, was an interest
in the community, as their readings suggest.

But pulling the community in another direction was the world outside
the convent walls. During the period of the Great Interregnum (1250–73),
Germany was particularly unstable. After the death of Frederick II and
before the election of Rudolph of Hapsburg, there were battles between
warring German lords, which put the monastery at risk of being attacked
and looted. In addition, the monastery was continually fighting debt, and
with that came the threat of ecclesiastic sanctions or of invasion from
creditors. These debts eventually led to a temporary interdict against the
convent. And, indeed, in 1342, the convent was invaded by Albert of
Brunswick. He had been elected Bishop of Halberstadt, but the Pope had
not confirmed his election. The Pope suggested alternatives, and the one
who was finally elected, Albert of Mansfield, was the brother of the current Abbess of Helfta, Luitgard. Albert of Brunswick, having been denied
the episcopacy by Luitgard's brother, attacked the convent, set fire to it,
and destroyed the vestments and decorations of the convent, along with
all its books.

But before all this destruction, the convent would provide shelter for
several outstanding women, and provide their texts for the world outside
the convent to learn about the life within. The nature and style of
Mechtilde's visions has yet to be fully studied; they are a beautiful amal-
gam of biblical imagery, details from conventual life in the thirteenth century, and liturgical imagery. The style in which her visions are written is
highly vivid and poetic, and they contain vivid, concrete details including

colours, hymns, clothing, liturgical settings and people. The *Book*'s structure roughly corresponds to the liturgical year.[4] A collect, antiphon, hymn, or one of the readings of the day will often prompt her visions, which serve to incorporate the visions within the corporate life of worship of her community. Thus, the convent becomes the setting in which God chooses to manifest the presence of Christ and other saints who appear in the visions. The *Book*'s early visions are set within Advent, and anticipate the coming of Christ into the world. As the *Book* moves through the liturgical year, the visions centre around the Marian and Christological feasts. Her visions are often set within the part of the liturgy of the convent that includes the Mass or Eucharistic celebration, and thus the presence of Christ, the sacrifice of Christ, and the overcoming of sin (because the Eucharist remits venial sins) all fit the venue. This Eucharistic devotion is a key aspect of the spirituality of the sisters of Helfta.[5]

Her visions are also composite visions, which included receiving an interpretation of the vision with the vision itself. When written down, Mechtilde's *Book* included these interpretations alongside the visions in order to help regulate their interpretation and application. Tight control on the meaning and application of the visions underscores the didactic function many of them offer her community. Additionally, the imagery of her visions sometimes incorporates the iconography associated with particular saints, particularly those with connections to the monastic tradition, with the intent to be showing that the community is part of a larger mystical body of Christ.[6] For instance, the sunbeam frequently appears as a symbol in her visions. This symbol identifies Saint Benedict, for whom, during a vision, 'the whole world, gathered together, as it were, under one beam of the sun, was presented before his eyes. In the sunbeam, Benedict saw the soul of Germanus, Bishop of Capua, in a fiery globe, carried up by Angels into heaven.'[7] Benedict was the saint credited with founding monasticism in western Europe and with writing the *Rule of Benedict*, which served as an organizing document to guide all monasteries in the western church. That her visions incorporated the person of Benedict presenting Christ's messages to the community and include details such as the sunbeam show the extent to which these saints were important to Mechtilde and her community, and the myriad details of her visions mirror her belief in the superabundance of God's grace and the variety of gifts that God gives to people.

It is hard to give a complete list of images that occur in Mechtilde's visions, because her imagery is so rich, that even one person, such as

Mary, can appear in multiple contexts and with an infinite variety of related details in the visions. The density of her descriptions includes myriad details such as rings, mirrors, angelic hierarchies, virgins, martyrs, saints, apostles, colours, gemstones, plants and musical instruments. In Mechtilde's spirituality, there is beauty and meaning associated with everything around her. Each of these details has a meaning or virtue that it is associated with and which it represents in the descriptions.[8] For instance, in one vision, she sees Christ robed in green and white clothing, and she glosses these colours to explain that the green signifies Christ's flourishing and the white represents Christ's virginal purity.[9] In another vision, she describes a vineyard in which water flows abundantly. The water is the flood of charity. In the water, fish that are gold in colour swim. The water tends the 12 trees, each with a different type of fruit. She glosses the 12 types of fruit to signify the 12 virtues that are from 'Paul's epistle': peace, joy, charity, patience, kindness, generosity, gentleness, mildness, faithfulness, temperance, continence and chastity.[10] This vision of paradise comes alive though her interpretations of such details.

Some of her visions require less interpretation of the allegorical significance of the details, precisely because they are meant to be stark reminders, and thus she uses very direct imagery to confront the audience. Such is the case when Mechtilde describes her vision of hell and purgatory. There, she emphasizes the pains and torments of punishment and how her prayers prove efficacious in removing souls from purgatory. She explains how she was given a sight of hell, in which the souls are tormented: 'she saw hell open under the earth and much painfulness and horribleness as there had been serpents and toads, lions and hounds, and likeness of all wild beasts cruelly raising and renting himself together and each other'. She describes how 'she saw also the purgatory where was as many kinds of pains as souls made them subject to vices in this life. They that were proud here in earth fell from slough to slough without ceasing. They that kept nothing or held nothing of the profession of their rule and of their obedience, walked around crooked as if they had been thrust down with a great or heavy burden.' The gluttons and drunkards are left to grovel in thirst. Like Dante's *Inferno* the punishments are visual representations of the besetting sin of each condemned soul. This and other visions of purgatory shows that those souls doing penance also undergo fitting punishments. She then prays for these sins, saying, 'our lord delivered a great multitude of souls for her prayers'.[11] In a vision of the souls of the departed, Mechtilde tells how 'she helps souls which are passed from the body that they be delivered out of pains, for by her merits many sinners, innumerable more have been converted, and many souls ordained to everlasting pains by my rightful doom are called again through her mercy and delivered from the fire of purgatory'.[12] Because Mechtilde emphasizes her own efficacy in releasing souls from purgatory (and hell!) her text is evidence of her optimistic theology. That she includes details concerning those who forgot their rule, suggests that it was a monastic community, and probably her own, that she intended to address.

These visions also confirm her own authority and relationship to the divine. Other visions that also reinforce her source of authority to God would be those in which she is told about her book:

> Wherefore she went to our Lord for help with a great trust, as she was want to do in each heaviness, and showed him her heaviness. Our Lord said to her: Give me forth in the freedom of my large heart, and give me forth in my goodness and not in yours. And she said to our Lord: Lord, what shall befall of this book after my death? Our Lord said again: 'All that seek me with a true and faithful heart shall be made glad in this book. And they that love me shall burn more in my love. And they that sorrow or mourn shall find comfort therein. and the book shall be called the book of spiritual grace'.[13]

In her visions, Christ and Mary appear in Mechtilde's visions for the comfort and spiritual direction of those souls to which Mechtilde has the greatest access, both living and dead. The purpose of revelations concerning Christ or Mary tends to be alternately consoling and didactic. Mechtilde's theology develops the role of Mary particularly robustly, seeing her as the pre-eminent example of an obedient and open follower of Christ.

Christ

When Christ came to Mechtilde in the first book of the *Book of Ghostly Grace*, He said to her that He desired all of creation to do homage to Him, but then He added that He will do that homage Himself.[14] At the heart of her Christological visions lies a reverence for Christ that wants to do full reverence to Him, but also probes the very character of Christ through the manner by which He treats humans. This also concretizes Mechtilde's vision of creation and the divine working in tandem. Creation's place is to praise God. Sin, which cuts short this ability, receives little attention from Mechtilde. She merely wants to show that where creation falls short; past that point, Mechtilde states that God steps in to help the creature.

The revelation of the person of Christ both to Mechtilde and to the community is a key theme in her visions. Christ serves a number of various roles: as the beloved, as a lordly person, as a comforter, and as a guarantor of promises. He is not merely an object of her visions, He is an object for her affections and her love, and, as such, He appeals to both her soul's virtues and to her human desires for a beautiful adolescent male. But Christ is not merely a human being in Mechtilde's thoughts: she very much still understands Christ is both human and divine. Even when Christ appears to her, he brings with him his divine powers, such as releasing people from sin. The divine nature of Christ receives attention alongside His human nature, for although Mechtilde's visions focus upon the physical Christ, most of the visions point to His divine acts (saving, restoring, atoning, turning wine into blood).

The Eucharist, with the real presence of Christ, provides a location for many of the visions and an impetus for their occurrence. When Christ becomes a living presence in the liturgy, He also becomes present in Mechtilde's visions. Thus, the visions reinforce the centrality of the sacrament of the Eucharist in the community. The spirituality of the Helfta nuns certainly bolstered the thirteenth-century devotional trends in which the clergy's power grew more central and in which their role as mediators of the sacraments and God's grace was stressed.[15] As Carolyn Walker Bynum explains, 'The overwhelming impact of Mechtilde's visions is to reinforce the monastic practice of her day, the power of the clergy, and the centrality of Eucharist and confession in Christian life.'[16] Mechtilde's visions also emphasize frequent communion. We see this particularly clearly when it clashes with the lived experience of the Helfta community; at one point the convent was under interdict and the writings of both Mechtilde of Hackeborn and Gertrude of Helfta from about this time show that Mechtilde and her community recognized the very serious nature of the absence of sacramental presence, and their visionary life as a community tried to address this situation.

The didactic nature of many of her Christ-visions directs the sisters how to show devotion to Christ, how to get the most out of the liturgy, and how to develop the virtues. For example, Christ explains to Mechtilde that four things please him in the religious: clean thoughts, holy desires, clean words in communing of ghostly sweetness, and in exercise of works of charity.[17] In these visions, knowledge comes to be associated with the presence of Christ intellectually in theological vision and in the real presence of the Eucharist.

One of the best-known and most-explored visionary images that Mechtilde receives is that of the Sacred Heart. In her description of the Sacred Heart, the heart of Jesus incorporates the human being into Christ, thus serving as a mediator for Mechtilde, who then serves as a mediator for the rest of her community. The human soul mirrors Christ's virtues. In a vision she prays for a devout sister and sees her sister's soul standing before her like a little child, holding the heart of Christ in her hands. Meekness is this child's key virtue. Christ tells Mechtilde how the sister should come to Christ. He promises to lead her to union of their hearts and virtues, and she holds the heart of Jesus in her hands.[18] She is taught how to give her heart to God in order to keep herself from sin: 'Our Lord gave his divine heart to a man's soul that a man should in the same manner give his heart again to him.'[19] Mechtilde explains that the person who gives her heart to Christ in this manner cannot fall into grievous sin after such a dedication of oneself. Mechtilde's visions evidence a close connection between Christ and the community of sisters. His solicitude does not end with his didactics. Christ demonstrates great concern for the individual members of the convent, particularly those dead and those with sins that need shriving. Christ also appears in the last part of the *Book of Ghostly Grace* in a vision, wearing clothing that is imprinted with the images of all the sisters (living and dead) of the community.[20] In this vision, Mechtilde confirms that the outward and inward lives of the sisters please Him.

Mary

Marian devotions were an aspect of Cistercian practice, because all of the communities of the Cistercian order were dedicated to Mary and looked to her as intercessor and protector. Mary also traditionally served as a role model for religious women of all orders. In dedication to Mary, Mechtilde learns the nine diverse meditations of Mary, which all centre around attributes of Mary's heart: virginity, meekness, devoutness, fervency in love to God and all Christians, steadfastness in keeping all knowledge of God, patience in Christ's passion, truth, busyness in prayers, and busyness in contemplation.[21] These virtues are characteristic of the Virgin Mary and seek to form the Cistercian sister who would follow Mary's example. Unlike the devotions to Christ's heart – which centred around reconciliation, final union with God in heaven, and human divinization – the meditations around Mary's heart focus on the example that the human must follow in order to approach Christ.

Mary serves as an example of the soul that follows the will of God unerringly through her response to the Annunciation. She serves as a model to Mechtilde, who then models for the community the Marian virtues such as meekness, obedience and love.[22] Her roles include queen and comforter, mother and mediator. Mechtilde repeatedly speaks of Mary as having been 'oned' to God,[23] and it is this sort of union of wills that she and her sisters seek. Mechtilde's vision of Mary is one in which she understands that 'she should rejoice in Our Lady with them forasmuch as that blissful lady represents the image of God in her uncorrupted and most fair and most seemingly appearance, surpassing any creature'.[24] Such passages echo the language of Augustine's theological anthropology, which states that the human is the image and likeness of God.[25]

Mary links humans and Christ because Mary was the most proximate human being to Christ (his mother) and because she was born sinless.[26] Medievals considered the grace that Mary received, through her intimacy with Christ, was available to all people who approached her through devotions.[27] Furthermore, devotion to Mary makes Mechtilde and her sisters present in Christ's heart.[28] Mechtilde explains that Mary leads people to touch the heart of her son, thus offering a model of how one should offer devotions to Christ.[29] Mary's prayers and intercessions also help release souls from Purgatory.[30] For women in the monastery, she is also the primary model for virgins; Mechtilde says that Mary was the first woman to take a vow of virginity.[31] Mechtilde further strengthens her identification of Mary and Christ by explaining that all humans should live in imitation of Christ, and she makes the claim that the person who does this pre-eminently is Mary.[32]

As an example, Mary offers guidance about how the human should respond to God. Mechtilde here uses the example of Mary feeding the historical baby Jesus to tell humans how they are to nurture Christ in their own lives:

> And to love this maiden [Mary] spoke and said, 'Oh dear sweet love, teach me to do suitable service to this

worthy noble child [Jesus].' Love answered and said: 'I, love, took him to me with my hands of virginity and wrapped him in clothes. I gave him milk of maiden's paps with his mother and nourished him in her lap. I ministered him and did him service of humanity with his mother. Ever yet I do him service without ceasing. Therefore whatever he be that will minister to him worthily, he must take me to be his fellow with him. And that is that he do all things in love and for love and that he be oned to him in that love by which God comes to humankind in himself and to himself. And if he do so then whatever he do may be pleasing and acceptable to God.'[33]

When Mary asks Lady Love for motherhood lessons, it is not for her own benefit that she asks. Rather, her question allows Lady Love to proclaim lessons in order for all humans to learn what is expected of them. Mary's obedience began with her *fiat* and Mary also obediently does what is necessary to foster the growth of Christ. Similarly, humans are expected to aim towards this Marian ideal even if they are not capable of responding with such dedication. Mechtilde hears Mary explain, 'The worshipful Trinity delighted and had joy in me because He would make such an image wherein the gracious working of all His mighty wisdom and all His goodness should passingly and curiously appear.'[34] In this statement, Mechtilde goes beyond saying that Mary is merely an example and makes her a conduit of the divine wisdom itself.

The liturgical and didactic role of Christ also fits Mary.[35] She teaches them proper worship and devotions. Even more, when the community of Helfta was under interdict, Mary communed the sisters even though priests were not allowed to offer the sacraments to the community. As the most perfect example of a human following the role of Christ, Mary can trump the temporal role of priest in order to ensure that the sisters of Helfta receive their sacraments. In the vision, Mary oversteps the authority of Rome, contradicting the church order that the sisters not receive the solace of the sacraments.[36] This vision boldly states that it is God's wish to continue to be available in any manner of ways to the sisters, even when obstacles such as interdict or lack of priests stand in God's way. Mary once again works as agent, saying yes to God's will as God acts unorthodoxly (much like God worked unorthodoxly in the Annunciation). That Mary appears in a priestly function in this vision also points to the theological significance of what Mechtilde's visions have told us about the virtues that these holy women have, and their proximity to Christ. Her ability to step outside constructed roles for women intends to embolden the rest of the community, if they act on behalf of the will of God.

Mary's blessedness and her presence in heaven is theologically confirmed by her Assumption into heaven. Mechtilde describes how 'that holy soul of the Virgin Mary, God's mother, passed from the body with unspeakable joy and without any pain and full gladly flowed into her son's arms and rested lovingly and highly pleasingly about his heart, and so was that blessed soul led forth with a festival mirth to the throne of that excellent Trinity'.[37] The Ascension of Christ into heaven was a common subject in Cistercian preaching. The Assumption received some attention among Cistercians, although not as much; yet Mechtilde's attentions to it here suggest that she understood its relevance in describing the quasi-divine roles that she would witness Mary playing. Mary's Assumption offered the structure by which Mechtilde could explore and understand the path by which humans spiritually advance towards God.[38]

Mary's knowledge of God begins with the Annunciation, and because she has stored secret knowledge of God in her heart from this experience, 'you shall salute her heart which was most steadfast in keeping of all that she had known of me'.[39] Mechtilde also says, 'when she beheld him first in his humanity she had full knowledge that he was truly God and that joy led her so that she might have a true and steadfast knowledge'.[40] Since this knowledge is what binds Mary so closely to God, knowledge of Christ by other humans is another way of helping to ensure their union with Christ. And, ultimately, this is one of the things that special revelations such as those contained in the *Book of Ghostly Grace* can offer – additional knowledge of Christ or God.

Love and the nuptials of the lamb

Love is the force that reorients the human back towards God and love is what prods the human to make progress. As the soul progresses, it continues to grow greater in love. Later on, as the soul progresses more, it will be Love from God in the form of grace that allows it to continue to make progress. As already mentioned, Mechtilde identifies love as that which animates the creation of the world, and love is the primary means of

Christ reconciling the world through the Incarnation and Passion.[41] Although Mechtilde does not explicitly draw on the courtly love tradition in the way that we have seen writers such as Hadewijch and Mechtild of Magdeburg do, she does draw upon a very wide range of studies including alchemy, love, music and poetry in order to probe the nature of love through a wide assortment of analogies.[42] This is not to say that Mechtilde does not engage the tropes of the courtly love tradition, as some of her images bear resemblance to it. Comparatively speaking, although Lady Love appears in Mechtilde's work, the courtly motifs remain at best a decoration when Mechtilde uses allegories to make her points known.[43] Lady Love in Mechtilde does not serve as a personification for an abstract virtue of love to be sought. Rather, she is a devotional object for the poor, enfeebled human to begin meditating on Love. Ultimately, Mechtilde has such a broad understanding of love, and one that is so ontologically rooted in her understanding of Christ, that the metaphors of Scripture are stronger in her hands than the metaphors of the courtly tradition.

In the course of the spiritual advancement described in the *Book of Ghostly Grace*, the human moves from a love expressed in human affections to a love that is divine.[44] Christ possesses such a love in its idealized form, and from this Mechtilde attempts to derive how humans should conduct themselves in order to cultivate such a divine love within themselves.[45] Her understanding of Love derives from the love she identifies within Christ. In a vision in which she describes the four pulses of the beat of Jesus' heart, she identifies the four aspects of Christ's love. The first pulse represents Jesus' acceptance of the Cross; this is a sacrificial notion of love. Second is the wisdom that governs Christ; this love is to be steeped in divine, not human, wisdom, and it should govern the human decisions. Third is a love that overcomes bitterness, but instead becomes sweet-tasting; she says, 'The marrow of the soul is that thing that is so sweet which a soul feels inwardly by infusion of love only from God / whereby it disposes all passing things truly [in favour of God].'[46] Finally, in the fourth pulse, is the solidarity that Christ shows through the Incarnation.

Christ the Incarnate is the gate to God, and the way to pass through this gate is love. God created the whole world in love, and it was through love that Christ's sacrifice on behalf of all humans took place. Love's connection with the Incarnation makes God's love accessible to humans once again. Love is also the bond between the Persons of the Trinity and is the unity that the human steps into in the beatific vision: 'Mechtilde's apostolate, primarily to individuals, manifests the infinite reaches of divine love accessible to every person.'[47] When the human is able to respond to this love, the possibilities that love opens include union in spirit with the Trinity. This conjoining will be a union of wills. God explains to Mechtilde, 'if you will all things that I will, you shall then always be oned to my almighty might'.[48]

Christ is both the object with which the human is unified and the foundation for hope in this union.[49] Christ says to Mechtild that he is that which makes all faith in God possible: 'All the desire that any man ever had was inspired by me, and that all Holy Scripture and speech of holy men come from me, and shall come from me without end.'[50] These are the gifts that make union with God a possibility. The heart of Christ opens with the key of love, Mechtilde declares. That is, to open the heart of Christ one is entering into mystical marriage with Christ, and this is done by the purest of loves that the human can have for God. Mechtilde uses other images as well to describe this union: several of her visions describe rings being exchanged; others include the detail of the intertwined fingers of Christ and the bride.[51] Still other places describe how Christ kisses his bride Mechtilde.[52] She engages in kissing and telling, saying that she 'kissed him full lovingly, through which kiss she was oned fully to the blessed trinity as much as ever it was possible any man or woman to be oned to God without personal union'.[53] In the Cistercian tradition, the kisses between the bride and bridegroom had received much attention from Bernard of Clairvaux, who began his Sermons on the *Song of Songs* by explicating the first verse: 'Let him kiss me with the kisses of his mouth.' Bernard explained how the kiss of the mouth was one of union and was the last kiss received in spiritual development.[54]

Community

Despite the fact that Mechtilde refused to tell of the existence of her visions for so long, they contribute insights for her whole community. Often, she received visions for sisters with troubled souls. Her visions also told of the afterlife state of a person when she and her sisters needed to pray in order to free them from purgatory. At other times, her revelations demonstrated that someone whose mortal soul was feared for was not in as much danger as first thought. Her visions sometimes had their impetus from the actions within the public sphere of the monastic liturgy. Because they functioned to console her as well as others, we must wonder why she stayed silent about her visions if they had such a public element. Perhaps such publicly addressed visions occurred only after she admitted to her sisters that she had been having them.[55] Perhaps she felt guilt over not having publicly admitted those visions meant to console more of the community than just her. Whatever the explanation, although many of her visions are expressed in individualistic terms of Mechtilde's relationship with Christ, the presence of those visions regarding other people underscores the fact that they were meant to be for the entire community.[56]

Mechtilde's affective response is as important as her imagery and theological message. It identifies Mechtilde as a model of Christian response to God; in her responses, we can read the responses that the visions are supposed to elicit for the rest of the community. Thus, we read how she views herself and her twin roles of mediator to her community and of nun. This latter role is one of prayers and offering an example (as opposed to teaching or preaching). Mechtilde fulfilled this role not only in her normal duties as a nun, but by offering herself vis-à-vis the revelations to show how to respond to special manifestations of God's grace. As a mediator, she also offered prayers for her community and others loosely associated with it, and she mediated the grace of comfort and assurance that some of the visions bring.[57] Her mediation lay between the figures of Christ and Mary and those still on earth; it entailed the angels and other saints as well who appear in her visions. She mediated grace in the way that a nun would do: she communicated information that Christ wished to pass on to the monastery; this was information not of a sacramental nature, however, but to guarantee the spiritual safety of the sisters.[58]

Conclusions

Mechtilde presents us with a clear example of a sister from a convent in her own context. Not inhabiting any role of leadership in her community, she sits alongside her sisters when offering these visions. Without the role of Abbess, she does not attempt to direct the community's reforms, development or future growth, unlike Hildegard of Bingen, and unlike the later Teresa of Avila. And yet it is within this only world she knew, the convent of Helfta, that Mechtilde's visions have their setting and meaning.

Her visions present a sense of the community of Helfta, not in terms of the individuals there, but in terms of how the community saw itself in the larger mystical body of Christ, connected to Christ, Mary, the saints and other monastic communities, as well as to those of their own monastery who had died beforehand. They also demonstrate the tenor of a community in which learning flourished, in which the nuns were familiar both with Latin and with the classical subjects of study, and they demonstrate the liturgical life of the community, which undergirds so many of the visions' settings. Mechtilde's visions present us with the lessons her community needed to learn at this time: reliance on the Triune God, the necessity of following a virtuous life as exemplified by Mary, the patroness of the Cistercian Order, and Christ's providential care for the Helfta community even in the face of ecclesiastic obstacles such as interdict. These visions, then, give us a sense of the concerns and hopes that this unusual women's community had in its thirteenth-century heyday.

7

Franciscan Penitent: Angela of Foligno

I was and am now drawn out of everything I had previously experienced and had taken such delight in: the humanity of Christ; the consideration of that very deep companionship which the Father from eternity in his love bestowed on his Son (in which I had taken such deep delight), namely, the contempt, the suffering, and the poverty experienced by the Son of God, and the cross as bed to rest on. I was also drawn to the vision of God in the darkness in which I used to take such delight. Every previous state was put to sleep so tenderly and sweetly that I could not tell it was happening. I could only recall that now I did not have these experiences. For in the cross of Christ in which I used to take such delight, so as to make it my place of rest and by bed, I find nothing; in the poverty of the Son of God, I find nothing; and in everything that could be named, I find nothing.[1]

Near the end of her devotions, this thirteenth-century *pinzochere* – a penitential woman in late medieval Italy – named Angela of Foligno (1248–1309) found in herself so rapt in God that even meditating upon the human nature of Christ no longer brought about the delight it once had. This loss, and its replacement with suffering, marks her union with Christ. Angela's book records how she came to embrace the suffering and poverty of the broken Lord through devotions that follow the spirituality of the Franciscans. Angela finds herself in an intensely emotional relationship with Christ; the text records her affective responses to his crucifixion and mixes these responses with a deeply erotic theology of spiritual marriage to Christ that she describes in highly physical terms. Angela's deeply affective and physical spirituality incorporates the Franciscan devotional emphases centred on the humility of Christ and seen through the lens of the poverty, suffering and penance in her writings, which document her life as a *pinzochere*.

Angela of Foligno's *Memorial* and *Instructions* purport to offer life directions to laymen and -women seeking a greater devotion to God through the Franciscan charism. Her book bases itself upon her own life, describes her conversion and her Franciscan spirituality, and it offers documentation of her ability to follow Christ even outside of traditional enclosure. Her book bears similarities to hagiography in the later thirteenth and fourteenth centuries, where saints' lives became a set genre unto themselves.[2] Her *Memorial* bears especial significance because it documents her wild behaviours and shows the extremes of lay penitential devotions in fourteenth-century Italy. The Franciscans specifically championed Angela as a model of medieval Franciscan spirituality and thus her writings serve as an example of Franciscan devotions. Furthermore, French intellectuals in the mid and late twentieth century – including Georges Bataille, Simone de Beauvoir and Luce Irigaray – used Angela as a model of mysticism, and knowing Angela's work is one necessary key to understanding modern French discussions of erotism and mysticism.[3]

Her life and writings

Angela's *Memorial* begins its tale *in media res*, telling her life from the inside-out, beginning with her conversion in 1285. At that time, Angela found herself afraid of damnation and wept extensively as a result of knowledge of her sins and fear of divine punishment. Previously, Angela had been a wife and mother, but unexpectedly her mother, husband and all her children died suddenly; Angela took consolation in this occurrence for she had prayed for it to occur.[4] Their deaths made a vocational change to religious life possible, which had not been possible for Angela while her family lived; although her rejoicing at her family's death may appear cold-hearted, it signifies that the call to religious life was stronger in

Angela than her ties to her family. Shortly afterwards, Angela experienced a conversion and the Franciscan character of her became stronger.

The Franciscan Order (Order of Friars Minor) had begun as an order following the charismatic leadership of Saint Francis. In 1209, Francis decided to devote himself to a radical poverty, and he was very quickly joined by others in his desire to follow a life involving moderate asceticism, voluntary poverty and evangelical preaching. The Franciscan wandering preachers spread a message encouraging conversion, which in medieval Christianity most often meant turning to a deeper Christian life. Franciscan preaching had a tremendous impact upon the laity, especially in Francis' native Italy and particularly around Assisi, his home town; this mendicant preaching served to stoke lay interest in the spiritual development of individuals and societies, and was especially popular among women. Similar to the beguines in the Low Countries were women who sought a life of voluntary poverty dedicated to the service of God and neighbour, and many women in Italy were attracted to the mendicant orders to serve the poor and sick of God through the ideals of the Dominicans and Franciscans. Women associated with the Franciscans primarily served the poor, focused on individual asceticism, and strove to live a semi-contemplative life.[5]

Clare of Assisi had also been attracted to the Franciscan ideal of renouncing all property, sharing in the life of the poor and ministering to them. Clare began by Francis' side, sharing in his mission of dignity for the poor and rebuilding the church through evangelical zeal, voluntary poverty and works of charity. Slowly, Clare and all Francis' female followers were required to accept limitations, and the women became encloistered rather than mendicant as the men were.[6] The *Rule* Clare received from the pope was essentially the *Rule of Benedict*.[7] From that point onwards, women would be enclosed in convents rather than out in the community living off of their begging like the men did. Yet, despite the limitations, Clare gained 10,000 female followers during her lifetime.[8] In Angela's Foligno, there were a number of women's penitential communities based on several different models.[9] Of these communities, three had become Poor Clare communities and several of the others had become institutionalized under the Augustinian Rule.[10] Still others would come to be under the tutelage or spiritual direction of Angela herself.

As early as the middle of the thirteenth century, houses had existed for 'regular' tertiaries – that is, those who lived under a rule or *regula* – and, starting in 1289, Pope Nicholas IV's papal bull *Supra montem* also made official the existence of 'third-order' communities of women within the Franciscan order.[11] These were penitential groups devoted to a combination of spiritual discipline, private and shared, practising works of mercy, caring for the poor, ill and despairing. Tertiaries (as members of these 'third order' communities were called) were generally older married or widowed women. Angela's persistence and spiritual depth finally convinced the Franciscans of San Francesco in Foligno to allow her to profess to the Franciscan Third Order in 1291 when she was 43. Angela professed as a third-order laywoman associated with San Francesco, a house of Franciscan men.[12] Thus, she lived in the larger Foligno society and not in a cloister.

Assisi was the spiritual home for Franciscans, as it was the home to Saint Francis and it was the location where he began his ministry, and it served as the centre of Angela's *Memorial*. It was on a pilgrimage to Assisi that Angela had an encounter which became central to her spiritual relationship with God. When Angela began her pilgrimage to Assisi, ten miles from Foligno, she desired to pray for three gifts: to feel the grace of Christ's presence in her soul; to better observe the *Rule* that she was bound to as a Franciscan Tertiary; and to help her become and remain truly poor, all of which were very Franciscan requests. During the pilgrimage, Angela had a vision of God's love for her while she walked the path between Spello and Assisi to the shrine of St Francis. She was told that the presence of the Holy Spirit would remain with her on the journey but would leave when she arrived in Assisi. When she reached the church in Assisi she did indeed lose the presence of the Holy Spirit. At the terror of suddenly losing her feeling of the presence of the Holy Spirit, Angela began shrieking inconsolably. Yet in this absence of the experience of the presence of God, Angela began to feel certainty about God's protective love and presence. It was also during this tumultuous experience that she met Brother A, who, although embarrassed and doubtful about her behaviour at first, eventually became her champion.

Angela's *Memorial* and *Instructions*

There are two texts associated with Angela. One is the *Memorial*, which was dictated by Angela and written down by an anonymous Brother A. In the text, his narratorial intrusions explain that much of the text was written down in response to questions he posed to Angela and her attempts to assuage his doubts about her visions. Much scholarly work is still being done to disentangle Angela's voice from that of her narrator-scribe, Brother A.[13] The *Memorial* covers the steps of Angela's mystical ascent, and although it contains biographical material it was written between 1291 and 1296, so it does not cover the last 20 years of her life. The other work associated with Angela is the *Instructions*; this book was most certainly written in the years around her death by various devotees of Angela who have not been identified. Because we do not know anything about the narrators of the *Instructions*, it is hard to know what relationship the ideas espoused in these compositions have to Angela.

The *Memorial*'s narrative opens with the moment when the comfort of the Holy Spirit left her as she entered the Shrine of St Francis in Assisi. Her behaviour at this moment – her shrieking in a near-incomprehensible voice – leads Brother A to be embarrassed and pursue her after they return to Foligno to explain the state of her inner life that led to the outwardly suspect effects. The narrative is thus born of Brother A's doubts, interrogations and promptings. After the first chapter briefly outlines the 19 steps before the liminal twentieth step, the second chapter consists of the narrator discussing his own role in the process of writing the *Memorial*. The remaining chapters discuss seven supplemental steps beyond the first 20. The first supplemental step is the same as the twentieth step, and the narrator became sufficiently confused with the last ten steps as Angela described them that he elided them into seven steps, of which six are new. With these self-confessed confusions on the part of the scribe Brother A, we have a text that we know is far from complete or accurate – yet it is also a text Angela knew of and nominally had some intellectual control over.

Of all the texts discussed in this book, the works of Angela of Foligno are undoubtedly the most compositionally complex. The narratorial intrusions into the *Memorial* mean that the text truly documents two things: Angela's spiritual journey, and the journey of an ecclesiastic figure who was supposed to present the sacramental church to her. Actually, the text documents how the lay penitential woman Angela teaches and transforms the representative of the bishop and church. Both Angela's spiritual experiences and the transformation to belief that occurs in Brother A as his conviction in her sanctity and spiritual depth grows constitute her authority. In other places, he records how Angela complains that his words did not do justice to her experiences. He explains:

> In truth, I wrote them, but I had so little grasp of their
> meaning that I thought myself as a sieve or sifter which
> does not contain the precious and refined flour but
> only the most coarse. Having experienced myself a spe-
> cial grace from God which I had never experienced
> before, I wrote filled with a great reverence and fear.[14]

Furthermore, he states that when he read back to her his version of what
she had described, it was practically unrecognizable. Later Angela commented that his rendition was accurate, although bland to hear: 'Your
words recall to me what I told you but they are very obscure. The words
you read to me do not convey the meaning I intended to convey, and as a
result your writing is obscure.'[15]

At times, Brother A's text certainly looks as though it attempts to
increase the uncertainty of the reader's response to Angela's messages. For
example, he says that when his conscience had unshriven sin, he could not
adequately compose after his meetings with Angela.[16] At other times,
Brother A could not think of the correct Latin words and would leave his
transcription in the vernacular. He says sometimes he wrote so fast he
would sometimes forget to change some of her first person pronouns to
the third person (and he reports that he has not corrected these even in
the final rendition of the text). From this list of editorial complaints, we
see that Brother A's compositional methods varied: at times, he composed
in front of her while listening to her. Other times, he composed the book
after his meetings with her. At least once, Brother A sent a young boy to
transcribe Angela's speech. Although Angela balked at the transcription,
Brother A included it in the *Memorial* anyway, even though he professed
he did not understand the piece the boy had transcribed and Angela
opposed its inclusion. Brother A also never mentions Angela by name, nor
the name of her town, and he refers to himself only by the letter 'A' and his
relationship to her as confessor and relative.[17] What we have is a narrator
who offers every excuse for his imperfections and who should not encourage our confidences. But Brother A is the only narrator we have, and the
Memorial is the closest text we have to Angela's own words. To go forward
with this text still places us closer to her own ideas, words and thoughts
than the *Instructions* written by her disciples at a greater remove.

Brother A serves multiple roles within the *Memorial*: he is the scribe,
the supposedly transparent vehicle through which Angela's words pass
into written form. But he is also the narrator who describes the events

through the lens of both what he has perceived in her outwards behaviour and what Angela has described to him of her inward states. Furthermore, he is one of the characters in the unfolding drama of the work;[18] he is responsible for the work's inception through his questioning and guides it along. This is especially true towards the end of the work: Angela's reflections become less narrative-based and more theological in their outlook in places where they are based more frequently upon the promptings of the questions Brother A asked.[19] Brother A also served a role of mediator, trying to explain to the reader (who he assumed was even less perfect than he in spiritual understanding) what it was that Angela meant. The *Memorial*'s editorial complexity does not end with the scribe's difficulty. Brother A says in the 'Approbation' at the beginning of the work that he submitted the book to Cardinal-deacon James of Colonna, as well as other Franciscan theologians, for approval.[20] The fact that Brother A sought ecclesiastic approval for Angela's writing shows the liminal position that Angela held as a Franciscan lay penitent, even in a place and time where such religious behaviour was commonplace and even encouraged. And her tenuous position would continue even after it received approval, because the approval that she received was from a cardinal who would soon be associated with the controversial movement of the Spiritual Franciscans, and therefore the connection with that movement spread doubts about the orthodoxy of her work. Additionally, in 1289, Angela was visited by Ubertino of Casale, the leader of the Spiritual Franciscans, a controversial group whose emphases were on spiritual poverty as opposed to the actual poverty.[21] Ubertino specifically cited Angela in his own treatise *Arbor vitae crucifixiae Jesu*, where he attributes Angela's teachings as the impetus for his conversion to radical asceticism.

Angela's spirituality

To discuss Angela's key ideas is to discuss precisely the spiritual emphases of Italy in her time. Angela was to become a figure with a cult following among Franciscans of the Italy of her time, and this status was in part predicated on the fact she was not threatening to the church hierarchy because 'Angela did not lay claim to any new belief, any new idea that challenged the prevailing world-picture of theologians in her time'.[22] In other words, Angela's innovations were merely in her mode of surrender to Christ, and not in what she was saying. Rather than being a shortcoming, her orthodoxy adds a certain value to what Angela's works tell us, for she is not a singular and different voice, but is one that is representative of her place and time.

Where Angela appears unique is not in her message, but in the medium by which she expresses it. She exhibited what Peter Dronke has termed '*topoi* of outdoing', in which she intended each of her actions to be more intense, devout, severe or noticeable than the actions of those holy men and women before her.[23] Thus, when Angela vowed herself to Christ, it was not enough for her to merely pledge herself to Christ or disavow her husband. Instead, she stripped naked in front of the cross, pledging her chastity to Christ alone from that moment forward.[24] Similarly, her shrieks and outbursts were over-intense. She did not merely cry at the loss of the Holy Spirit in the Assisi church. She howled as if she were dying. But these are not innovations as much as they are merely exaggerations of the spirituality that was already present. They express her *reactions* to the spiritual stimuli of the day.

The main focus of her spirituality and her theological discussion was the example of Christ, seen through the lens of the Franciscan movement, and the subsequent union that could be brought about via penitential acts, which would benefit not only her but the souls of others as well. The thoroughly Franciscan spirituality of Angela appears most clearly in three aspects of her teachings. First, St Francis, *Il Poverello*, was the centre of several of her visions and his example is at the centre of her spirituality; his guiding influence helps to give Angela a sense of identity and direction. Second, the town of Assisi, which was the home of St Francis and a pilgrimage site of Franciscan importance, was a key place for her conversion. Among women associated with the Franciscans, two trends have been noted: living with the poor and serving them, and focusing on individual asceticism, eremeticism and a contemplative life.[25] Third, the main Franciscan spiritual foci on poverty, devotion to the crucified Christ and evangelical zeal for service to the neighbour are all central to her book and her life, as is the devotional practice of cultivating an affective response to a Biblical passage or a set prayer. For example, Angela documents her affective responses of penance, consolation and sweetness by describing how one day she 'recited the Our Father so slowly and consciously that even though, on the one hand, I wept bitterly because I was so aware of my sins and my unworthiness, still, on the other hand, I felt a great consolation and I began to taste something of the divine sweetness. I perceived the divine goodness in this prayer better than anywhere else, and I still perceive it better there even today.'[26] In this case, the act of reciting a common prayer, the Our Father, elicits in her an emotionally charged response.

The steps

Angela bases her teaching about the spiritual life on a series of steps. The twentieth step is the pivotal step, for Angela is in this state when Brother A first meets her. Unlike women we have seen previously, Angela describes a clear ascent towards God, which structures her entire message. Through the attainment of this twentieth level Angela also garners authority in the eyes of her scribe. However, the steps in Angela's narrative are not all given equal attention by her scribe. The first 20 steps are condensed into the first chapter. Starting with the third chapter, the first supplemental step is then explained in much greater detail than the first 20, and the rest of the book unfolds the six or seven supplemental steps. The scribe clearly emphasizes the supplemental steps as 'more important' compared to the first ones, suggesting that what matters is the highest spiritual attainments rather that just any spiritual growth.

Even though Angela introduces a ladder of ascent, the way forward is one that is fraught with unease and vacillation between the poles of deep contrition and doubt on the one hand and rapturous visions on the other. This buffeting comes to a head in the sixth supplemental step, where she encounters a dark night experience. Angela's experience of suffering is very different in character and in depth from what we have seen before in the discussions of suffering from people such as Hadewijch's. For Angela, suffering is a very real phenomenon, and she appears quite inconsolable at times. The reason for this difference in depth of character is that Angela's understanding of suffering is allied to the knowledge of the absence of God. Her suffering is one in which the only source of meaning and hope in her life is no longer present, with no sense that it will return. It is thus at the absolute depths of something beyond despair.

Christ

Angela focuses upon the person of Christ in the multiple roles of a devotional object, an example, bridegroom and provider of graces. That is, Angela's spirituality engages Christ according to both his divine and his human nature. Her visions incorporate a number of representations of Christ in visual or bodily form. Angela's visions of Christ exhibit a strongly imagistic quality, in which she clearly envisions Christ as he was depicted pictorially in artwork of her time. Like other Italian women of her time, Angela often had strongly affective responses to iconography in which Christ was depicted.[27] Such images led to Angela entering into the picture and envisioning herself holding the broken body of Christ, as if she were the Virgin in the *pietà*. Often, visual objects influence Angela, providing a basis for her consideration of the life of the human person Jesus of Nazareth. She explains that once during the liturgy she reflected upon a crucifix, which led to an interior vision:

> While I was thus gazing at the cross with the eyes of the body, suddenly my soul was set ablaze with love; and every member of my body felt it with the greatest joy. I saw and felt that Christ was within me, embracing my soul with the very arm with which he was crucified … The joy that I experienced to be with him in this way and the sense of security that he gave me were far greater than I had ever been accustomed to.[28]

But joy is not the only response that Angela had to her visions. More often, her response would be one of empathy for the suffering man nailed to the crucifix. In fact, these visual reminders became too difficult for her to navigate eventually, because of the emotional response that she would have. She notes how these responses escalated to include crying and howling after her pilgrimage to Assisi. She explains that 'this fire of the love of God in my heart became so intense that if I heard anyone speak about God I would scream'. Her reactions grew more intense, and she reported that 'whenever I saw the passion of Christ depicted, I could hardly bear it, and I would come down with a fever and fall sick. My companion, as a result, hid paintings of the passion or did her best to keep them out of my sight.'[29]

Even when her images are not directly related to art work, devotional objects or visual stimuli, Angela's devotions to Christ often appear in very physical terms. She embraces Christ in her soul, using bodily terms to describe the encounter. She enters the side of Christ. She lies in his tomb and kisses him in the tomb on Holy Saturday, as she describes:

In a state of ecstasy, she found herself in the sepulcher with Christ. She said she had first of all kissed Christ's breast – and saw that he lay dead, with his eyes closed – then she kissed his mouth, from which, she added, a delightful fragrance emanated, one impossible to describe. The moment lasted only a short while. Afterward, she placed her cheek on Christ's own and he, in turn, placed his hand on her other cheek, pressing her closely to him. At that moment, Christ's faithful one heard him telling her: 'Before I was laid in the sepulcher, I held you this tightly to me.'[30]

Angela's vision occurred on Holy Saturday, which is the day between Good Friday and Easter Sunday. The liturgies from Holy Thursday to Easter Sunday liturgically recreate the events of the last days of Christ's life from the Last Supper on Holy Thursday to the Resurrection on Easter Sunday. On Holy Saturday, Christ's body lay in the tomb and he descended into hell, in what was known as the Harrowing of Hell. In this event, he permanently broke the gates of hell and offered salvation to the righteous who were detailed there. In Angela's vision, she sees herself lying in the tomb, lying down with Christ and embracing and kissing in the tomb. She startlingly combines the imagery of death and the tomb with the intimacies of embracing and kissing her beloved, just as she combines the erotic and the grotesque in other places. For instance, she describes a vision where

Christ on the cross appeared more clearly to me while I was awake, that is to say, he gave me an even greater awareness of himself than before. He then called me to place my mouth to the wound in his side. It seemed to me that I saw and drank the blood, which was freshly flowing from his side. His intention was to make me understand that by this blood he would cleanse me. And at this I began to experience a great joy, although when I thought about the passion I was still filled with sadness.[31]

Placing her lips on Christ's side (like a kiss), along with the imagery of drinking the blood of his wound (with implied Eucharistic overtones and nursing overtones), combines forcefully to show how the bodily aspects of her visions support the theological visions she has. In this vision, the physical union is a concrete manifestation of the spiritual union she and Christ share. The shared tomb is a shared marriage bed as well.

Nowhere does Brother A question Angela about her use of physical language, so we do not have her own reflections on her use of physical and erotic language. In the course of Angela's *Memorial*, it becomes clear that at least one role that the bodily metaphors and language play is to show how the human's body is engaged in the work of divinization. The body engages in a very real and physical imitation of Christ – through poverty and works of charity – so that the imitation of Christ can be fully borne. Yet, for Angela, imitation of Christ does not merely imply being devoted to Christ or feeling joy. It means taking up, quite literally, the toughness of Christ's life, especially the suffering, humiliation and radical poverty of Christ. Physical bodies, such as Francis' stigmatic body, or the afflicted bodies of lepers, the dirty bodies of the poor and the broken bodies of the wounded, imitate Christ in a way the mind alone cannot.

In Angela's examination of Christ's virtues, she develops a picture of Christ that is in conformity with the Franciscan ideals of poverty and suffering for others. The *Instructions* explain how Christ had three companions that helped him to achieve perfect love of God: voluntary poverty, suffering contempt from others, and an extreme suffering.[32] This work asserts that because Christ is the head of the mystical body of Christ and he exhibited these behaviours, the rest of the mystical body of Christ (all Christians) must follow in the same manner. The mendicant orders made the suffering, rejected Christ, their devotional focus. *Il Poverello* saw the face of Christ in the suffering, poor, sick and outcasts of society, and to minister to them was to minister to the one who had no place to lay his head, the prophet rejected in his own country and crucified for the sins of others ('whatever you do to the least of these, you do to me').[33] To encounter the leper, the outcast, the widow or the poor and respond was the beginning of conversion according to the Franciscan charism.

Penance

Penance is, of course, also tied to the model of the suffering Christ, for acts of penance sought to imitate Christ's saving work by helping the penitential soul atone for its own sins and the sins of others. Angela explains that 'the sign that true love is at work is this: the soul takes up its cross, that is, penance as long as one lives, penance as great and harsh as possible'.[34] Just as Christ's suffering and death redeemed the whole human race, suffering by penitents helped loose the souls of other humans from the punishments in Purgatory.[35] Penance was not merely a means of personal self-satisfaction, but a means of church reform through the energies of everyone who was able and inclined. It had a communal focus in terms of whom it atoned for and the reform of the will of both the practitioner and those in community.

Angela's works indicate that penance is a lifelong activity. She asks, 'How long does penance last and how much of it is there?' And the answer that she gives is that it lasts, 'as long as one lives. And as much as one can bear. This is the meaning of being transformed into the will of God.'[36] Penance began for Angela when she felt that what she strove for in life (motherhood, honours among the women of Foligno and socializing with other women of the town) were not enough. Her turn to penance was a re-ordering of her life from things that had served her desires to things that would serve God. After her conversion she serves other humans, particularly the sinful in need of penance, and the sick and poor, and she does so for the service of God. At the end of penance is rest in God for Angela as well as for those she serves. Love is transformative not just because it encourages penance; love also begins to shape the human into the object of its loves. When the soul begins to love God, it wants to possess and taste God. In so doing, 'the power of love transforms the lover into the Beloved and the Beloved into the lover'.[37] The ultimate goal is the divinization of the human, where the person will be 'transformed into God, without having lost its own substance, its entire life is changed and through this love it becomes almost totally divine'.[38]

The presence and absence of God

But before this state of union, Angela experiences some frightening moments where God seems utterly absent. In fact, a particularly noticeable trait of Angela's spiritual life is her alternation between intimate perception of God's loving presence and her utter despair of abandonment when God withdraws. (Yet she does not say that God is not present, but that God *feels* absent.) This oscillation marked her initial journey to Assisi and would continue to mark her experiences of God through her life. Even in her sense of her calling, Angela vacillates between extreme doubt and confidence depending upon whether she knows God's consolation or not. It was, ironically, only with the removal of the presence of the Holy Spirit at the cathedral in Assisi that Angela came to have full faith in God (which is also where the narrative of the *Memorial* begins).[39] In the end, her understandings of the presence and absence of God lead her theologically to emphasize the radical unknowability of God. With the absence of God comes certainty of God's presence and beneficence towards her.

The idea of union with God, possible only in snatches in this lifetime, only serves to increase Angela's frustration with this oscillation between the poles of presence and absence of God. In her visionary moments, she receives temporary and imperfect union with God, which she knows will not last; in these moments she sees imperfectly what one the beatific vision will offer. These moments point to an even better, wonderful and perfect union with God in the afterlife and therefore offer Angela the joy of hope. It is towards this perfect union that everything aims: she describes it in terms of love, saying, 'The perfect and highest form of love, one without defects, is the one in which the soul is drawn out of itself and led into the vision of the being of God.'[40] Her vision here is one of unity, not just of the individual soul and God but of the entire universe. In Angela's writings, this vision does not only occur at the moment of death; her perception is of a love that the soul can experience here and now, and Angela discusses its continuing effects on the development of other loves. This vision induces its own consummation, for it encourages the growth of love through which the soul's love is perfected towards creatures. The ineffable nature of God also leads Angela to realize that if God is beyond scripture, then her experiences themselves, which are of something that cannot be contained within language, are also beyond the limits of her own text.

Conclusions

Angela's discussions of the ineffability of God incorporate the use of words such as 'blasphemy' or 'transgression'. Although she is quite orthodox in almost all of her work, she holds on to a trope of blasphemy as indicative of her project. Angela relies upon this trope to suggest a number of ideas: her humility in the face of great spiritual gifts; her reticence at being recorded. But at the centre of her words about the transgressive nature of her work are the twin ideas that God just cannot be fixed in language, and language is too limited, fragile and fine a vehicle to match God's might.

In the last chapters of the *Memorial*, Angela moves from a position of merely dictating her visions to answering questions that Brother A has raised. In so doing, Angela moves from a role of reporting mystical experiences to one that approaches the actual doing of theology, a role that was off-limits to women. It is in this role, of theologian and teacher, that Angela steps from the margins into the centre, and most fully embodies the Franciscan ideal, one that tried to restore the disenfranchised and abandoned within high medieval Christianity.[41] Angela's value filters down to our own times in several important aspects: first, she represents the Franciscan ideals, showing the charismata of the mendicant orders that grew up in her time. Second, she represents one such way that a woman with none of the traditional trappings of power and authority could in fact come to have some of these through the careful collaboration of a male whose devotion to and recording of her life and experiences lifted her up as a model of Christian behaviour. Finally, Angela represents the audacious nature that characterized many of the forms of spirituality in her time. In this last regard, Angela shares certain characteristics with another woman we shall read about later, Margery Kempe. Margery was also a wife and mother who felt the call to religious profession, albeit that her own negotiation of this had a slightly less professional twist to it. She also engaged, like Angela and like Christina before, in an overstatedly emotional or 'hysterical' manner, although Margery, unlike Angela, is not so easily tied to the spirituality of only one order.

8

Annihilated Soul: Marguerite Porete

> This Soul, says Love, is totally dissolved, melted and drawn, joined and united to the most high Trinity. And she cannot will except the divine will through the divine work of the whole Trinity. And a ravishing Spark and Light joins her and holds her very close.[1]

In her book *The Mirror of Simple Souls*, Marguerite Porete (d. 1310) describes how a soul comes to be radically reliant upon God through a gradual spiritual asceticism. She relates an allegorical dialogue between the Soul and Love that describes how the work of annihilation of the soul is a work of love inspired by God in the soul. At the end of this journey, all that keeps the soul from union with God has been destroyed and the soul is utterly enveloped within God. Marguerite's writings on the annihilated soul push the religious vocabulary of union and the limits of language to talk about life with God past their breaking point.

Of Marguerite's early life we know little, save what comes from fourteenth-century chronicles surrounding some of the events in her late life. She was identified as Margarita de Hannonia, which probably refers to Hainault, south of Flanders and Brabant, in the proximity of southern Belgium and northern France. She was most likely a beguine, and probably a wandering one not connected to a beguine enclosure. Rather than begin this chapter, however, with the usual biography, I would like to begin with her works, and their literary and theological significances, and then turn to her life, in order to put its events into perspective.

Writer and text

Reading *The Mirror of Simple Souls*, we are immediately met with a challenge: Marguerite Porete's text was not meant for the average Christian but for an advanced audience only.[2] She did not equate an advanced audience with official ecclesiastic status, for she herself neither lived in a monastery nor was instructed in scholastic theology. Although she appears to be highly educated and familiar with the *Minnemystik* and courtly love traditions, she displays disdain in her book for the scholastic tradition and other officially sanctioned devotions and theologies. The fact that she was a woman did not keep her from addressing those whom she felt were truly spiritually superior. In fact, as we shall see, Marguerite believed that being in a clerical position often hindered true spiritual development. She also wrote in the vernacular (old French), which was not the traditional vehicle for theological reflection.

The Mirror of Simple Souls consists of two parts of uneven length: the first 119 chapters are an extended allegory in which Love leads various characters such as the Soul, the (sometimes-absent) Reason and FarNear in a dialogue. The last 20 chapters break free of this dialogue, and include a new, more personal narratorial voice, which scholars have suggested is the voice of Marguerite Porete herself. Quite possibly, these last chapters were not written until after the book's initial burning at Valenciennes in 1306.[3] Allegorical models were common in the courtly love tradition, but Marguerite Porete uses allegory differently; she uses it as a didactic tool to map the progress of the soul to God, thus establishing seven steps the soul must take. In Hadewijch, allegory served a descriptive purpose in giving concrete imagery to the soul's quest. This use of allegorical didactics aligns Marguerite within the tradition of philosophical allegorical dialogues, such as Boethius' *Consolation of Philosophy*, which was a dialogue in which Lady Philosophy consoled the philosopher when he was imprisoned and taught him about the natures of virtue and happiness. Another contemporary example of allegory was the medieval French *roman* by Guillaume de Lorris and Jean de Meun, *Romance of the Rose*. Thus, allegory in Marguerite has different roots from that in other writings we have seen by medieval women thinkers.

Within Marguerite's work, we find relics of other literary traditions as well. The theme of Marguerite's prologue uses the *Roman d'Alexandre*, a thirteenth-century writing of Alexander of Bernay, as an *exemplum*. This story, which was very popular with medieval writers, has roots back to the second-century Greek author Pseudo-Callisthenes and other classical authors. In the high middle ages Alexander's story was sung by the troubadours of the courtly love tradition. The legend describes a king named Alexander and his romance with a woman named Candace. In Marguerite's hands, Alexander was identified by his kindly giving and became a symbol of divine love and giving. But while Alexander was out in battle and travels, he was separated from his beloved Candace. During Candace's long-distance romance, she used a picture of Alexander to keep him in mind. Marguerite shows that this example parallels the human situation: the human soul is estranged, distanced, from its lover, God, who exists across an unfathomable epistemological and ontological gap, and must rely on memory to keep God in mind. Marguerite planned for *The Mirror of Simple Souls* to discuss how this gap can be overcome.

The dramatic trajectory of *The Mirror of Simple Souls* is the gradual movement of the soul through seven stages of development. Porete glossed over the first three stages quickly as if they are self-evident, characterized by grace, supererogatory devotions and good works. Here, Marguerite's idea of union is one effected by faith, not works, since works pass out of her schema in the early stages.[4] The fourth level in Marguerite's schema is spiritual poverty, and at the end of this level the soul takes leave of the virtues. After this level, the fifth and sixth levels mark the soul's progress beyond most earthly aids such as sacraments, virtues and works. Marguerite describes the fifth level as offering the soul a 'freeness of charity' given by gentle FarNear. In the sixth stage, she begins to receive glimpses of the seventh stage as a perception of the ultimate gift. In the seventh level the soul is annihilated. It is worth noting that she explicitly develops a scheme of ascent similar to the spiritual writings of men such as Bernard of Clairvaux and William of St-Thierry. Developmental schemes were common among the speculative theology and mystical theology of men, particularly in the monastic traditions (Victorines, Cistercians, Benedictines) and within the Neo-Platonic traditions of the early and high middle ages.

But a scheme of development is an aspect of only the first part of *The Mirror of Simple Souls*. The last section of the *Mirror* also deserves attention because of its radically different and more personal voice. The two parts of *The Mirror of Simple Souls*, with their differences in voice naturally lead to questions about whether the more personal parts of the book (in the second part) are meant to be autobiographical or not, a question that has met with a variety of answers from scholars. A number of scholars such as Peter Dronke and Elizabeth Petroff read these last chapters to refer explicitly to Marguerite Porete herself. The argument in favour of this is that the tone changes and appears to refer to the example of Marguerite Porete's life rather than just abstract argument, as the previous 119 chapters do. Porete avoids using a narratorial voice of her own (as opposed to Mechtild of Magdeburg, who merely masks it by various tropes) by using extended allegory for most of the work.[5] The argument in favour of the end being autobiographical relies upon the sudden shift in narratorial voice away from allegory throughout the second section, suggesting that Porete herself is a spiritually advanced soul who wished to offer her own lived life as a proof of the doctrine of *The Mirror of Simple Souls*.

Love and the soul

Porete knew aspects of the courtly love lyric tradition, for traces of it appear in her work. Besides the content borrowing from *Alexander* discussed above, she uses two poetic forms in the *Mirror* that were common to the courtly love tradition, including a *canzone* in her Prologue and a *rondeau* at the end of the work. Highly lyrical passages occur at pivotal points in the text, particularly in the final 100 lines of the text, indicating Porete's familiarity with the linguistic style of courtly love lyrics, which used lyrical intensity at climaxes in the dramatic development. The purpose of *The Mirror of Simple Soul*'s dialogue is to probe the ways in which God interacts lovingly with the soul in order to woo it into responding lovingly to God. If this is done, love becomes both a flight from the world and a liberation of the soul through the annihilation of oneself in God, being therefore transformed into God. This is not a typical trope of any courtly love genres. And unlike other beguine writers such as Hadewijch and Mechtild, Marguerite does not use the language of the courtly love tradition to focus on the attaining of love. The character Love directs the dialogue, but the courtly love tropes do not. Marguerite ultimately aims to show that love is not enough (nor is any human language) to contain what happens to the soul in union with God. The character Love appears flatter, more like a philosophical idea. The text's vision is an apophatic one, and it is to speechlessness that Marguerite in the end passes. The trope of ineffability underscores that the reader must become more involved in Marguerite's text than in others: for it is in the fact that

Marguerite cannot fully describe what is occurring that the reader is encouraged to discover it for herself.

As is quite obvious in the other chapters dealing with women writing in the tradition of *Minnemistik*, the nature of Love is an essential component for understanding the female thinker's theology and has a number of uses and meanings. Though, having done much of the work unpacking the concept in Hadewijch's case, Marguerite's use of the term will seem much simpler. At the heart of Marguerite's idea of love is a selflessness that she says has 'only one intent alone, which is that the Soul love always loyally without wishing to have anything in return'.[6] This selflessness will result in the pure annihilation of the human being when the soul gives way to the divine will in place of her own will. Love sustains these elite souls, and Marguerite says that they are known as part of the 'Holy Church the Greater'. Love is the bond between the Persons in the Trinity, and thus it is also the connection between God and the elite soul. Such souls seek a union with the Trinity that can only take place through this love, in effect unifying the soul and the Godhead. For Marguerite Porete, nothing is complete until the beatific vision in heaven, and she explains that 'the soul does not possess sufficiency of divine love, nor divine love sufficiency of the soul, until the soul is in God and God in the Soul, of Him, through Him, in such a state of divine rest. Then the Soul possesses all her sufficiency.'[7] In this final state, the soul is in union with God, a state which Marguerite describes in a multiplicity of ways. Marguerite sees the soul yielding to a force bigger than itself (the sea, fire) and allowing the larger force to consume it however it will.

Marguerite Porete describes the average God-fearing Christian soul as a soul enslaved to the virtues and God's commandments; the soul must move from enslavement to freedom or 'nobility'. The soul begins enslaved to the virtues; doing what it is told will increase the virtues and direct it towards the heavenly afterlife. When the soul becomes bound up with love, it finds that it must take leave of the virtues, in order to move towards becoming one with God.[8] By forsaking the virtues, the soul finds a new freedom because it no longer responds to anyone but God. It is at this moment that the soul takes a big step towards God, and at this point it no longer needs the ministrations of Holy Church the Lesser – good works do not help. Sacraments are unnecessary, because although they help bring souls to God, they are a mediated form of relation with God. This freed soul is closer to God, in a less mediated fashion, than the ministers and their sacraments. Once the soul is rapt into the sixth state, even if it stumbles, it cannot fall below the fourth state, and thus it still will never use the virtues again. Her concern with the workings of the soul lies in the power of the will. Such a soul is freed 'when Love dwells in them, and the virtues serve [the soul] without any contradiction and without labor by such souls'.[9] Such souls, Porete says, have 'perfected the virtues'. Here, the soul does not serve the virtues, doing what the virtues require out of fear of afterworldly punishment or reward; rather, such freed souls get the virtues to do the soul's bidding, which is directly congruent with the will of God.[10] From this point onwards, the soul works towards becoming annihilated in God's love. The annihilated soul's understanding is not found in scripture, nor is it apprehended by the senses. The annihilated soul reverts to a precreated state. It is here that was seen most clearly the Neo-Platonic metaphysics of emanation from God and return to God in Marguerite. Her cosmological vision relies upon an order of emanation and return, and asserts that the human has these skills hard-wired into itself. Other theological influences include the influence of the Cistercian William of St-Thierry, who we saw also influenced Hadewijch. In the *Nature and Dignity of Love*, William explained that Love and Reason work to know God through radically different paths. Reason sees discursively, and does not ever really 'grasp' God. Her approach is the *via negativa*, in which she most clearly sees what God is not. Love grasps God through the *via affirmativa*, for Love is one of the means God has of communicating what God is. We see those two paths in *The Mirror*. In the two main characters of Love and Reason, we have a portrait of the two faculties of the soul as opposites: Reason chatters on and on, often being reproached for misunderstandings. Reason's excurses usually divide. Love's excurses seek to unite, and she is ultimately the one in control of the dialogue.

The soul, guided by love rather than reason, strives towards a freedom that Marguerite identifies with the annihilated soul. God and the human soul are finally united in her annihilation. She also describes this interaction between the soul and God as a courtly exchange, in which the deity gives the soul the goodness of the deity, and the soul gives its will to the deity.[11] Annihilation is a fusing much more than a mere giving-up or getting rid of. Love is ultimately that which God is for Marguerite. As the character Love says, echoing 1 John 4.16: 'I am God, says Love, for Love is God and God is Love.'[12]

Such freed souls no longer possess will or desire. In the medieval view, will or desire propels the soul towards God or towards whatever the soul seeks. Ultimately, Marguerite says that the soul is to live without a will and even 'without a why'.[13] To deny the existence of will either implies the soul cannot seek God of its own capacity any more or it implies the soul has already attained an inseparable union with God and therefore does not need to keep sustaining her efforts towards God by means of her own will (God's grace alone will lead her). This cannot happen until the soul rests in God completely and ultimately in the afterlife. To say that the soul must live 'without a why' implies a total dependency upon God for the trajectory of her life to be determined, for the 'why' (final cause) is what propels the will in its direction towards God, and even this trajectory of the soul is to be given over to God.

The dialogue of *The Mirror of Simple Souls* strains towards the apophatic and this shows the inherent difficulty of explaining lofty spiritual achievements at all. Often, Porete's language seems more abstract than most speculative theology of her day because of the highly allegorized nature of her dialogue and the circular argumentation that this form provides. Porete's theological ideas – such as the soul not willing, the annihilated soul and the lack of virtues in the unencumbered soul – appear well beyond the grasp of the average seeker. But this highly abstract feel of her writing further bolsters her whole point that the union is an achievement beyond human means alone (and especially beyond human reason alone). At the heart of her calls for a surrender of will is a radical unknowing, rooted in creaturely humility, that leads to a *fiat*: the soul simply says 'God's will be done'.

Body

The body and all material objects to religion are tools for the weak only, according to Marguerite. Her spirituality dislikes the body as an 'enfeebling encumbrance'. Other stumbling blocks that Porete lists include the historical Jesus, sacraments and the visible church. And her theology shows an apparent lack of reintegration of the soul with the body in the final unity with God. Marguerite states that the purpose of the sacraments and good works is mediatorial for weaker members. This even leads to Porete's own book being unnecessary once the soul has progressed sufficiently far.[14] Writing the book has transformed Marguerite; reading it should begin the work of transformation in others; but, to Marguerite's mind, the book – like all material aids – ultimately must be surpassed, and therefore it really sums up nothing.

Some of Marguerite's reflections on the body do exhibit similarity to several of the beguine traditions we have previously seen. For instance, she has a feminized Love figure who represents the divine. Her language also uses the tropes of love and courtly romance to explain her ideas of the relationship between God and the soul. But she rejects the bodiliness and asceticism that we see in other beguines. Marguerite stands apart from most of the women in this book in the absolute lack of bodily knowledge in her work. In place of the body, we find Marguerite has an emphasis on a spiritualized asceticism, namely the annihilation of the individual's will, which is arguably a much more difficult form of asceticism than the bodily feats we see in others. There is also a greater move towards the apophatic, which was suggested in the work of Mechtild of Magdeburg but which finds a fuller expression in the *Mirror*. And with this move to apophasis, there is a move to subvert the traditional associations of femaleness and female ways of experiencing God, particularly bodily forms of knowing, loving and experience.

Anticlericalism

One of the more distinguishing characteristics of Marguerite Porete's writings are her hostile barbs against the institutional church. We saw in Hildegard how she identified failures within the clergy in order to justify her role as God's prophet. As with other aspects of Marguerite's writing, her derogatory comments rise to a new level of anticlericalism. In places she will refer to 'Holy Church the Greater' and 'Holy Church the Lesser'; the former identifies the proficient mystic's experience of God, and the latter refers to clerical and scholastic elements in the church. In her dialogue she notes that she will be condemned by scholastics who are guided by reason rather than love.[15]

In her critique of scholasticism, Marguerite expresses her dislike of a tradition guided by reason in which love, experience and the affective responses – in other words, her own emphases – had little or no seeming place. In her critiques of scholars and priests, she also belittles both groups, saying that each is merely going through the motions without having the appropriately deep experience of a life truly given up to God. Included in one of her lists of those who will disagree with her teachings are the major orders of the church:

> Beguines say I err,
> priests, clerics, and Preachers,
> Augustinians, Carmelites,
> and the Friars Minor.[16]

Yet even the established beguine communities fall into a group from which Marguerite distances herself. Here Porete separates herself from any and all institutionalized or regularized forms of religion, which she sees as limiting the scope of the way in which adherents to these traditions can experience God.

Porete undoubtedly angered church officials when referring to Holy Church the Little, the church militant governed by Reason, which is equivalent to the church on earth.[17] Her alternative, Holy Church the Great, is governed by Divine Love and includes unencumbered souls. God alone – who exiles, annihilates and forgets these special unencumbered souls – knows who is where and understands them. Because these souls are so cut off, in their own internal isolation, only God can enter and hence probe them. Although many medieval mystics criticized the church, to do so required that one have certain protections. Marguerite Porete spoke without the protections that people such as Hildegard of Bingen had, namely speaking as recognized to be the voice of the divine light, and ecclesiastic approval of her visions.[18] And this last point, when viewed with her anticlericalism and her finely nuanced theology, undoubtedly added to her trials.

The trial and death of Marguerite Porete

The production and distribution of a text were not what granted it authority; rather, the reception of the text provided the basis of its authority. As we saw in Hildegard, the Rhineland mystic campaigned to have her writings authenticated by those in clerical power, cementing its approval. She used connections within the spiritually powerful Cistercian Order to obtain papal approval for her writings. Once this happened, she used this power to consolidate other opportunities not normally open to women. Other women we've seen received posthumous authority based on lives written about them, as in the case of Christina the Astonishing. In the case of Marguerite Porete, it appears the readers of her works fell into two camps: those who found a sublime, doctrinaire position; and those who found it scandalously heretical. Unfortunately for Marguerite, those in the latter group triumphed, and she was condemned as a heretic and burned to death in an auto-da-fé in Paris.[19]

In 1274, the Council of Lyons reiterated the thirteenth Canon of the Fourth Lateran Council, which stated that no new orders were to be allowed or established. About this time, pamphlets began to surface in Paris and other cities condemning the beguines. The Franciscan friar Gilbert of Tournai vocally condemned the beguines, and he expressed a number of allegations including an account that the beguines had unauthorized scriptural translations into the vernacular (only the Latin Vulgate being the official version). Some time between 1296 and 1306, Porete wrote *The Mirror of Simple Souls*. At this time, Guy II, Bishop of Cambrai, condemned her manuscript. At the heart of Guy's allegation was the growing concern that vernacular theology and lay devotional movements offered too much power to the laity and had caused too much democratization of religion, which in turn meant that the clergy feared their power slipping away and chaos (and heterodoxy) ensuing.[20] Her book was burned, and she was ordered to stop disseminating her ideas upon pain of execution. With this stern warning, she escaped her first clash with the ecclesiastic authorities. However, she did not stop advocating her ideas: instead, she sent her book to prominent churchmen, all of whom agreed to varying extents that her ideas were both orthodox and so extremely subtle as to be hard for the average person to understand correctly. The three individuals whom Marguerite explicitly mentions approved her book were Friar Minor John de Querayn, a monk named Frank of the Cistercian Abbey of Villiers, Brabant, and Godfrey of Fontaines (in Flanders), an ex-regent of the University of Paris, which was the central continental university for the study of theology at the time.[21] In 1306–07, Guy II's successor, Philip of Marigny, had Porete brought before him, where she was then accused of heresy and of leading the common people astray by her teachings. By late 1308, Porete had once again fallen into the hands of Papal Inquisitor and Dominican William Humbert. William's notoriety was on the increase, as he had just concluded the same year the Templar trials in which 54 men were sentenced to death.

After her arrest, Marguerite Porete steadfastly refused to defend herself, she refused to ask for absolution, and she remained silent the entire time. She would not even swear the oaths necessary for her to go to trial during her 18-month imprisonment. Undoubtedly, this attempt to act just like Christ (who had also remained silent at the hands of his own questionable condemnation and political manoeuvring) made Marguerite infuriate her own captors even more. At the time of Porete's arrest, Guiard de Cressonessart, a wandering contemplative, tried to offer her support, and as a result he was also arrested in Paris, where he was tried and condemned with Marguerite. De Cressonessart held questionable beliefs that, while different from Marguerite's, concerned the investigators: he held millenarian views similar to Joachim of Fiore and Bonaventura.[22] In the end, he retracted his support for Marguerite and spent the rest of his life in prison, thus avoiding death by burning.[23] While she was still in prison, the authorities sent excerpts from Marguerite's *The Mirror of Simple Souls* to 21 theological regents of the Sorbonne. Normally, the authorities would have asked Marguerite to explain the work herself, but as she would not talk, they had to rely solely on the readings of the regents, who saw only the excerpted passages. This group of investigators included many important names in scholastic theology at the time, such as John of Ghent and Nicholas of Lyra. On 11 April 1310, the regents returned an opinion that at least 15 articles were deemed heretical, and the canon lawyers delivered a unanimous verdict against Marguerite. On 31 May, Marguerite was released to secular justice as a lapsed heretic, to be burned at the stake in the first public auto-da-fé in Paris, alongside a converted Jew who had been convicted of spitting on an image of Mary.[24] She was burned as a heretic, and not as a beguine, but the bishops on her jury also served the following year on the Council of Vienne; this council issued the Clementine Decrees of 1311–12, which persecuted beguines, and their documents identified beguines as examples of the so-called heresy of the free spirit. Marguerite's trial has been seen by scholars as the beginning of the end for beguines and other extra-religious groups, even cloistered ones.[25] The movement that sought control by not allowing further orders to be created moved another step forward by clamping down on extant groups that did not have official status as orders.

Since Marguerite's writings were addressed mainly to women, the burning of her book and the subsequent burning of its author are read by some scholars to have been a warning by the church authorities against women.[26] The extent to which her prosecutors went to prove her unorthodoxy by contacting leading theologians shows that she was considered a serious threat; these actions also directly confronted her own method of having tried to obtain authority. Marguerite had appealed to theologians to guarantee the validity of her ideas; because authority was something that had to be given to her, the inquisitors found they could remove her authority by simply finding other theologians who would deny the orthodoxy of her ideas. As a result, the proceedings highlighted her extremely tenuous position and was a direct challenge to women who would seek such granting of authority in the future.

In 1312, the Council of Vienne promulgated the decree *Ad nostrum* in which it announced it had decided that the Free Spirit heresy was evident among the beguines and beghards.[27] Church officials considered the discussion of theological matters to be especially perilous among lay people, and this concern would become the basis for the bull's condemnation of beguines and beghards.[28] In fact, Marguerite's own work, *The Mirror of Simple Souls*, was the 'quarry for certain suspect statements condemned in *Ad nostrum*'.[29] This official document condemned a number of beliefs, all of which dealt with the perfected souls who were still in this life. *Ad nostrum* took some statements from very few people (sometimes out of context), and wove a 'widespread' heresy out of them. As several modern scholars have noted, the Heresy of the Free Spirit was certainly never an organized movement, nor was it advocated by any identifiable group.[30]

Conclusions

The condemnation of the beguines and beghards underscores that there was a difference in the behaviour, actions and beliefs allowed within the enclosed community of the nunnery and what was allowed outside. Many of her thoughts, her claims of revelation, and even her explication of the Scriptures, might well have been ignored if Porete had only written for an enclosed, all-female audience. It was Marguerite's act of going outside the walls of the Paris beguinage and propagating her work that led her into trouble within the world of the theological men who were safekeepers of orthodoxy.[31]

Yet it is fair to suppose that, despite her unfortunate end, Marguerite Porete might not have minded the abuse hurled at her or her book. Ultimately, the book that Marguerite wrote is a book that she meant to help people start out on the road to God, but the book, just like any other material aids – sacraments, crucifixes, visual meditation, or the body – must be overcome in order for the soul to progress. In this way, Marguerite suggests that the book is a concession to help people, and is not really a summary of the higher levels of what the soul can attain, for that is beyond the descriptive power of language and schemas, and her attempt to explain these higher levels is really just discourse with the world; it is not the practice of union with God. She says:

> Now I understand, on account of your peace and on account of the truth, that [this book] is of the lower life. Cowardice has guided [this book], which has given its perception over to Reason through the answers of Love to Reason's petitions. And so [this book] has been created by human knowledge and the human senses; and the human reason and the human senses know nothing about inner love from divine knowledge.[32]

In fact, the book moves beyond cataphatic theology to apophatic theology, and beyond apophatic theology to include an entire apophasis of desire. As was commented, 'The *Mirror* brings together the Apophatic paradoxes of mystical union, the language of courtly love – as it had been transformed by the beguine mystics of the thirteenth century into a mystical language of rapture – and a daring reappropriation of medieval religious themes.' The result is an 'apophasis of desire',[33] which in the end is a melting of the divine and the human into a unity, no longer separated or divided.

9

Bodily Mystic: Julian of Norwich

More so than any other woman in this book, Julian of Norwich (1343–1413) is a female thinker who has come to be regarded as a cornerstone of women's mysticism in the middle ages. She combines mystical visions based upon the crucifix with nearly 20 years of deep theological meditation upon them that would result in the Long Text of the *Shewings* (or *Revelations*, as the work is also known). In her writings, Julian pictures Jesus in a number of images, including Jesus as a mother, and these images provide a visually stunning set of 'texts' from which Julian further derives her theological reflections on God and the human. 'Pictures' is a key word when discussing Julian, for her descriptions of her visions incorporate a strong visual component, and her explanations of the theological significance of the details of her visions solidifies her strong descriptive feel.

Julian represents two distinct trends in medieval English spirituality: the bodily representation of Christ common in the English affective traditions and the contemplative tradition, which focused on moving the mind beyond physical images; uniquely, she combines these two very well. Part of the brilliance of her work as a thinker is that her text, like many others, has both literary merit in its composition as well as theological merit. In particular, Julian provides an example of how practices of memory and contemplative practices such as those of the work of *lectio divina* (divine reading) can result in profound theological reflection upon visions received from God.

Background and life

Julian's life is rather obscure; even her name we do not know. It is an odd contrast to a woman we come to know so intimately through her writings. 'Julian' undoubtedly refers to the church to which her anchorhold was attached; it was customary for anchorites and anchoresses to take the name of the church to which they were connected. What we do know about her comes from only a few veiled references within her own works, from some wills and other testimonies that people left behind, and from what we can infer from knowing the religious milieu of late medieval Norwich. In her writings, Julian describes how at the age of 30 she suffered a serious illness in which the priest was called to give her last rights, and her mother was present, because they thought she was dying. Yet she never mentions where she was living, or what she was doing, at the time of her sickness, so it is unclear whether she had already entered her anchorhold before the time of her sickness.

During her lifetime, Norwich was second in size and population only to London, and she lived as a contemplative in a rather large urban environment. Medieval Norwich contained houses for all the major orders of the middle ages, including the Franciscans, Dominicans, Augustinians, Benedictines and others. The anchorhold of the Church of St Julian was under the benefice of the Benedictine convent of Carrow, located just outside the city of Norwich. Many scholars have speculated about the possibility that Julian had either lived or been educated at Carrow before her enclosure at the Church of St Julian. There are no clear ties to support this, but Julian's ability to write, and her knowledge of theological writers, would be consonant with her having connections to this convent. If Julian were to have a connection to Carrow, it would tell us about her social class, for it was a convent that educated the wealthy daughters of Norwich.

Her writings give us a strong sense of her inner relationship with the Christ who revealed Himself to her, even though she gives us little idea of what her outer life was like. For a sense of her outer life, we need to turn to any of a number of rules for anchoresses, hermits and other solitaries which exist from the middle ages; on a day-to-day basis, Julian's life would have involved the spiritual direction of lay people and visitors, intercessory prayers for those who asked, and the conduct and behaviour she was expected to exhibit.[1] Rules such as the *Ancrene Rewle* suggest that the anchoress was not to gossip with those who came to visit, and, for modesty's sake, she should talk to visitors through a double curtain. For errands that involved going into the city, such as shopping, she should employ a servant who would neither cause strife in her life nor would entice the anchoress to gossip. She was not to hold possessions for safe-keeping, nor was she to get involved in legal disputes. From her cell, she had a small window or door through which she could view masses in the church and receive communion. She also had a door or window to the outside through which she could talk with people who came seeking spiritual advice. In exchange for her prayers and advice, people provided offerings that would have allowed the anchoress to live a modest life in her cell.

Julian was born in 1342 or 1343, and during her childhood the stir-rings of civic unrest had begun, caused by several years of high taxes and labour shortages due to bad harvests and epidemics; during her child-hood and adolescence, the first bouts of the Black Death ravaged England. In epidemics such as the Black Death, the toll that the disease had on the population of Norwich and on the stability of the church and countryside was considerable. Medieval Norwich, like all cities in the middle ages, was closely built and infested with vermin, and had little or no sanitation. Notions of disease prevention and hygiene did not yet exist, so the popu-lation had no way of controlling the disease, whose method of transmis-sion was not yet known. The disease was so contagious that people who had been healthy one morning might be dead or near-dead by evening. Those who were sick often died without last rites; the priests who minis-tered to the sick usually came down with the disease themselves, or were quarantined for the fear they might spread contagion. The souls of those who died without last rites were thought to be sent to hell for not having received final reconciliation; their bodies were often sent as piles of bodies on carts that navigated the city every evening to unmarked, mass graves on unconsecrated soil. This turmoil, and the desire for some type of comfort or assurance of God's providential care, forms a backdrop for Julian's theological reflections in the *Shewings*. But the *Shewings* was also born out of her desire to live a life more deeply conformed to God. At age 30 she prayed for three special gifts: 'the first was recollection of the Passion. The second was bodily sickness. The third was to have, of God's gifts, three wounds.'[2] Julian says that she then forgot about this three-fold prayer until she became sick six months later and nearly died. While on her deathbed, she received the sacrament of Extreme Unction, or Last Rites, which was given to those about to die, and following this Julian had a series of 16 visions, which she then wrote down. She wrote down her first reflection immediately following the visions, which is known as the Short Text. She spent the next 20 years reflecting on these visions, and in 1393 wrote a longer version, known as the Long Text. Between these two writings, the Peasants' Revolt of 1381 occurred as a result of all the unrest, adding to the period's tenor of instability and danger.

Julian as a writer

The Short Text of the *Revelations* describes Julian's visions in careful sensual detail and includes explanations of the meaning of each vision. The text's order follows the chronology of the 16 visions. This text also provides the rudiments of the structure for the Long Text, which offers more extensive commentary on the meanings of her visions. The meditative process that gave birth to the Long Text also helped Julian see connections between the individual visions, which indicates that she saw the 16 revelations as a whole. As the editors of the critical edition of the *Revelations* show, both the Long Text and Short Text provide the same sense of Julian's doctrine and content of the revelations, although the Long Text is the more stylistically enhanced.[3] Julian's commentary on her visions in the Long Text is particularly illuminative because it shows the process by which she acquires meaning for the revelations she received. Whereas the visions are a divine revelation, the meanings are a joint combination of divine gift and human construction; sometimes meaning is passed on directly by God, but more often it is constructed from Julian's careful rumination upon the visions. As the recipient of the visions and as the primary commentator, Julian has a particular authority concerning the interpretation of her visions and she claims this authority through linking the visions and interpretations closely in the Long Text. Because the process she used was akin to the processes of memory and of *lectio divina*, Julian uses her practices to reinforce the sacred nature of the visions, insisting that no detail is too small to be insignificant.[4]

For Julian, language was not merely a vehicle: her style is consistent with the refinement of her thought. Julian's style evidences conscientious use of metrical cadences, rhythms, compositional complexity and abundant rhetorical devices, which shows that she was a writer knowledgeable of composition.[5] Many other writers, such as Chaucer and Langland, also stretched the spectrum of the English language at the same time as Julian, discovering how English could express divine secrets.[6] One way this happened was to reinvent literary devices and apply Latin compositional devices to middle English. Authors also found ways to create new literary devices for composition in English from the classical literary devices used in Latin. One favourite device of Julian's that has left us perhaps her most memorable passage is that of *complexio*, which involves repetition of first and final words in several successive clauses, as when God says to Julian, 'I will make all things well, I shall make all things well, I may make all things well, and I can make all things well.'[7] One can also find parallels between Julian's writing style and the rhythms of the preaching styles of the day. Although Julian calls herself 'unlettered', this does not mean that she is not a good and trained reader; this merely means that she was not educated in Latin composition. Based on the similarities between her Short Text and the Long Text written two decades later, she must have been able to read her middle English text in order to compose an elaboration whose text tracks so closely to the original text where passages parallel that text.

The *Shewings* purport to be based solely on the 16 visions she received, but much of her material has at least some of its sources in the Latin spiritual treatises of the time, and her ideas have analogues traceable to English vernacular translations of the twelfth century.[8] Devotional texts and popular spirituality works that have analogues in Julian's works include the *Ancrene Riwle* (a treatise that was a rule governing the lives of anchoresses), a collection of five related religious writings known as 'The Katherine Group' (which contained lives of three saints: Katherine, Margaret and Juliana), and two treatises: *Hali Haidenhead* and *Sawles Warde* (which were writings for or about women and which exalted virginity).[9] Other parallels show that Julian was also familiar with continental mystical writings:[10] 'Vernacular devotional literature focused intense meditation on the humanity of Christ, and particularly on the Passion, with the goal of achieving sorrow for sin, through which one attained a kind of subjective appropriation of Christ's objective atoning work by participation in his redemptive pains.'[11] Julian's writings purport to do the same, but move from the affective sphere to a more theologically abstract speculation on the nature of sin. Her writings also show she had a thorough knowledge of the Vulgate and was especially fond of the Pauline and Johannine epistles.[12] Finally, there are passages that show clear influence from a number of patristic and medieval Christian thinkers in the Long Text, including Gregory, Augustine and William of

St-Thierry, as well as the English treatises *The Treatise of Perfection of the Sons of God*, the *Cloud of Unknowing* and Walter Hilton's *Scale of Perfection*, and a translation of Boethius' *Consolation of Philosophy*.[13] Thus Julian's texts show she did not work in anchoritic isolation; rather, her writings engage the trends of her theological and literary times.

Julian's spirituality

Julian's writings present a spirituality meant to provide comfort and hope, and a theological insight that wrestles with a number of difficult questions before it can reach such comfort; questions such as the relationship between God and humans, the nature of God and the Trinity, the nature of the human, and sin. Julian's works are studded with examples of close connection between God and God's creatures: Julian says that God creates creatures through love and God's providential care sustains creatures, who come to fruition in salvation. God and creatures are complementary, and God suffers when creatures suffer. Conversely, all creatures also suffered when Christ died on the cross. Julian explains that she

> saw a great unity between Christ and us, as I understand it; for when he was in pain we were in pain, and all creatures able to suffer pain suffered with him. That is to say, all creatures which God has created for our service, the firmament and the earth, failed in their natural functions because of sorrow at the time of Christ's death, for it is their natural characteristic to recognize him as their Lord, in whom all their powers exist.[14]

Julian further explains, 'God wishes to be seen, and he wishes to be sought, and he wishes to be expected, and he wishes to be trusted.'[15] God longs for humans, and the human, in response, when it knows God, should long for the love of God in return.[16]

The fact that there is an intimate relationship between God and creatures does not mean that there will never be any problems; creatures can and do still suffer as a result of sin, feeling isolated from God, or other causes. But she tells in one vision how she vacillated between feelings of weal and woe, and in the end she found that, in both situations, God was providentially caring for her.[17] The most obvious nexus of the human and divine, and the strength of this relationship, is to be found in the person of Jesus, both human and divine: 'For Julian, God's self-disclosure in Christ, in the order of redemption, is inseparable from his love on the order of creation.'[18]

Christ in the centre of Julian's spirituality

Julian's visions start at the nexus of her own physical body's suffering and the sight of the suffering body of Christ on the crucifix in front of her. Her body responds as she looks at Christ's suffering body: her own bodily pain passes, and feeling returns to her upper torso.[19] From there, Christ's body becomes the centre of her reflections. Gazing on the body of Christ both heals her and leads her to a deeper understanding of God; her reflections on the physical body of Christ serve as a backdrop on which other ghostly revelations are displayed, such as Mary (4.28–40), the hazelnut representing creation (5.9–33), and lessons on prayer (6.1–28), and ultimately leads her to a revelation of the immaterial Triune God. Christ appears as the loving, bleeding redeemer who is willing to die on behalf of creatures to ensure their return to God.

When she talks about her process of receiving the visions, Julian refers to both bodily sight and spiritual sight; Julian's use of these terms is unclear and it has caused much discussion among scholars about what Julian may have meant, and whether 'bodily' referred to seeing a likeness of Christ's body or referred to her means of reception. Bodily vision may refer to those visions that use as a starting point her gaze upon a physical object such as the crucifix.[20] Alternatively, by bodily vision, Julian may intend that some semblance of the physical senses is involved, and, by spiritual vision, Julian means a more hidden vision and meaning. Both of these interpretations of 'bodily vision' find evidence within the text and the ways in which Julian approaches her own visions. Perhaps more important than a clear definition of bodily vision is the recognition that although Julian uses the categories of bodily vision and spiritual vision, they do not contradict one another but stand together as different parts of the same process, both capable in their own unique ways of helping to lead her to God. The bodily does not work against the 'spiritual' but work with it and bolster the connection between God and creatures, fostering their longing for one another.

The visions in and of themselves are not beneficial except in the effect they produce in humans. She says, 'I am not good because of the revelations, but only if I love God better; and inasmuch as you love God better, it is more to you than to me.'[21] Physical descriptions in her texts underscore the sensual nature of her visions and continue to depict Christ's body in his last moments, and focus on details such as the manner in which the blood falls from his crown of thorns:

> The great drops of blood fell from beneath the crown like pellets, looking as if they came from the veins, and as they issued they were a brownish red, for the blood was very thick, and as they spread they turned bright red. And as they reached the brows they vanished; and even so the bleeding continued until I had seen and understood many things. Nevertheless, the beauty and the vivacity persisted, beautiful and vivid without diminution.[22]

In this light, she thoroughly describes the physical appearance. Julian's spirituality is different from the spirituality of most mystics because of its ability to incorporate the analytic with such a deeply sensual element. She manages to do this through a structure where she describes the visions and then analyses their significance. Thus, the text also encapsulates two different modes of the devotional life: the visions are presented first and in these lies most of the sensuality; her analytic skills are evidenced through the ruminative method. In her case, the theological insights that she pursues are much more in a vein with Anselm's *faith seeking under-standing* than they are similar to Walter Hilton's or Margery Kempe's emotional responses to God.

Her theology: sin in particular

Julian's writings about sin are one of the starker contrasts between her and her era. During her unstable, uncertain times, medieval theology had begun to show a preoccupation with some of the 'darker' aspects of theology and human experience, especially human sin and God's retribution. Much of the popular preaching of this time focused upon the conversion of sinners, atonement for sin and penance, and multiple passages in Julian's texts read as a response to this focus.[23] When she reflects on the nature of sin and how it affects relations between God and humans, Julian presents a view of sin that makes humans look like disobedient toddlers who do not know what they are doing wrong. In this view, sin is something that God as Mother can look past to teach the child correct behaviour.

Yet Julian looks into God and she does not see any sin. She interprets this to mean that sin has no existence from God, and therefore is 'nothing', and if it is nothing then it will not thwart God's plans. She does not deny that sin is real in human experience; what she denies is that it has any eternal reality: it has no part in God, who is the source of all existence.[24] Julian identifies a tension between what she sees as the all-encompassing love of God and the emphasis that humans put on sin. This is a difference that runs parallel to the difference between the human and the divine perspectives and is not a true contradiction between sin and love.[25] She explains, 'I did not see sin, for I believe that it has no kind of substance, no share in being, nor can it be recognized except by the pain caused by it.'[26] By the conclusion of her meditations on sin, all that Julian can do is remain confident in the mystery that is God, and assure herself and her reader that sin will not prevail. She says, 'in these same words I saw hidden in God an exalted and wonderful mystery, which he will make plain and we shall know in heaven. In this knowledge we shall truly see the cause why he allowed sin to come, and in this sight we shall rejoice forever.'[27] In perhaps her most famous words, she once again reassured herself and her reader that 'sin is necessary but all will be well, and all will be well, and every kind of thing will be well'.[28] Julian explains that the human's emphasis on sin in some ways misses the point when it focuses on God's punishment of sin, because sin itself is a type of penance since it makes the person who committed it feel so bad. She reflects:

> Sin is the sharpest scourge with which any chosen soul can be struck, which scourge belabours man or woman, and breaks a man, and purges him in his own sight so much that at times he thinks himself that he is not fit for anything but as it were to sink into hell, until contrition seizes him by the inspiration of the Holy Spirit and turns bitterness into hope of God's mercy.[29]

Julian's ruminations on hell, damnation and distance from God always lead beyond punishment to an assurance that this will not be a permanent state, but God will help this be overcome in short order. Her theology of sin takes sin seriously, but places it within the much larger perspective of a loving God who will unify all creatures with Godself.

Jesus as mother

The motherhood of God is one of Julian's most memorable images, but the strength of the image lies not in the mere image but in its context within Julian's work. The image of God as mother dates back to the patristic era in Christianity, and the image continued to appear in the writings of many writers through the high middle ages. Spiritual and theological writers, and religious such as Anselm of Canterbury, Bernard of Clairvaux, Aelred of Rievaulx, Hincmar of Rheims, Bonaventure, Aquinas, Richard Rolle and William Flete, all used the image of Christ as Mother in their prayers, treatises and sermons.[30] In Julian's time, the image of Christ as a mother correlated with the rise in affective devotional piety. These devotional traditions were based on the sense of the human being created in the image and likeness of God (a common inheritance from the Augustinian tradition), and the humanity of Christ served as a guarantee that humans can look forward to being joined with God. There were three basic stereotypes that the role of Christ as mother was predicated upon: first, the mother was seen as generative, producing the new child out of her own matter; second, the mother was loving and tender, and could not help but love her child; third, a mother nurtures her children, as when she feeds her child with her own body. In Julian, we find clear echoes of the second and third notions of motherhood. But we also see Julian reflecting on the motherhood of the Trinity, and she connects the Trinity's motherhood (rather than Christ alone as mother) with generation. God's motherhood serves to stress the way in which God continually keeps an eye on God's creation, acting in such a way as to protect God's children. This supported and reinforced her statements that sin was not as serious as humans think it is; God as mother can see that human's sins are like the mistakes of a toddler who does not have the cognitive abilities to know any better. Her imagery also emphasizes the physicality often found in the second theme.[31]

Julian first introduces the image of God as mother by saying that both Fatherhood and Motherhood are images that refer to God. She explains that she 'saw that God rejoices that he is our Father, and God rejoices that he is our Mother, and God rejoices that he is our true spouse, and that our soul is his beloved wife. And Christ rejoices that he is our brother, and Jesus rejoices that he is our saviour.'[32] Here, divine motherhood is just one of many roles that Christ plays, echoing the myriad forms of relationships that humans have with Christ and the incomprehensible plenitude of

God. But His motherhood highlights some of the aspects of the providential, nurturing care that Christ provides for all humans. She explains:

> Our Mother in nature, our Mother in grace, because he wanted altogether to become our Mother in all things, made the foundation of his work most humbly and most mildly in the maiden's womb. And he revealed that in the first revelation, when he brought that meek maiden before the eye of my understanding in the simple stature which she had when she conceived; that is to say that our great God, the supreme wisdom of all things, arrayed and prepared himself in this humble place, all ready in our poor flesh, himself to do the service and the office of motherhood in everything. The mother's service is nearest, readiest and surest: nearest because it is most natural, readiest because it is most loving, and surest because it is truest. No one ever might or could perform this office fully, except only him. We know that all our mothers bear us for pain and for death.[33]

Here, and elsewhere, Julian uses the image of motherhood as an aspect of God which counteracts the terrifying aspects of the lordship and fatherhood of God. Associated with motherhood are tender, loving characteristics which related not only to Christ but to the entire Trinity.[34] Motherhood is tied to God's appearing accessible. It invites a childlike trust associated with the spiritual life.

Here Julian consciously plays with the notion of Christ as a child of a mother, Mary, in order to then discuss how the other 'parent' of Christ, the Godhead, is also a mother. But God is a mother to all humans, as opposed to Mary, who is the parent of one particular child. She continues to explain, through the metaphor of nursing, how

> The mother can lay her child tenderly to her breast, but our tender Mother Jesus can lead us easily into his blessed breast through his sweet open side, and show us there a part of the godhead and of the joys of heaven, with inner certainty of endless bliss.[35]

The water and blood that come from the side wound of Christ are like the breast milk of a mother, and offer nourishment. Julian carries this image further when she also talks about how a mother feeds her child, and Christ does so through the institution of the Eucharist:

> The mother can give her child to suck of her milk, but our precious Mother Jesus can feed us with himself, and does, most courteously and most tenderly, with the blessed sacrament, which is the precious food of true life; and with all the sweet sacraments he sustains us most mercifully and graciously, and so he meant in these blessed words.[36]

The image of God as mother is not at all unique to Julian, however. It too is a tradition that she has inherited, although she incorporates it into her theological vision much more than others, in whom it appears as an image not fully integrated. Within the English homiletic tradition, Anselm uses the image in his devotional prayer but he does not apply it to the Trinity like Julian does. Christ's motherhood is for Julian an expression of the Trinity's love and belongs to Christ because of the Incarnation.[37] She says, 'I contemplated the work of all the blessed Trinity, in which contemplation I saw and understood those three properties: the property of fatherhood, and the property of motherhood, and the property of the lordship in one God.'[38] In another place, Julian probes:

> But often when our falling and our wretchedness are shown to us, we are so much afraid and so greatly ashamed of ourselves that we scarcely know where we can put ourselves. But then our courteous Mother does not wish us to flee away, for nothing would be less pleasing to him; but then he wants us to behave like a child. For when it is distressed and frightened, it runs quickly to its mother; and if it can do no more, it calls to the mother for help with all its might. So he wants us to act as a meek child, saying: My kind Mother, my gracious Mother, my beloved Mother, have mercy on me.[39]

Here Julian stresses the emotional closeness of the mother, and the imagery suggests that, as children, it is not correct for humans to try to be independent of their 'mother'. The import of the mother image here is to emphasize the idea that the mother constantly tries to put things right for the errant child. The anthropology here is one of human fear of God, and wanting to hide one's sins. Julian's image of the Motherhood of God tries to correct for such a misperception by emphasizing the ability of a mother to bring all things back together.

Bodily metaphors

Much of the research that has been done on Julian notes how the body plays an important role in her spirituality and theology. Her texts focus upon the vision of the body of Christ in intricate detail during the Passion. But she reflects upon human bodies as well. Her visions start when her own body 'failed' her and she was on the brink of death. Julian uses enclosure metaphors to describe how the bodiliness of the Incarnation encloses the divinity of Christ, and similarly how human bodiliness is a vestige of human relationship with God; she likens the human body to a purse, saying, 'A man walks upright, and the food in his body is shut in as if in a well-made purse. When the time of his necessity comes, the purse is opened and then shut again, in most seemly fashion. And it is God who does this, as it is shown when he says that he comes down to us in our humblest needs.' She then continues, 'For as the body is clad in the cloth, and the flesh in the skin, and the bones in the flesh, and the heart in the trunk, so are we, soul and body, clad and enclosed in the goodness of God.'[40] Enclosure or enfleshment is a type of divine protection.

Julian received her visions, as visual images, directly from God. These visions were then followed with a sense of God's outpouring of the Trinity in order for her to understand the divine perspective in which to put them. Finally, this outpouring of the Trinity helped to guide Julian to an immediate response, as well as to the longer-term task of writing down her visions and interpreting them:

> I perceived, truly and powerfully, that it was he who just so, both God and man, himself suffered for me, who showed it, to me without any intermediary.
>
> And in the same revelation, suddenly the Trinity filled my heart full of the greatest joy, and I understood that it will be so in heaven without end to all who will

come there ... And this was revealed in the first vision and in them all, for where Jesus appears, the blessed Trinity is understood, as I see it. And I said: Blessed be the Lord! This I said with a reverent intention and in a loud voice, and I was greatly astonished by this wonder and marvel, that he who is so to be revered and feared would be so familiar with a sinful creature living in this wretched flesh.[41]

Her *Shewings* follow the chronological order of her visions. This image of how she received this first vision points to Julian's insistence in the majesty and sheer greatness of God. But it also points to Julian's stance that God is never far away, and is always watching out for, protecting and caring for the human. Her audience are all Christians, she says, but this may be slightly disingenuous, as her treatise presupposes the reader will have some theological background.

Conclusions

'For Julian, what she sees – Christ's body – is like an inexhaustibly detailed landscape that requires more than a lifetime to comprehend.'[42] Like Hildegard of Bingen, the visionary becomes a text which Julian interprets and which serves as a basis for other gifts. In Hildegard's case, these further gifts included preaching, prophecy and leadership within the church outside her convent. For Julian, this gift manifests itself in her interpretive work and in the integrative aspect of her visionary vision, which roots itself in both the affective and contemplative prayer traditions.

The exact nature of Julian's mysticism is striking precisely because it does not fit neatly into any of the stock categories. Rather, the fact that she incorporates more than one set of devotional trends offers both challenges to interpreting her and an unexpected depth to her own works. Based on what Julian tells the reader about the circumstances upon which she received the revelations, as one scholar remarked, 'Julian takes affective piety's emphasis on the suffering body of Christ and transforms it into a Christocentric theology of revelation and redemption.'[43] Along a similar line, another scholar suggested that the first and second desires 'indicate clearly that at the time Julian's piety was of an affective, devotional kind', which she transcends and makes a more elevated form.[44]

In essence, his argument is that he finds from this one line a movement from affective spirituality to a more distanced (and therefore higher) spirituality in the theological reflections of the Short and Long Texts. In Julian, we probably do not have enough evidence to discern a trajectory of her spirituality as it might have developed from this request until the writing of the Long Text. What we can note in her text, though, is the way that the hierarchies and schemata we have seen in others such as Angela are not present. Rather, the progress is a going inwards, in which one finds oneself more easily able to probe, through Christ the gate, first his body, then his life, his theological significance, and ultimately the Trinity itself.

10

Papal Advisor: Catherine of Siena

> But I have already told you how I desire and long for
> you to be nailed fast to the cross, where we find the slain
> Lamb. Bleeding from every member, he has made him-
> self cask and wine and cellarer for us. Thus we see that
> his humanity is the cask that encased the divine nature.
> The cellarer – the fire and the hands that are the Holy
> Spirit – tapped the cask on the wood of the most holy
> cross. And this wisdom, the incarnate Word, sweetest of
> wines, tricked and defeated the devil's malice, for he
> caught him on the hook of our humanity.[1]

Drinking deeply of the Christ's blood-wine, tapped by the Holy Spirit, is
just one of many characteristics of the writings and actions of Catherine
of Siena (1347–80); this Italian mystic has captured the attentions of
medieval scholars because of her role as advisor to popes, as well as
because of the extraordinary extremes to which she took her ascetical
practices. Although we have already seen extremes in religious behaviours
before in people such as Christina the Astonishing and Angela of Foligno,
Catherine's extremes, such as subsisting solely on the Eucharist for years,
have led her to be a central figure in investigations concerning the madness or sanity of medieval women's devotional practices such as extreme
fasting.[2] At one end of this spectrum is hysteria and madness; at the other
end is utterly obedient devotion to God. These investigations question to
which end of the spectrum her extremes have belonged. But if it is the

practices of her daily life as recorded by her confessor Raymond of Capua that initially presented her as an object of study, then her writings clarify why she was deemed a doctor of the church. Her writings offer strong Christological reflections through the prism of vivid imagistic language. Catherine of Siena provides us with a very rich example of the combinations of personal piety and outward ministry, as well as theological writings that help to show evidence of the wide range of women's spirituality in fourteenth-century Italy. Her life as a Dominican tertiary (a life similar to the Franciscan tertiary Angela of Foligno) and her writings about Christ undergird a deeply action-oriented spirituality that informed her political activities as well as charitable works.

Her life

Catherine of Siena was born Caterina Benincasa in 1347, the same year that the black death began its sweep across Europe. She was the twenty-fourth of 25 children born to her mother and the only child that she nursed at her breast; her twin died shortly after birth. Precocious from an early age, Catherine had her first vision when she was a little girl of six and made a vow of virginity by the age of seven.[3] At 15, she had a vision in which she became mystically married to Christ.[4] While still young, Catherine also started the strong ascetical practices that would last a lifetime, including fasting, praying for hours on end, and hours of flagellation. As a young girl, she took the Desert Fathers as her model and refused to eat meat.[5] By the age of 16, she would only eat bread, water and raw vegetables. By the time she was 23, this asceticism strengthened so she would only take the Eucharist, drink water and eat herbs and bitter greens. These fasting practices reinforced other ascetical practices such as her renunciation of marriage, and the long periods she spent kneeling in prayer.

Catherine's desire to not marry rooted itself in her earliest days. In addition to her early vow of virginity, she fought her parents over their marriage expectations when she was a teenager. She went so far as to cut off her hair (thus rendering her 'ugly' and less marriageable), and when taken on a vacation away from Siena that was meant to make her more favourable to a marriage proposal she had received, she scalded herself in the hot baths. At 17, with the question of marriage still a war within her house, she caught a pox that she refused to treat and which left her disfigured, physically undesirable and hence unmarriageable. Before this, Catherine had tried to join the Dominican tertiaries, but they had been unwilling to consider her for membership because she was a young and lovely woman (whom they thought ought to marry). Tertiaries in Siena were older widows who had a stable home life. After catching the pox, however, Catherine successfully used her disfigurement to leverage her way into the community. And although her family was frustrated with her refusal to marry, Catherine was allowed to live at home when she joined the community, but she was reduced to a position of servitude by her parents.

Thus, Catherine's desires for a religious life finally came to fruition when she received the Dominican habit at age 18. She joined the Mantellate, who were widows affiliated with the Dominicans. The Mantellate wore a habit, lived in their homes, and served the needs of poor and sick under the direction of a prioress initially, then under direction of friars. After joining the Mantellate, Catherine only went out of her rooms at home to attend Mass at the Church of San Domenico, just down the street from her parents' house. In the silence of her solitary existence, she spent the three years from 1364 to 1367 praying in solitude, performing household chores as a servant, and learning to read. In 1368, this time of solitude led to a spiritual climax: Catherine experienced a mystical espousal to Christ on the last day of Carnival.[6] Following this momentous event, she felt she could return to the world, and she started actively joining the Mantellate in its ministry to the poor and sick in Siena, which she actively pursued from 1367 to 1370. From the moment of this vision, what had been a very private spirituality became a public and church-focused ministry for Catherine.

Catherine lived through her works to benefit other souls, particularly the sick. Her prophetic voice was one that was also meant to heal the sick, namely a sick church governed by men who were not properly living out their vocations and were renting the body of Christ through their schism. Raymond writes that Christ assured Catherine at the start of her mission: 'In these latter days there has been such an upsurge of pride, especially in the case of men who imagine themselves to be learned or wise, that my justice cannot endure them any longer, without delivering a just chastisement upon them that will bring them to confusion.' Having identified the problem, Christ then said he would send a solution: 'To confound their arrogance, I will raise up women ignorant and frail by nature but endowed with strength and divine wisdom. Then, if they come to their senses and humble themselves, I will behave with the utmost mercy towards them.'[7] Catherine's role was to be a conduit, a 'chosen vessel' for Christ's reforming grace to those who would receive His doctrine. The fact she was a female meant she was more humble than a male (who is supposed to rule the female, according to the medieval worldview). Christ's use of Catherine both chastises arrogant men and offers an example of humility and submission by which to guide the straying church.

In 1368, Catherine met Bartolomeo de'Domenici, who would become her second confessor and lifelong friend. It was around this time that she began to have more frequent and more intense mystical experiences, and she felt more and more compelled to intervene when she saw truth compromised, whether by individuals or in larger political and ecclesiastic arenas. A couple of years later, Catherine experienced a mystical death and return to life. These experiences caught the attention of the Dominican leadership, and in 1374, when she was 26, Catherine was formally questioned by the provincial chapter of the Dominicans. As a result, Catherine received a spiritual director, the Dominican friar Raymond of Capua, who would remain her spiritual director until her death. A year later, on 1 April 1375, Catherine received the (invisible) stigmata and prophesied the schism that would take place four years later.

Catherine's works as a church leader took several forms of humanitarian work on behalf of the poor, the foundation of women's religious houses, and her political work designed to end the Great Schism. After years of the popes residing in Avignon rather than in Rome, Catherine asked Pope Gregory XI to return to Rome, which he did. Unfortunately, he died there shortly after his return. In order to try to keep the papacy centred in Rome, the college of cardinals elected an Italian to the See of Peter; Urban VI was thus elected the successor to Gregory XI. However, Urban VI quickly turned into an overbearing, temperamental leader, and his conduct annoyed and angered the cardinals who had elected him. Less than half a year later, the cardinals re-convened and on 20 September they elected another pope, the cardinal of Geneva, who became Clement VII. Clement could not occupy Rome, so he lived in Avignon. Although there had been previous anti-popes, or multiple claimants to the papal seat, this time the two rival popes were both elected by the same body of cardinals. Catherine's role in this would not last long, for she died only two years after the controversy began (it would last until 1417, and she died in 1380). But from the time of Gregory's return to Rome, Catherine took an active role in trying to keep the papacy in Rome and reconciling the rival popes.

Her writings

Catherine left behind a large literary legacy, which includes over 382 letters from the early 1370s to 1380, a book entitled *The Dialogue* and a number of spontaneous prayers recorded by friends during the last year and a half of her life. All of her writings show the same difficulty to the interested newcomer: their style is incredibly intense in imagery, in theology, and in the very concrete circumstances of Catherine and her correspondents.[8] The letters show her correspondence with a wide range of people that she either knew personally or who wrote to her asking for advice. Her correspondents included popes, prostitutes, abbesses, friends, queens, relatives and neighbours. At the core of the majority of her letters is a kernel of biblically-based advice, which responds to the question the interlocutor asked or represents the advice Catherine wishes to pass on to the person.

In addition to hundred of letters, Catherine wrote *The Dialogue* as a long, flowing narrative without divisions.[9] She wrote it between November 1377 and October 1378, by dictating it to multiple scribes simultaneously (just as Saint Thomas Aquinas, a Dominican friar and theologian, also dictated the *Summa theologica*, his great 'introductory' work of theology, to a team of scribes). The core of *The Dialogue* is a mystical experience outlining the four petitions that she made while gazing on 'Truth, her Spouse'.[10] These four petitions were for the reform of holy Church and salvation of all the world. Catherine also structured *The Dialogue* with a number of recurrent stylistic patterns – petition, response and thanksgiving; all circle around central themes, and each pass adds layers of thought that deepen her reflections on particular aspects.[11]

Her writings show a spiritually precocious young woman with multiple visionary gifts, a view that is supported by Raymond of Capua's writings. In Catherine's own writings, we see a mind that works in images rather than in logical categories, in contrast to Raymond's more organized presentation. Raymond organized the *Legenda* according to logical categories in which he groups Catherine's charisms and then documents each with examples from her life and the stories her friends told. In Catherine's own *Dialogue* and *Letters*, we hear an impassioned writer whose writings introduce us to turbulent mystical experiences. Richard Kieckhefer noted about hagiographic writings of her era that 'The hagiographers of the fourteenth century ... often recapture an Augustinian fascination with the inner life and an equally Augustinian sense of disquietude'. The saint becomes the ground for the demonic hosts and divine grace to battle with one another, and as a result 'the holy life appears as a strenuous and uncertain groping toward a goal not fully perceived, let alone conceptualized. The saint is a figure overwhelmed with grace and devotion, overwhelmed with adversity, overwhelmed with feelings of guilt and penitence.'[12] Both Catherine's and Raymond's writings illuminate Kieckhefer's central points well. When Catherine writes about herself, she writes with a pen that is full of self-scrutiny. She writes about her need to do penance, and her doubts that her devotions are frequent or intense enough. When Raymond writes about her, he emphasizes the adversities she has overcome from family, church and temptations. But he also glosses over her shortcomings, writing much more about her gifts, her special attentions to prayer, and her desires to help intercede for others, as well as her ability to preach and pray. One of the similarities between the writings of Catherine and those of Raymond is that they share a similar intensity.

Raymond describes her process composing *The Dialogue*:

> She had asked her secretaries, who were used to taking down the letters she sent to various places, to take care not to miss anything when she was taken up into one of her customary ecstasies and to write down carefully whatever she said …

During all the time she was in ecstasy her eyes could not see, her ears could not hear, her nose could not smell, her tongue could not taste, nor could she feel anything with her hands. And yet in this state she could dictate this book; which shows that it was not composed by any natural powers, but by the power of the Holy Spirit working within her.[13]

This passage describes a number of classical images for mystical inspiration, all of which Raymond claims for Catherine: she writes according to the inspiration of the Holy Spirit; she writes in a trance, all of her senses unaware of what is going on around her. And yet she writes coherently, able to communicate her ideas to the secretaries who write down her text for her. And her secretaries model the 'proper' response to divine inspiration: obedience and service. The mystical aspects of the process underscore the divine nature of the messages that Catherine recorded from God. The whole emphasis of this passage is on Catherine's passivity in the visions, showing that the message was merely God's will.

Her spirituality and emphases

The spirituality that shaped her life is the nexus between the action she engaged in and her writings. Her emphasis on community and the social aspects of her theology resonate throughout her *Letters*, which seek to answer the questions of Catherine's wide circle of acquaintances. Her *Letters* show the fiery spirit with which Catherine tackles the problems placed in front of her, acting as a resource and authority for anything that she is asked to help solve. Catherine lived during a time when a few exceptional women were beginning to take up roles of spiritual advisors with international importance and political roles, such as was the case with Birgitta of Sweden.[14] The wider vocational opportunities did not only change her self-perceptions, but also changed the very way she envisioned Christ. Christ was not merely bridegroom, and she was not merely bride. Love was important to Catherine, but sexual union and nuptial metaphors were not the predominant metaphor for her relationship with Christ. He to her was the suffering saviour, her teacher, the object of her ecstasies, and bridegroom.[15] Catherine represented Christ through a multiplicity of images: the tree of life, a fountain, a lion, a knight, an eagle, a lamb, a book, a bridge and a bed. Her *Letters* describe her tasting Christ's blood in her mouth for several days and smelling the stench of sin. In *The Dialogue* she pictures Christ as a bridge, and describes her image in minute detail, explaining the significance of things such as the stones and steps. These images brought a physicality to her very concrete descriptions to her visionary life.

For Catherine, Christ is, first and foremost, the saviour of all people. The role of saviour was the one that Catherine reflected upon most often, and many of her images directly reflect this focus, including her images having to do with the lamb, sacrifice, the cross and blood. The Incarnation served to restore the relationship between God and humans, by means of restoring the image of God in people. She describes Christ as having presented a bond for the release of humanity, playing off of the imagery of a bond written on vellum, the sheepskin used for writing in the medieval world, blending that imagery with the imagery of Christ as the sacrificial lamb:

> The bond [of payment for human sins] was written on nothing less than lambskin, the skin of the spotless Lamb. He inscribed us on himself and then tore up the

> lambskin! So let our souls find strength in knowing that
> the parchment our bond was written on has been torn
> up, and our opponent and adversary can never again
> demand to have us back![16]

She begins by identifying the bond written on sheepskin and the body of
Christ, the lamb of God. The act of tearing up of the lambskin both suggests
that the bond is secure – no one can now have a claim again against humanity – and it also evokes the image of the body of Christ being torn by the
scourging on the way to the cross and by the nails during the crucifixion.

In *The Dialogue*, the largest unit of the text, spanning chapters 26 to 87,
describes Christ as a bridge. In order to understand this central image, it
helps to have an understanding of what a medieval Italian bridge would
have looked like. Catherine's image is of a bridge such as the Ponte
Vecchio; this medieval bridge in Florence is more than a river crossing. A
medieval bridge was a self-contained community. In Catherine's image,
the bridge is a structure that spans a river, has walls, a roof, shops and
dwellings lining it, and has steps that lead up to it.

The bridge symbolizes Christ's providential care for humans, and His
ability to serve as a way by which the human can approach God. It also
serves to show and tell the reader about humans as well, for her spirituality aims to bring the human to God, and it is to this end that her visions
orient themselves. Catherine's visions give instructions of the steps
involved for humans to conjoin to God. Here, in the example of the
bridge, she explains:

> The first stair is the feet, which symbolize the affections.
> For just as the feet carry the body, the affections carry
> the soul. My Son's nailed feet are a stair by which you
> can climb to his side, where you will see revealed his
> inmost heart. For when the soul has climbed up on the
> feet of affection and looked with her mind's eye into my
> Son's opened heart, she begins to feel the love of her
> own heart in his consummate and unspeakable love. ...
> Then the soul, seeing how tremendously she is loved, is
> herself filled to overflowing with love. So, having
> climbed the second stair, she reaches the third. This is
> his mouth, where she finds peace from the terrible war
> she has had to wage because of her sins.

> At the first stair, lifting the feet of her affections form
> the earth, she stripped herself of sin. At the second she
> dressed herself in love for virtue. And at the third
> she tasted peace.[17]

Three-part structures provide an architecture for Catherine's reflections on Christ here and in other places. Catherine meditates on the body of Christ, seeing three particular parts that it will focus upon: the feet, the side and the mouth. These three meditations correspond to the three traditional 'stages' of spiritual growth: purification, illumination and union. They also correspond to stages of humans' relationship with Christ: servant, friend, and child of God.[18]

Detailing other aspects of Christ as a bridge, Catherine documents how all the architectural elements correspond to the model of Christ who directs humans towards Him. She says that 'The bridge has walls of stone so that travelers will not be hindered when it rains.'[19] She then says that these stones were hewn before the Passion but Christ builds them into a wall through the Passion, commenting that 'they are all stones of true solid virtue'.[20] Similarly, the roof of the bridge is a roof made of Christ's mercy. For tired travellers, the Holy Church serves as a hostelry. These travellers are fed with the bread and blood of Christ so they do not grow weary on the journey.[21] The image of the bridge is her pre-eminent example of how she can probe a mystical image in order to understand the theological depth of the symbolism found in her visions.

Elsewhere, she describes the body of Christ as a ladder to be scaled. This image incorporates biblical imagery such as the statue of Nebuchadnezzar's dream, turning it into an image of how the abbot can climb into the heart of Christ. To the Abbot of Monteoliveto, she writes:

> He has made the stairway in his own body. Lift up your
> affection to the feet of God's Son, and climb up to his
> heart, which is opened and consumed for us. And
> [then] you will come to his mouth, the kiss of peace,
> and you will begin to eat and savor souls. Then you will
> be a true shepherd, one who will lay down your life for
> your little sheep.[22]

To nestle into Christ's heart is to find a place of solace and rest against the throws of the world, like the dove nestling into the cleft of the rock in the *Psalms*.

Contemplation and action

One basis for Catherine's spirituality is a strong sense of self. Catherine credits this to her notion of a cell of self-knowledge. In this interior space, the person arrives at a cell in which God can be present with the person. Rather than being a physical cell, it is an interior place where a person can escape, distant from all things that distract and intimately present to God. It nurtures both knowledge of self and knowledge of God. Catherine explains that the work of this self-knowledge is both a human and divine enterprise when she explains how 'we cannot, in fact, nourish others unless we first nourish our own soul on true solid virtues, and we cannot do this unless we cling to the breast of divine charity and from that breast draw the milk of divine sweetness'. She continues: 'through his flesh we shall draw the milk that nourishes our soul, charity's offspring, the virtues … . And we cannot be nourished on this milk without suffering.'[23]

But Christ is not just provider; He is also the model for the virtues, suffering and action that Catherine finds to be proper objects of human imitation. She questions the would-be follower:

> Do you know how you ought to act? Just as you do when you go to your cell at night to sleep. First you go to find your cell, and you see that inside is the bed. It is clear that you need your cell, but your cell isn't all you need. No, you turn your glance and your longing to the bed, where you'll find your rest. And this is what you have to do: go to the dwelling, the cell, of self-knowledge. There I want you to open the eyes of your understanding with loving desire. Walk across the cell and get into bed, the bed which is God's tendergoodness, which you find within this cell, yourself. (Surely you can see that your existence has been given you as a favor and not because it was your due.) Notice, daughter, that this bed is covered with a scarlet blanket dyed in the blood of the spotless Lamb. Rest here, then, and never leave.[24]

As with others, the contemplative life is meant to be one which feeds into other activities. It helps to orient the person to God and orients them to a life of serving Christ. It is not until one has confronted Christ and self in the cell of self-knowledge that one can follow Christ fully. But this confrontation is not something that remains only in the contemplative moment; it is to animate the person once again to seek the outside community.

Catherine the ascetic

If the cell of self-knowledge is meant to direct the person ultimately outward again, the challenge of understanding her ascetical practices must surely make us wonder about the interior orientation of these bizarre practices. Certainly the most well-studied aspects of Catherine of Siena's life and legacy have been her austere ascetical practices. They captured attention beginning with her Confessor Raymond of Capua's biography of her. He credited the Desert Fathers, with their strict asceticism, as the role model for Catherine's fasting practices from a very early age, when she pledged to not eat meat and ran off to live in a cave.[25] He even stressed how, under obedience, she was required by a former confessor to eat, and it nearly killed her.[26] Whereas in her own work she talks some about her body, Raymond focuses upon her eating rituals even more than Catherine does.

Central elements in Catherine's practices included her obsessive fasting and her Eucharistic piety, which appear not only in Catherine's own writings, but in Raymond of Capua's *Life* as well.[27] Fasting and feasting became not merely metaphors for how Christians were to act, but were lived metaphors for Catherine: 'Sympathetic scholars have sometimes suggested that she progressed from viewing ascetic practices as an end to seeing them as a means to kill the will, and her letters suggest this.'[28] She fed the destitute, she ate the filth and pus of those she tended, and through her hunger she united with the agony of Christ on the cross. She used these actions as a penance for the salvation of the world. In these ways, food takes a frontal stance on her practice both devotionally and as lived charity. Mary Magdalene was a model to Catherine, because the Magdalene fasted for 33 years.[29] Furthermore, gluttony in the middle ages was a sign of inordinate lusts towards things other than God. To control one's appetites in eating, one could show control over inordinate lusts. We see in the vision she had where Christ gives her a drink from his side that surpasses all earthly drinks that her earthly thirst (and hence earthly lusts) has been replaced by a heavenly appetite.[30]

Her ascetical practices also serve to show the sincerity of Catherine's devotional practices. Catherine's family thought that her lack of eating and her purging after eating was a diabolical trick. Thus, through Raymond's telling of the stories, eating served to symbolize either God's power or the devil's power; it could not be neutral once the claim that it was a diabolical trick had been offered by her family. Catherine also saw her suffering as a means of and sign of her merging with Christ on the cross, and a means by which she could help save souls by means of the purgative effect of her suffering for others. Oftentimes, Catherine included others in her suffering, as when she drank the pus of sick victims. She also united herself to the example of the suffering Christ by living solely off the Eucharist. Catherine saw her suffering as service: Mary assures Catherine that Catherine's suffering and pain help to free souls from purgatory.[31] Just as her eating could involve a voluntary suffering for others, suffering held other roles for Catherine. And, like Hadewijch, it was in the suffering that she could identify with Christ. Catherine did not identify with the triumphant Christ of his Resurrection, but in the process by which the triumph can take place, namely in the suffering on the cross.

Catherine believed that taking in meant to love something, and that whatever a person loves becomes a part of them: 'Catherine understood union with Christ not as an erotic fusing with a male figure but as a taking in and a taking on – a becoming – of Christ's flesh itself.'[32] In this context all her emphasis on food and her thoughts 'You are what you eat' come into focus as subservient to this desire. Or, rather, they are further developments of this desire to become one like Christ, her own theosis. Thus, Catherine really did think that spiritual eating replaced all forms of physical eating. Eating and hungering have the same meaning for her because eating can never fill one perfectly.

Reflections on Catherine's relationship with food and eating do not deal only with her ascetical practices. Many passages in her writings offer her ideas on what substitutes spiritually for physical food. The Eucharist and the pus-water of the neighbour she attends replace physical food, but spiritual food also forms a centre of her prayers and informs the way that she views Christ feeding people with the breast of mother Charity.[33] Breast milk in Catherine's day was said to be blood. So a lactating Christ was synonymous with a bleeding Christ who sacrifices himself in order to be able to give (heavenly) food to his children. Blood takes on an even more poignant place in her thought when one realizes that the laity were not allowed to receive the cup in Catherine's day; only the priests could.[34] Because her primary referent for the blood of Christ was the Eucharist, in which the blood is spiritually present but not seen, Catherine treated this as a spiritual food, not a physical food. Its prominence, though, suggests that Catherine's insistence on eating only the Eucharist was a very literal and physical attempt to rely exclusively on the spiritual food of the suffering Christ. Some of the images that Catherine associated with the Eucharist are also related to feeding and food: Christ as a nursing mother, whose milk is not entirely pure, but symbolizes mixed pleasure and pain.[35] Her visionary world also included visions of fruit trees from which she could feed, and she conceptualized the Trinity to be a trinity of table (Father), food (Son) and server (Holy Spirit) that is unique to her.[36]

Conclusions

In her article about the requirements to become a doctor of the church, Suzanne Noffke provides a very useful rubric for considering Catherine's theological contributions. The requirements for canonization include outstanding holiness, testimony of popes or general councils, and distinguished teaching. In exploring Catherine's natural gifts, Noffke unearths the nature of Catherine's theology: first, she is not scholastic, although she belonged to an order whose theology was heavily invested in scholastic developments; she is much more imagistic than most writers of her day; and she is in keeping with the teachings of the magisterium.[37] The imagistic nature of her relationship with God drove the way she expressed her ideas in her letters, using the imagery she found in scripture and in the Christian tradition to direct the advice she gave.

Much like the Franciscan woman Angela of Foligno, Catherine's life was one in which the way she lived her life influenced what she taught. Angela's experiences in Assisi were the starting point not only of her conversion, but of the conversion of Brother A; Catherine's years living in her parents' house, perfecting her ascetical practices, were the beginning of her own reflections of the work in which she was to engage both in her town and in the larger Roman church. But they were also the years in which she established the close relationship to the crucified one whom she married, and this close relationship was what led her other pursuits: zealously leading her correspondents back to God through her letters, using her prophetic voice to correct the practices of leaders of the church, nursing the sick and lame, and trying to reconcile the schism in the Roman papacy.

11

Contemplative Pilgrim: Margery Kempe

And when last we came to Mount Calvary, I fell down, no longer able to stand or even kneel; and there I lay, writhing and struggling in my body. I reached out wide with my arms and cried aloud as though my heart would burst. For in the city of my soul I saw truly and freshly as if for the first time how our Lord was crucified. … I was quite unable to prevent myself from crying out loud, a kind of roar it was, even though it might have been the death of me.[1]

If Julian was the retiring, contemplative English anchoress, then Margery Kempe (1373–1439) has traditionally been read as her polar opposite. Margery, who once visited Dame Julian in Norwich seeking spiritual advice, lived a life of pilgrimage, upset fellow churchgoers with her violent outbursts, crying and howling, challenged the church authorities with her desire to wear penitential clothing, and was accused several times of being a heretic Lollard. Margery can be a difficult figure to appreciate, because many of her spiritual behaviours can seem melodramatic, insincere or downright fake. Often this has led scholars to see her as a self-confessed masochist, generally hysterical, or at the very least mentally unstable.[2] I do not plan to read Margery this way; rather, I think that in Margery's book both the affective and the meditative devotional traditions combine to teach the material world's ability to bring people to God. Margery is far from being abstract, speculative or otherworldly, but she is also far from being hysterical, masochistic, shallow or 'merely' affective. *The Book of Margery Kempe* documents how she brought the affective meditative tradition, nuptial theological metaphors and other popular devotional practices such as pilgrimage together within her spirituality. In Margery's time, vocation was synonymous with inherited social position and occupation. The social milieu of a late medieval woman tended to be highly regulated: thus, Margery herself begins with her inherited role of wife and mother, but she eventually finds a way to add to these roles the additional roles of pilgrim and mystic.[3]

Margery Kempe was born into a family of minor nobility, the daughter of the four-time mayor of Lynn. At age 20, she married John Kempe and bore him 14 children. After her first child's birth, she was quite weak from some sort of illness, and she feared that she would die with an unshriven sin on her soul. From this time onwards, Margery continued to be plagued by what she describes as temptations of demons for 'half a year, eight weeks, and a few odd days'.[4] Feeling called to religious abstinences, Margery Kempe gave up meat first and looked for ways to give up other things such as sexual relations with her husband. Following lengthy negotiations over her fasts from meat and her husband's desire that they continue to have sexual relations, her husband agreed to her request renouncing further sex in 1413. After years spent trying to free herself from the obligations of being a wife to a businessman and the mother to 14 children, she also won her sought-after freedom to pursue what she thought was her calling to go on pilgrimage. Shortly afterwards, Margery visited Julian of Norwich and made her first pilgrimage out of England, to Italy and the Holy Land.[5]

Having been freed from family obligations, Margery travelled to Rome, Santiago de Compostela, and many English shrines including Canterbury and Walsingham. In chapter 2 we explored the significance of pilgrimage in medieval times. By Margery's era, the pilgrimage routes to Jerusalem had re-opened, even though Jerusalem was once again under Saracen control. Her extensive journeys attest to the safety and travails both of travel and of a woman travelling abroad at these times. It is what she experiences when she travels – spiritual experiences of the presence of Christ and her experiences on pilgrimage – that she focuses upon in her book and which provide the structure to her loose narrative. But, even more significantly, in Margery's book we learn about the era in which she lives more clearly because she introduces us to many of the people she comes across, whether they are friendly to her or try to hurt her. And it was a pivotal era in England's history, for Margery lived in King's Lynn, in East Anglia, at a time when the rise of cities had begun to break the bonds of feudalism; England's ties to the Low Countries had grown stronger through the cloth trade. Because of the French presence in the English Channel, and thus the French blockades of southern ports, the port of Norwich had become a centre for much of the shipping between England and the Low Countries and Germany. The church was a source of authority, but it too was being eroded by the presence of commerce, as people began to organize themselves in guilds; social status and relations with those who worked in the same trade mattered. Margery becomes quite aware of who perceives her and how she is perceived. In this respect, she mirrors the rivalries and upstart natures of both the commercial and religious environments of her time much more clearly than Julian's peaceful approach.

Margery dictated *The Book of Margery Kempe*, widely held as the first autobiography in English, to a series of scribes. This vernacular exploration of a new genre of writing is just like her new vocation: mother, wife, pilgrim, active woman, ascetic, and public apostle.[6] One aspect that makes Margery's story so important in English literature is precisely how it introduces a new genre. It is an autobiography, and it does not entirely follow the model of previous spiritual autobiographies. Augustine's *Confessions* served as the primary model of a spiritual autobiography. In his story, the middle-aged Augustine looks back on his life leading up to his conversion, and the year or so after his conversion up to the death of his mother, and then reflects on the beginnings of the book of Genesis in order to put his story in cosmological perspective. In so doing, his story becomes a universal story leading from personal estrangement from God to community with God; on a cosmic level, his story symbolizes the return of all creatures to God. In Margery's own time, the fourteenth-century Henry Suso's *Life of the Servant* was another primary model of a life of a spiritual person's quest; it was written by Suso himself and devoted to the internal life more than the external.[7] Another similar type of writing were hagiographies. Although these texts were written by others, they are similar to spiritual autobiographies because they focus on inner states, yet their outward purpose varied considerably from that of spiritual autobiographies. Hagiographic lives were usually written by male confessors, and presented the women as paragons of virtuous living, usually to promote the woman for canonization. They accomplished this through documenting the efficacy of her prayers, ascribing miracles to her and showing that others revered her as holy. These lives (such as that of Christina the Astonishing) explained how the confessor came to understand that the woman was holy, and would offer attestations from others, incorporating their stories into the text. Many lives documented the new vocations to which women were called. Margery Kempe's book does not come from the hands of any confessor or narrator who vouches for her holiness.

In the case of Margery, her autobiography records her attempts to convince authorities that she is indeed not a fake, not a heretic, and not hysterical. And it ends without clear proof that she has done so. As such, her autobiography shows the tenuous character that many female mystics must have felt. Yet Margery did not see herself as separate from her quest for God, and therefore her story and her way of telling about her life bears much in common with how Augustine viewed himself primarily as one of God's creatures on the route back to God. A further challenge to understanding Margery's writing comes in the form of autobiography itself and the way that modern scholars in various disciplines have read this genre and its focus. Autobiography, some scholars posit, means that the spiritual is de-emphasized in order to focus on the individual.[8] Others have argued the opposite, stating that since Margery constantly refers to herself as 'this creature' she de-emphasizes the individual nature of her new genre of writing, the autobiography. Whether one decides to read it as an individual's narrative or the narrative of a person who sees herself as a creature of God affects whether one finds a coherent spirituality in the work.

The Book of Margery Kempe consists of two books of uneven length. The first book, which comprises the majority of the work, is structured around five contemplative visions that track her increasing spiritual progress. The first vision occurs during Advent;[9] it is one in which Margery sees herself within the Holy Family. This vision provides a bridge to connect her life as a mother and the life she desires as a holy woman, and it shows her able to attend first to Anne's birth of the Virgin Mary and then Mary's birth of Jesus, serving in the role of a nurse at the Incarnation. The image of Margery as nurse within a contemplative vision combines the active life (nurse) with contemplation (gazing upon the infant Jesus). Four other visions follow this, helping to structure the book's tales about Margery's wanderings. The second structuring meditation occurs during her pilgrimage to Jerusalem and describes her mystical marriage to Christ (once her marriage to John Kempe is renegotiated).[10] The third experience continues the themes of the second, and it is a meditation of the Passion of Christ in the context of the Easter liturgy.[11] In this meditation, Margery Kempe's devotion unites the liturgical actions that occur during the Triduum and Easter celebrations with meditations upon the historical events that these liturgies commemorate. It is here that the affective and historical come together. The fourth vision provides a meditation on the purification of the Virgin.[12] Book One closes after the fifth and final vision: a mystical discourse between Margery and Christ at Communion in chapter 86.[13] Other elements of structure in *The Book of Margery Kempe* can be seen in the things that Margery says structure her life, her prayer and her actions, things such as the liturgical calendar, places of significance in Christian history, and the practice of imitating Christ. For instance, Fridays are the setting of many of the notable events in the book, and they were a date set aside as fast days, to mark the memorial of Christ's passion.[14] In her actions being set on Fridays, Margery aims for her life to take the form of the imitation of Christ, both literally and symbolically. She literally traces the route of Christ when she visits the Holy Land. She visits places associated with Christ's mother Mary and offers herself in her prayers as a nurse to Christ. The book also provides her influences: a priest read to her works including the Bible, commentaries, Bonaventure, Bridget of Sweden, Richard Rolle, Walter Hilton and others.[15] Thus her reading list was influenced primarily by late medieval writers and by the English affective tradition. After Margery receives the gift of crying, which causes her much trouble, she mentions learning about Marie d'Oignies' similar gift. Dorothy of Montau was most likely an influence as well.[16] In short, *The Book of Margery Kempe* is far from being a chaotic narrative of a hysterical woman.

Writing her own story is not the only way Margery challenges many of the notions about her place (and a woman's place more generally) in medieval society. She records her business start-ups and losses. She also challenges the clothes that she is allowed to wear, back in the days when one's clothes were a uniform determined by one's social status and work. Choosing to wear white clothes moves her out of the uniform that defines her as John Kempe's wife and as her children's mother, redefining her as a holy woman. For Margery, to petition to wear white clothes was to attempt to wear the uniform or habit of a different profession, allowing others to see her in a different role at first sight.

The writing of *The Book of Margery Kempe* had its own set of problems, in part because Margery's first scribe was not exactly literate and the text he recorded was mainly a bunch of incomprehensible notes.[17]

This first scribe wrote the entire first book of the text, but he had written the manuscript initially in a language that was neither German nor English, and the reading of it could only be accomplished by her second scribe through the grace of God.[18] Her second amanuensis was most likely a priest she knew. He revised Book One under Margery's direction after the miraculous translation and wrote the much-shorter Book Two. Yet if the miraculous translation is not enough to suggest that Margery believed God wanted the book to be written, she also records other examples of divine favour; the act of Margery working on the book also inspired signs and wonders, and miraculous phenomena, sounds and ineffable melodies.[19] She relates these in order to show divine inspiration for her efforts and to prove that she was not trying to enhance her own standing; the miracles also show that she had divine favour and was thus not a heretic.

Margery's spirituality

Margery's spirituality is both very intense and very sensual in its focus. The senses played a key role in the person's experience of God: Margery experienced a number of mystical sensations, such as smelling odours and hearing pretty music or awful music from a celestial realm.[20] She could discern the divine origin of this music by its sweetness and the way it surpassed the beauty of earthly music. The melodies have a strong effect on her: every time afterwards that she hears any laughter (a sign of joy) or music, she sighs or cries. Doubtless, this crying at music would have proved frustrating to others at Mass with her.

Her spirituality also enhances the enigma of her persona for modern readers; scholars alternately describe her spirituality as typical of continental devotional practices in vogue at her time (though not yet common in England), or as being atypical of her times.[21] Often modern scholarly judgement as to whether Kempe was typical of her times or not relies upon evidence of how her contemporaries perceived her; the underlying assumption is that, if Margery is an example of well-known and orthodox devotional patterns, she would have been respected rather than maligned by her contemporaries; in other words, many of the interpretations of Margery Kempe depend not merely on her text of life but on how others of her age viewed her. In response to the assumptions that are rampant in modern scholarship about Margery's reception (that it was all negative), one scholar documented the reception Margery received, and found that previous scholarly insistence that Margery frequently received rebukes are not particularly accurate. One-fourth of the male religious she meets rebuke Margery; female religious tend to treat Margery well. The rebukes were not based on theological concerns or devotional differences, but on perceptions that Margery was a socioeconomic threat to women of her class based on her challenging the social norms of women's roles.[22] Ultimately, the reception she received was not the most important aspect to Margery; her relationship with Christ is more important than her relationships with the humans who surrounded her.

Personal relationship with Christ

The Passion of Christ serves as a central focus for Margery's devotions; at the heart of her often confusing spirituality is a very strong sense of the personal nature of her relationship with Christ.[23] As with many other women we have investigated so far, Margery sees the culmination of her relationship with God in the form of a mystical marriage. But, unlike others, the idea of mystical marriage creates problems in Margery's often-literal mind, since she is already married to John Kempe. When Christ mentions mystical marriage, Margery protests to Christ that because she is not a virgin, having borne 14 children, and because she has a husband, she cannot be a bride of Christ. She assumes that only those under a vow of virginity – by which she primarily meant cloistered nuns – can be brides of Christ. Her marriage and childbirth make this impossible. Her first assurance of her new sense of vocation came when Christ appeared to Margery in a vision and invited her to be His bride. When she was in Rome, Christ offered Margery the option to become mystically married. She had just travelled from Jerusalem when she received the vision, and her movement completes a journey in which she symbolically moved from the place of the Passion of Christ to the existence of the physical church on earth, in its seat of power. Christ's offer to be her bridegroom comes to Margery on the celebration of the feast of the celebration of St John Lateran, making her mystical marriage a culmination of her pilgrimage and its focus on the person of Christ, a celebration of her place within the church on earth, and an opening up of her personal relationship with Christ to include God the Father.[24] The vision represents both an individual relationship (personal marriage with Christ) and a corporate one (Margery within the church).

Although this mystical marriage is the most dramatic exposition of the relationship between Margery and Christ, there are plenty of other indications of their relationship. For instance, Margery Kempe has frequent conversations with Christ throughout the book, on all manner of subjects, and these conversations show Christ's regular presence to Margery and demonstrate how he helped to guide her day-to-day activities. Margery sees herself in solidarity with the example of Christ because she has to endure feelings of contempt from others around her. Christ's response is to infuse Margery with more grace so that she can endure; the taunts, blows and mockery of others bring her even closer to Him. The picture Margery presents is of a Christ who is her best friend, sticking beside her and offering advice and companionship even when she is hurt by others.[25]

It is important to note, though, that this separation from those who mock her is mainly a separation from the laity she meets on pilgrimage, and from selected corrupt priests and friars. This separation is not one that removes Margery from the church, but rather it separates her from other lay people whom she perceives are not as spiritually serious as she is. This separation, in fact, allows her to love Christ more, but also to love and work with selected Christians better.

What is remarkable about Margery's theology is how absolutely truly basic it is: over and over again, Christ tells her that love is what matters. Basic here does not indicate a lack of depth; rather, basic means that her spirituality focuses on this key idea rather than trying to write a comprehensive system for spiritual growth. The continued dialogues between Margery and Christ underscore that the personal relationship Margery has with Him is at the heart of her spirituality. The continual frenetic activity of the story suggests that Margery either does not hear Christ's insistence that love is key, or cannot fully accept this and put it into action.

This emphasis on love counterpoints with the very real sufferings of Margery as well as her more imaginary sufferings. She indicates that trials and tribulations will follow her. As she says when she sets out on her first pilgrimage, 'I took leave of my husband. I also said my farewells to my confessor, the anchorite, but not before he had given me ample forewarning of the trials and sufferings I would encounter on my journey; for he told me that every one of my travelling companions would desert me, but that a man with a hunchback would become my guide and, with our Lord's help, lead me safely on my way.'[26] In Christ she finds the model for the sufferings she will undergo. Further along in the same chapter, she explains that her companions tore her clothes, made her put on sackcloth, and would make a fool of her, much like what happened to Christ during his arrest. Part of Christ's love is in having trod this path of sufferings before. The love Christ instructs Margery in is one that both engenders sufferings and provides comfort. And like her other spiritual gifts, it has its negative side as well as its positive side.

Crying and howling

Spiritual gifts such as crying and howling seem extraordinarily odd until we realize that Margery was not the only woman in the middle ages who possessed these gifts; crying was frequently attested to in the lives of holy women. In some forms, it was associated with the gift of tears and with the mourning of women over the dead Christ.[27] Marie d'Oignies, who lived two centuries before Margery, was one such woman who experienced such outbursts of uncontrollable crying, and Margery attests to knowing of Marie and her sobbing.[28] Tears of compunction were also a gift to saints who saw their sins clearly before themselves. Jesus himself wept, upon hearing the death of Lazarus, and Jesus saw Mary weeping at his tomb.[29] All of these forms of crying are gifts that result from a recognition of the tenuous place of God's sinful creatures or from a recognition of Christ's sacrifice on behalf of creatures.

Margery's own crying fits occurred over the course of at least ten years. She would sob for five to six hours every Good Friday.[30] Julian of Norwich counselled Margery on her weeping, saying it was the 'unspeakable groanings of the Spirit'.[31] Unlike the gift of tears, which was based upon the sorrows of the Blessed Virgin Mary and the Man of Sorrows (whose purpose is to inspire others to sorrow and share in the tragedy of the killing of Christ), Margery's weeping was a purely affective response to Christ.[32] At first, it was a response to how distant her beloved Christ was, but as it developed, it became a stronger reaction of howling in response to the Passion after she had visited the Holy Land and retraced the steps Christ took to his death.[33] Her crying paralleled the rest of her spirituality, which revolved around the fact that she was emotionally moved by the stories of Christ. This affective movement of her soul became even greater in places where Christ had once lived.

Besides Julian's explanation of Margery's crying, *The Book of Margery Kempe* includes several conversations between Margery and Christ on the subject, which give us further theological reflections on how she viewed her gift. Christ explains to Margery that the gift of weeping is not only a very old gift, evidenced through the Christian tradition (based on the authority of Jerome, speaking over a millennium before Margery), but is also a divine gift, saying it is the work of the Holy Spirit.[34] Margery cannot control her weeping if it is a divine gift; she would only be able to control it if it were human artifice that was making her cry. Christ also explains to Margery that her tears are a form of spiritual warfare against the devil and forces of evil. For a woman living shortly after the end of the largely unsuccessful crusades, who had visited the Holy Land, this would be a particularly poignant image.

But crying was by far not the most nerve-wracking gift Margery received. When she was in Rome, she also received the 'gift' of howling, although she does not develop a theological explanation of this gift. At times, she suggests that her howling is a more violent form of the gift of crying. In these places, depth of emotional intensity suggests a parallel deeper meditative or spiritual intensity. In other places, the howling seems to be something wholly other than crying, a forlornness more akin to Christ's cry from the cross, 'My God, my God, why have you forsaken me?'[35] Again, in Angela of Foligno we saw another instance of howling, and in Christina of St Trond as well, where the affective responses guided their sense of vocation and relationship to Christ.

Pilgrimage

As has been discussed above in chapter 2, pilgrimage was a common form of devotion, and East Anglia, continental Europe and the Holy Land sported a wide range of places to which the penitent could travel. When Margery went on pilgrimage, it added layers of significance to her life story: first and foremost, the pilgrimage was a reorientation of her life, and a liberation. It reoriented her life so that her family was no longer its focus. Rather, the physical city of Jerusalem represented the freedom that allowed her to make the heavenly Jerusalem the focus of her life. Physical freedom from family, allowing her to travel, also suggested the freedom to uninhibitedly focus on Christ.

Margery's Jerusalem pilgrimage is the centre of the book. Literally, it figures near the midway point; but this pilgrimage is also a point where Margery obtains a much clearer sense of her identity and that of Christ.[36] The medieval view of the world placed Jerusalem at the centre of the world, both geographically as shown on maps, and spiritually; Calvary was the sacred *omphalos*.[37] The reorientation of Margery's life parallels the iconic representation of the world as her time knew it. On the Jerusalem pilgrimage, Margery undergoes a remarkable transformation of her spirituality. Previously, her affections had been centred on the Incarnate Christ, but on the baby and on the living Christ. Here in Jerusalem she comes face-to-face with the suffering Christ as she walks the *via dolorosa*. The pilgrimage intensifies her responses to material objects, and this transformation appears most clearly in the outward changes in her affective behaviour: she now wails.[38]

After Jerusalem, Margery continued to wander the earth and went on pilgrimage to many other places, including Assisi (the home of St Francis), Rome, St Brigit's House and Santiago de Compostela (which held the bones of the apostle St James), and to many local and regional shrines in England, including Leicester, Lincoln, Ely,[39] London and York. She also visited the anchoress Julian of Norwich.[40] If the purpose of pilgrimage was a penance for sins, then one would think that the shape of a semi-permanent pilgrim's life would be perpetual penance. But this is not the case for Margery. In these other pilgrimages, Margery Kempe spends less time talking about her spirituality and more time discussing the wider church. Much more of her attention at places of pilgrimage is given over, in a Chaucerian sort of attitude, to the people she travels with, their shortcomings, and the group interactions. She also complains about the clergy who treat her badly or malign her, as well as those who defend her. This fits with the larger picture of Margery's spirituality, which was primarily a social spirituality. She envisions herself in the midst of the Holy Family; she goes on pilgrimage with other people; she holds continual conversations with Christ. She even has revelations about the states of other people's souls, particularly those in purgatory.[41] Hers is more of a social apostolate in which she evangelizes, rather than a penitential life.

Lollardy

Margery's book is also marked by clear conflicts that arise around her personality. These conflicts can be attributed to her behaviours, as mentioned above. But they can also be attributed to her status. For Margery Kempe did not benefit from having a church-appointed confessor who could rally on her behalf. She also was not associated with a particular order. Her status as a woman who did not have these benefits shows just how tenuous the position and authority of the laity was at her time. Many of the conflicts also have roots in external issues of her time, such as the Lollard controversies and the hunts for heretics that ensued. Church authorities ordered her to stop parading around, as if her outbursts were merely for attention and not from God. The purpose in telling each of her stories and placing them within the context of people who did not believe was both to show how the people of God always face persecution when exercising the gifts God gives, and to demonstrate that the gifts that God gives are wider than the narrow definitions of acceptable religious behaviour. More so than any other woman we have met in this book, Margery's travels by herself, her insistence in emotional prayer, her standing up to the church authorities about clothing, her rights to go on pilgrimage and her orthodoxy stand out as the most recognizably 'proto-feminist'.

When reading Margery Kempe, it is easy to be caught up in her seemingly endless disputes with the local clerics and with figures that represent the church. It is because there are references to her clashes with priests and confessors that scholarship on Margery often tries to find a relation between Margery and Lollardy. In Margery's time, before the Reformation, many different groups of people had concerns that priests did not adequately do their duties and were often lax, living off the tithes collected from the people, or corrupt. Even the mendicant orders of the Franciscans and Dominicans had been among those calling for evangelical piety and preaching to the people for reform of corrupt church practices. Indeed, as we have seen, neither calls for reform nor anticlericalism was anything new. But the Lollards were another group calling for a reform of the church, who were condemned as heretical for a number of their doctrines. Originally founded by Jean Wyclif, Lollards held that priests were corrupt because they lacked vital piety. Because they lacked this, they could not effectively consecrate the Eucharist. Wyclif went so far as to say that a lay person with vital piety could more effectively consecrate the Eucharist. This, of course, crossed the line: a similar heresy had been viciously condemned by Saint Augustine in the fourth and fifth centuries when he argued against the Donatists. The Donatists, like the Lollards, held that it was the moral character of the minister that determined whether the sacraments administered by that person were effectual. The Catholic position was that the power of the sacrament lay in the power of Christ, who instituted the sacrament, rather than in the person.

The Lollards, however, did not merely lapse into an old heresy; they also posed other serious challenges to the church in Margery's time. Lollards believed that a number of medieval church practices were wasteful, unnecessary or doctrinally unfounded. They protested against the uses of images and ornate decorations in churches, calling them alternately wasteful or distracting. They protested against pilgrimage and the cult of the saints, and the powers that shrines were supposed to have. Pilgrims and the monies made from them cared for many shrines, and a call to end pilgrimage amounted to a threat to the survival of some shrines, such as Becket's tomb in Canterbury and Walsingham. Additionally, the Lollards called for church property to be taxed. Although consonant with the evangelical piety of the mendicant orders, the way the Lollards broached the taxation of church property both cut into church authority and challenged the church's wealth, and thus appeared doubly dangerous. It was not accidental that this type of attack occurred at a time in which the bourgeoisie had unprecedented amounts of power, and as society was becoming restructured not only as feudalism ended but as trade and movement of people grew; Lollardy was an attack on the traditional loci of authority from several vantage points.

Because of the focus on piety over church hierarchy, Margery's particularly ostentatious piety and her requests for unusual marks of her piety (her clothing, regular communion) were suspect.[42] And so she came under suspicion of being a Lollard.[43] Every time she was mocked, people responded with mixed reactions: some were amazed at how pious and forthright she was; others thought that she should not be travelling; still others thought her verbal prowess meant she must be a heretic. Time and again, Margery was released from her bond only to find herself in trouble in the next town, as in this case: after a trial, a prison sentence of 40 days, and final release at the river's edge, she found herself accused of Lollardy in the next county.

Part of the contentiousness of Margery's statements about religion may be that she demanded some authority based on her life and her statements. In this, she is part of a small but growing trend during her time in which laywomen such as Birgitta of Sweden or Catherine of Siena took on roles with political and religious significance. Perhaps Margery just missed the political mark and wasn't quite as successful as she wanted to be. If she had been more successful, her positions would not have been questioned, as they were not in the case of Catherine of Siena.

Margery also claimed to be an intermediary for God; Christ supports this role, telling her, 'Daughter, do not be afraid, I shall take away your pride. And those who honor you, honor me; they that despise you, despise me, and I will punish them. I am in you, and you in me.' He continues, explaining that Margery will be an intercessor for those who listen to her: 'And those who do listen to you hear the voice of God. Daughter, if any living person, no matter how sinful he might have been will leave his sin and listen to what you tell him, I will show my love for you by giving him whatever grace you promise I will give him.'[44]

Margery here sees herself as a living intercessor, both for people in purgatory and for those still living a familiar role, based on the other women we have seen so far. But to this traditional role she adds an evangelical slant: she is an intercessor for the living as well as for the dead. For those in purgatory, she can pray for them; for the living, she can both pray for them and actively try to convert them to better living.[45] As a living intercessor on behalf of the living and the dead, she is reminded by Christ that she is in the company of some well-known men and women with the same grace, such as Saint Paul, Katherine, Margaret and Barbara.[46] Here, Margery claims some well-known saints as her fellow workers.

Margery's role as intermediary can also be seen as pseudo-clerical, putting her in opposition to the priests and bishops of the church, whose sacramental actions mediate the divine to the people. Not only did her role challenge the traditional role of clergy, but she added her own insult: Margery envisioned part of her task to include encouraging leaders of the church to reform themselves and the people around them, in their monasteries and households. She criticized monks by telling a parable (how Christ-like!) of how they despise people; worse yet, in her book Christ turned their spite to his reward, and in another instance she criticized the Archbishop of Canterbury for the state of his household.[47]

Margery's relationship with the ecclesiastic authorities of England was an everchanging wonder. She repeatedly went to the authorities to ask permission: to wear white, to go on pilgrimage, to recognize that she was no longer bound by marital obligations to her husband but would be chaste, for recognition of her gifts from Christ, and for explanations of her sobbing and other behaviours. She asked for regular confession and weekly communion. These visits to church authorities often were what landed her in trouble. In her constant visits to clergy for approval, she appears to be a submissive woman, always seeking the approval of men for her activities and visions rather than relying on her own judgement. But, as we have seen before in women such as Hildegard, Julian and others, the approval of men carried with it a lot of weight and ultimately provided a lot of freedom. Margery certainly took advantage of the freedoms provided to her by the support of various bishops, archbishops and leaders within orders, even while accepting the accusations of Lollardy. But she also shows her respect for the authorities of the time by continuing to ask permission, even if her requests seem to place her outside of the mainstream.

Conclusions

When reading *The Book of Margery Kempe*, it can be hard to figure out what Margery's influence as a great medieval woman thinker actually is, since the person of Margery Kempe with her larger-than-life personality overwhelms so much in the book. As a result, her writings have suffered much at the hands of history and scholars. Even in recent years, Margery has routinely been dismissed as a mystic or as a religious woman. Drew Hinderer wrote in favour of Julian of Norwich as an appropriate and devout medieval religious woman, and he described Margery as anxious, insane, hysterical and preoccupied with herself.[48] Hinderer is part of a common move to declare certain women mystics as exemplary of women's mysticism, and hence these characterizations lead to certain behaviours or attitudes being 'acceptable' not merely as theological or as female, but as patterns that limit what counts as religiously worthwhile for women. But, as reading Margery confirms, there is much more to her than the mere hysteria with which she has so often been charged; Margery's spirituality rests not on hysteria, but on deep experiences of the person of Christ that come to her through contemplative prayers and through her own consciousness of her affective responses to these prayer experiences. It is a recognition of this basis – which Margery herself used to structure her book – that serves to show her significance in medieval spirituality; and it is this basis that is so often missed when dismissing Margery's example.

12

Carmelite Reformer: Teresa of Avila

From the cross the bride
To her Beloved says
This is a precious palm
Upon which she has climbed,
Its fruit tasting
Like the God of paradise:
It alone is the road
Leading to heaven.[1]

All of the great monastic traditions in the western church were founded as a means to reform the church, reform its practices, and entice believers to a more ardent faith. Whether it was Benedict's establishment of a *Rule for Monasteries* in the sixth century, the Cluniacs of the tenth century, or the Cistercians of the eleventh century, all these groups aimed to improve the state of the church and protect it from lax practices that the reformers feared. Teresa of Avila (1515–82) was no exception. Her inner quest to have a deeper, less superficial relationship with Christ parallels her outward work in reforming the Carmelite order of her day by establishing the Discalced (barefoot) Carmelites in Spain with her friend John of the Cross. Her writings reflect a vision of reform and document the spiritual life that led her desire to found the Discalced Carmelites and her work to reform their own practice.

Teresa was born in Avila on the Spanish plateau in the kingdom of Leon-Castille on 28 March 1515, when Spain was at the height of her imperial power. She was born into a family of new Christian converts, or *marranos*, Christians of Jewish origin. Her family had financially succeeded in their trade business, and had bought a title of nobility. To make a new start, they moved from Toledo to Avila; this claim to nobility was challenged when they applied for tax-exempt noble status in Avila.[2] In addition to this family turmoil, when Teresa was 12 years old her mother died, and she was placed in a school for noble girls run by Augustinian nuns. Teresa thrived in this environment and started to believe she had a vocation. It was while reading the *Letters* of St Jerome that she experienced a conversion and decided that she wanted to become a nun. Her father tried to prevent her from joining the convent and tried to force her to marry, but she fled to the Carmelite monastery of Incarnation in Avila, which she entered on 2 November 1535. At this point her father acquiesced, and two years later, in 1537, she professed her vows. But a year later Teresa fell ill. After the convent had unsuccessfully tried all the treatments available, Teresa was sent to Becedes for an experimental treatment from a famous medical woman. At the climax of the experimental cure, she was in a coma for three days. Eventually she revived, but her return to health took a long time and she was unable to walk for nearly three years. Parallel to this physical debilitation was a deep spiritual one as well; until age 39, Teresa felt a struggle because she lived a worldly life but felt deep faults in her prayer life. It would be the coming together of both her physical health and her spiritual life that would initiate her period of great activity, spiritual leadership and Carmelite reform.

In 1554 her life in the convent changed again when she had two visions. The first occurred when she was praying near a statue of Jesus Christ and the second happened shortly after reading Augustine's *Confessions*. Both of these visions offered the same sort of message: they showed her a way towards true conversion and following Christ. Through both visions, Teresa said that she experienced liberation through Christ. Following this year's visions, the experience of passive prayer and union became more frequent to her, and the combination of the visions and prayer development led her to also take on ascetical practices.[3] At this point, the community also called in a local preacher to consult about Teresa's visions, for fear that they might be caused by the devil rather than by God. The man she talked to, Gaspar Daza, was known throughout the region for his preaching and his role as confessor for the area.[4] After talking with Teresa, he judged Teresa's gifts were caused by the devil, but he sent her onwards to the Jesuits of the College of San Gil in order for her to be more fully examined by spiritually advanced clergy. There, the Jesuits who examined her disagreed with Daza's estimation, and declared her to be led by God. This provided the first authentication for what was to become a life of visionary experience.

In 1561, Teresa received a vision of the devils and the place in hell that they had prepared for her. This vision caused her to want to live the *Carmelite Rule* more correctly or perfectly. She founded the Monastery of St Joseph in Avila that same year with a small group of nuns. She wrote of her decision to found the monastery, that she had received divine assurance that it was divinely requested, and that it would receive protection; that

> One day after Communion, His Majesty earnestly com-
> manded me to strive for this new monastery with all my
> powers, and He made great promises that it would be
> founded and that He would be highly served in it. He
> said it should be called St Joseph and that this saint
> would keep watch over us at one door, and our Lady at
> the other, that Christ would remain with us, and that it
> would be a star shining with great splendor.[5]

On 24 August 1562, Teresa entered San Jose with four of her close acquaintances who were also enthusiastic about her reforms: Antonio del Espíritu Santo, Ursula de los Santos, María de la Cruz and María de San José.

She composed her first book this same year. Called *The Book of Her Life*, it attempted to explain the gifts and visions she had been given. The impetus for this book was the mixed results of her preliminary attempts to explain to spiritual directors what was going on in her spiritual life. It was written at the request of her confessor, and this audience caused her to adapt a rhetoric in which she justified each of her actions before this intended ecclesiastic leadership. This book's readership was even wider than her confessor had anticipated, including Dominican and Jesuit theologians, secular priests, laywomen and -men, and even the Bishop of Avila. This book helped begin the process of crystallizing in a set structure her spiritual progress. Teresa wrote her second book, *The Interior Castle*, also in obedience to her confessor but also at the request of her spiritual sisters to clarify certain aspects of mental prayer. At the time of Teresa's writing, there was general suspicion of the practice of contemplative prayer by women; the general assumption was that it was too easy for women to be led astray by the devil in the practice of such unguided prayer.[6] *The Interior Castle* sought to explore the inner life of prayer and the soul as a meeting place between the human and Christ, who dwelt at the very centre of the soul. In the process of inward movement that the book records, Teresa explored the various forms that contemplative prayer could take.

In contrast to the more public audiences her early works had, Teresa's next work, *The Way of Perfection*, was requested by the nuns for their own community. After receiving permission from her confessor to write 'a few things about prayer', Teresa was under the obligation to write in this book for an audience of women who were under her own authority. Her goal was to live with 11 nuns in a small community dedicated to serious contemplative life according to the *Carmelite Rule*. *The Way of Perfection* sought to provide the sisters with an example and directions for a life of prayer for the service of the church. Many of the instructions in this book try to get to the heart of one of the aspects of prayer life that Teresa herself found most difficult: the peace of soul necessary for the life of prayer. She taught how to achieve this peace of soul through detachment, love of neighbour and humility. Teresa wrote two versions of *The Way of Perfection*. The first and less inhibited form dates from between 1562 and 1566. The second version is much more restrained and less lively, and dates from 1569, after censors objected to parts of the original. The censorship also points to the public nature of even the act of writing for one's own community in Counter-Reformation Spain.

By 1567, Teresa had attracted the attention of Church officials: Fr Rubeo, general of the Carmelite Order, visited Spain and was impressed with her and St Joseph's. Following his visit and favourable impression, he gave her the order to found as many contemplative monasteries as she could, and he gave her permission to found similar communities for the friars as well. After this second commission, she arranged to meet with John of the Cross for help with establishing houses of Carmelite friars. Teresa became a part of the missionizing fervour of her time, which saw the Northern European churches splitting from Rome and the discovery of lands in the Indies that had not yet been evangelized.[7]

In her *Book of Foundations*, Teresa described the beginnings of her new Carmels. She wrote this text for a dual audience of sympathetic people, mainly nuns, involved in the reform, and a host of potential political enemies.[8] Establishing these monasteries meant travel and involvement with the various leaders of the world's biggest empire to date. The process and these political contacts together mean that we also possess a large body of correspondence from Teresa. She claimed more authority as a chronicler of her own reform than she claimed as a teacher of prayer, even though, even as a historian, her authority was not completely guaranteed.

Although Teresa worked to establish a community of nuns that grew out of a particular order, there was nothing small or isolated about her theology or convictions. Teresa was influenced by theological writings from the patristic period right up until her own times. Classical Christian sources mentioned in her writings include Gregory the Great's *Morals*, Jerome's *Letters*, Augustine's *Confessions*, selections from the *Vitae Patrum*, Cassian's *Collationes*, as well as pseudo-Augustine's *Soliloquies* and *Meditations*. Other influences come from medieval writers such as De Voraigne, the *Flos Sanctorum*, Ludolph of Saxony's *Life of Christ* and *The Imitation of Christ*. Also influential were many contemporary Spanish writers, including John of the Cross.[9] Teresa's knowledge of these writers and their ideas shows the truly cosmopolitan nature of her reading and testifies to the fact that she knew she needed to speak to the tastes of a wide audience. But Teresa also lived at an anxious time. The Inquisitor General, Don Fernando Valdés, compiled *The Index of Prohibited Books* in 1559; Teresa possessed a number of books in this index, which she had to dispose of.[10]

During the Counter-Reformation in Spain, both women and men were encouraged to read more works of spiritual direction, and Cardinal Ximénez Cisneros (d. 1517) helped to make sure that translations into Castillian were made of spiritual classics such as the works of Catherine of Siena, Clare of Assisi, Juana de Orvieto, Jean Gerson, Johannus Climacus and others. He also made sure these were distributed to monasteries and convents for spiritual reading. But following his immediate reign, the Spanish Counter-Reformation became suspicious of women's roles in the church, became suspicious of lay attempts at teaching and piety, and became suspicious of vernacular translations, particularly of the Scriptures.[11]

Teresa's theology and her writing show that she is given to integration of things often considered opposites. She believed that experience and doctrine were interwoven, and her writing style itself shows the same balance between impetuous outbursts of passion and ideas that are followed through gradual logic. Her language is natural, direct and often colourful. In a way that we don't for most of the women in this book, we still have autographs (handwritten manuscripts signed by her) of many of her major and minor works.[12] Teresa was a prolific writer, which also adds to the variety of her own works, and allowed her to explore responses to a number of different contemporaries and their ideas. Her works spanned a number of genres, including history and autobiography, spiritual advancement treatises, poems, and meditations on scripture. In all of these works her determination, notoriously sharp wit and constant striving towards God come out.

Teresa's experiences of God

It is to the internal life that Teresa's work keeps returning, for her own inner life is what gave her outer life its direction and purpose. This inner life was driven by her will to learn how to discern God's will for her and her community and then to assent to that divine will. In one place Teresa writes that Christ said to her, 'While one is alive, progress doesn't come from trying to enjoy Me more but from trying to do My will', and this is the spirit in which Teresa worked.[13] The results of her assent had profound effects both on her soul and on the shaping of her community and Christianity within Spain. Teresa explains that any soul in a state of grace is given a power by the Trinity in which it receives dominion over the whole earth.[14]

Before she could acknowledge or accept her experiences of God, Teresa first needed to understand what constituted prayer. Furthermore, types of mental prayers were suspected of leading the weak minds of women easily astray because of their lack of concrete referents to 'anchor' them. Teresa spent many of her early years after her 'conversion' trying to understand mental prayer in a way that could lead her to God rather than to fear of her own prayer life. Eventually she settled on the idea that 'Mental prayer in my opinion is nothing else than an intimate sharing between friends; it means taking time frequently to be alone with Him who we know loves us.'[15] In Teresa's Spain, books outlining meditative practice were also popular. These books offered schemata by which people could follow guided meditations that would lead to a resultant state of prayerfulness and contemplation. Teresa balked at such overly restrictive schema, saying that these books were great for methodical people, but not for people like her who are unmethodical.[16]

Her visionary experience helped reinforce her belief that she was doing God's will. In *The Spiritual Testimonies*, she related a vision of Mary in which Mary said that she would be present with the rest of the women in their praises of Christ in the choir.[17] Mary's promise shows that Teresa's community and its prayers had received the approval of the Mother of God. Teresa received another vision of Mary in which she said that she was there for the renewal of the vows of the women in the community. Again, Mary's involvement with the community in its liturgical celebrations confirms divine approval of Teresa's reforms. Teresa's visionary life offered her some deep understandings of the nature of God that she could not fully express in words. For example, she wrote about having received an infused knowledge of the Persons of the Trinity in which she understood how the three Persons are one. But the exact mode by which she knew, as well as how to express the content of what she knew, were beyond the scope of her language.[18]

Many of her visions have either liturgical or sacramental origins; her visions are often prompted by liturgical celebrations, and they stress the importance of sacramental participation. This is similar to Mechtild of Hackeborn, the difference being that Teresa's visions also provide a sense of care for a community that she has worked to establish, whereas Mechtild's relationship to her community was less leadership-oriented. For Teresa, the Eucharist was an opportunity to understand the nearness of Christ, the indwelling of the Trinity in the human soul, and other mysteries of God, because it is in the Eucharist that the real presence of Christ is made present to the congregation. The sacraments grant Teresa the opportunity for supernatural grace of the sacrament which surpasses her intellect and leads to a unified knowledge that the first humans had before the fall. Unlike Mechtild's visions, which focused both on the persons of Christ and the saints as well as members of the community, Teresa's visions probe the unspeakable depths of God more frequently, probing the members of her community, past and present, much less frequently than Mechtild.

The earthly end result of Teresa's visionary life is an authoritative voice, by which she gathers the power to be able to carry out her reforms. The heavenly end result of her visionary life is a dear closeness to God. This closeness of the soul to God is reflected in her innate belief in the nobility of the human soul because of her belief in the capacity for the human to receive these visions of God and extraordinary knowledge about God.

The stages of the soul

It is in her work *The Interior Castle* that we see how Teresa builds upon this knowledge of the nobility of the human soul to show that the soul can properly return to God. This return occurs first through joint efforts of the human and God, and by the last stages it occurs through the work of grace alone. It is this work of reuniting humans and God through internal prayer that *The Interior Castle* attempts to describe. This work contains many of Teresa's most memorable images. She explains that her view of the progress of the soul is not one of hierarchical climbing; the path she envisions involves going deeper and more internal into the soul itself. She says, 'We consider our soul to be like a castle made entirely out of a diamond of very clear crystal, in which there are many rooms, just as in heaven there are many dwelling places. For in reflecting upon it carefully, Sisters, we realize that the soul of the just person is nothing else but a paradise where the Lord says He finds His delight.'[19] She continues, explaining that these rooms or mansions that the soul will go through are within each other: 'You mustn't think of these dwelling places in such a way that each would follow in file after the other; but turn your eyes towards the center, which is the room or royal chamber where the King stays, and think of how a palmetto has many leaves surrounding and covering the tasty part that can be eaten.'[20] Each of these layers represents a different 'mansion', with the first being the outermost, and the seventh the most interior and the most intimate with God.

The process of unwrapping these layers will involve many different types of work, including both works of charity and various types of mental prayer. Teresa warns the reader at the beginning that prayer is not a matter of simply saying words, but will require all sorts of various faculties of the body and especially the soul. She says, 'Insofar as I can understand the door of entry to this castle is prayer and reflection. I don't mean to refer to mental more than vocal prayer, for since vocal prayer is prayer it must be accompanied by reflection. A prayer in which a person is not aware of whom he is speaking to, what he is asking, who it is who is asking and of whom, I do not call prayer however much the lips move.'[21] Teresa does not intend to initiate a new form of prayer, but rather intends people to become more conscious of what they are doing in prayer.

Prayer leads to knowledge of God as well as knowledge of self.[22] The fallen human knows little or nothing about her nature, where she came from, and where she is going. As a result, she does not know what she is capable of. But, perhaps equally bad, she does not know what she is not capable of.[23] The virtue that is associated with the human knowing its place and abilities is humility, and she says it is one door through which to enter into the first mansion.[24] But humility does not mean shrinking back; rather, it means to find one's rightful place an aspect in order to discover what one is capable of.

Teresa's descriptions offer concrete and vivid descriptions of the obstacles that belie the movement inwards. In the first mansion, we are introduced to the reptiles, beasts and snakes which represent those forces within the human that attempt to block his spiritual progress. These animals can sometimes represent things outside the castle which distract the person from moving inwards, and sometimes they represent those things that block the light of God coming to meet the person.[25]

In the second mansion, Teresa begins to build impetus for the spiritual progress of the person by explaining the necessity of pushing forward. She says that this second stage 'pertains to those who have already begun to practice prayer and have understood how important it is not to stay in the first dwelling places. But they still don't have the determination to remain in this second stage without turning back, for they don't avoid the occasions of sin. This failure to avoid these occasions is very dangerous.'[26] Prayer becomes a time for Christ to teach these souls.[27] In so doing, the soul is fortified and shown how it should progress. But as the soul begins to progress, suffering increases because souls in this state do not yet start to understand more clearly their peril, and they start to sense more clearly the distance they still must go.[28] At the same time, their distress is balanced with an even stronger sense of Christ coming as a neighbour and a friend to meet those souls who have begun to move inwards in the castle of the soul.

In the third dwelling place, Teresa explains that the souls have had a great favour given to them by the Lord, namely his help in getting them through all the difficulties attendant to the first levels. Teresa explains the virtues that are found in these souls, saying:

> I believe that through the goodness of God there are many of these souls in the world. They long not to offend His Majesty, even guarding themselves against venial sins; they are fond of doing penance and setting aside periods for recollection; they spend their time

> well, practicing works of charity toward their neigh-
> bors; and are very balanced in their speech and dress
> and in the governing of their households – those who
> have them.[29]

But this is still one of the early stages, and these souls are still outwardly focused in these works of charity.

In the fourth mansion, we begin to see the melding of both natural attempts at prayer by the human and supernatural work by God through humans in their prayer. It is at this stage that God's grace begins to become indistinguishable from what the creature herself always wills, inasmuch as the creature naturally begins to will what God would will for her. In the fifth mansion onwards, Teresa focuses on describing states of the soul as it approaches union with God. It is in these last three stages that the soul receives manifold supernatural gifts. Her last three mansions show how 'the truth is that the treasure lies within our very selves'.[30] In these stages, the soul experiences things at a much deeper level than the normal surface-life. She says, 'It doesn't matter where those spiritual or earthly joys come from, for the feeling is very different as you will have experienced. I once said that the difference is like that between feeling something on the rough outer covering of the body or in the marrow of the bones.'[31] In this depth of feeling, the soul loses its bearings and ability to follow what God has given it. Also at this point, the soul beings to know things about God that are too deep for human reason and so the understanding fails.[32] She explains that God does not ask the soul to understand at this level: 'God so places Himself in the interior of that soul that when it returns to itself it can in no way doubt that it was in God and God was in it.'[33] But although the human can know God was there, God 'desires that, without its understanding how, it may go forth from this union impressed with His seal. For indeed the soul does no more in this union than does the wax when another impresses a seal on it. The wax doesn't impress the seal upon itself but remains still and gives its consent.'[34] At this stage, Teresa likens the soul to a silkworm, basing her comparison on the life of the worm, who builds a home in which it dies. This home is the home of Christ, built up by prayer, the renunciation of self-love, and self-will:[35] 'This silkworm, then, starts to live when by the heat of the Holy Spirit it begins to benefit through the general help given to us all by God and through the remedies left by Him to His Church, by going to confession, reading good books, and hearing sermons, which are the remedies that a soul, dead in its carelessness and sins and placed in the midst of occasions, can make use of.'[36]

The next stage, the sixth mansion, comprises nearly a third of the entire text. Here her nuptial theology comes to the fore and Christ is now called the Bridegroom. Now, the soul is only one chamber away from union with her beloved. In this mansion, the soul's interior trials multiply. She catalogues the trials, tribulations and diseases that the Lord sends as a series of nearly final tests for the soul.[37] But just as the torments increase, the gifts increase. It is also here that the paramystical phenomena such as locutions take place (although Teresa gives warning that their source must be discerned before they are to be trusted).[38] She explains the type of rapture that can occur at this stage, saying, 'One kind of rapture is that in which the soul even though not in prayer is touched by some word it remembers or hears about God. It seems that His Majesty from the interior of the soul makes the spark we mentioned increase, for He is moved with compassion in seeing the soul suffer so long a time from its desire.' She continues explaining the effect on the soul: 'All burnt up, the soul is renewed like the phoenix, and one can devoutly believe that its faults are pardoned. Now that it is so pure, the Lord joins it with Himself, without anyone understanding what is happening except these two; nor does the soul itself understand in a way that can afterward be explained.'[39]

In the seventh mansion, the soul is led into the presence chamber, or the bridal chamber, before 'consummating the celestial marriage'.[40] It is in this mansion that Teresa fully experiences the earthly union of her relationship with God and expresses it in the imagery of a spiritual marriage. In this stage, the willing soul experiences, finally, 'a forgetfulness of self, for truly the soul, seemingly, no longer is, as was said. Everything is such that this soul doesn't know or recall that there will be heaven or life or honor for it, because it employs all it has in procuring the honor of God.'[41] This stage is the culmination of the mystical experience of the soul, in which it is finally united with its beloved in a promise of what is to be fulfilled in the beatific vision after the earthly life.

Mystical experiences

Teresa's writings about mysticism are reinforced by a lifelong series of mystical visions and experiences. Her life was one in which mystical experiences often provided the impetus for her to change her own ways or for her to encourage others to change their ways. God's prompting served to motivate Teresa from the place where she was to continue her work of reform within the Spanish Carmelites. Her early years before she began her active reforms were characterized by a period of reflection on the experience of prayer, attempts at a number of different types of prayer, and a gradual acceptance of God's omnipresence as well as guiding love. Her mystical experiences started when she felt the presence of God,[42] but she was concerned about how this was possible when she was not in a state of grace. A priest, Fr Vicente Barrón, explained to her that God is omnipresent, regardless of the particular state of her soul. When her writings received approval, implicitly the experiences upon which some of the passages in the texts were based received approval as well.

Characteristic of Teresa's approach to prayer was her questioning of the types of prayer she experienced and her doubts concerning the origins of her prayer experiences. In her early years, she was concerned about her experiences of passive prayer. She had been taught that passive prayer was a 'higher' form of prayer that required her to move beyond reflection on Christ as a human being, and to stop using the aid of physical artefacts in a quest to move towards a more spiritual understanding of God. She soon realized that this was a mistake.[43] Her own writings about prayer show that even in the innermost stages of *The Interior Castle* the soul's expressions come through physical experiences, imagery, and the use of concrete analogies to demonstrate her points. For instance, in 1556, Teresa had her first experience of rapture in which she had a spiritual sense of hearing Christ speak to her.

Around 1558, Teresa had what she described as an intellectual vision, without external or internal image. In this vision, Jesus was by her side. This vision did not pass. Rather, the constant presence of Jesus next to her formed part of her everyday life. From this point onwards, she continued to have imaginative but transitory visions of Christ, in Christ's glorious risen body. These appeared in stages. First she would see his hands, then, a few days later, his face. The final stage of Teresa's visionary experience was when she experienced the mystery of the Trinity. In this intellectual vision, Teresa perceived an area reserved for communion with members of the Trinity, and the presence of the three Persons of the Trinity. These visions served as the basis through which the rest of her work flowed. All of her writings bear evidence of Teresa's prayer life and rest upon it as the foundation from which they spring forth. The visions that she received were not intended as prophecy, as in the case of Hildegard. Nor were they meant to provide evidence of her holiness; rather, they were what moti-vated Teresa to seek out a life of reform and they helped sustain her work on behalf of the Carmelite order.

Conclusions

Teresa died reciting verses from the *Song of Songs* on 4 October 1582. In this picture of her last moments, we have a summary of Teresa's life. The *Song of Songs* was a scripture that describes the ardent love between a bride and her beloved. It also describes the longing that these two charac-ters have for one another. This love, longing and the ardour, all character-ize Teresa's spiritual life. Many of Teresa's writings on prayer were in response to the theological trends of her times and prayer trends, and from her unease with the ways she was being told to pray. And it is this legacy of prayer that helped to establish the order's reform, which she ini-tiated and saw through. It is also this legacy of prayer that gave her the experiences which were the basis for her actions and her writings. Like Catherine, much of Teresa's lasting importance was not merely in the scriptorium, but it was also in the activities that she pursued. As a founder of monastic houses for women, she found that she could provide a new, more intense and more directed form of religious life for women who ardently wanted it. As such, her work in establishing the Carmelite houses brought about a renaissance of women's religious organizations and necessitated her writing in order for the new religious communities to have a directing voice guiding them.

Conclusions

From the feudal days leading up to William the Conqueror's invasion of England to the height of the Spanish empire, we see these women filling an incredible variety of roles. We see women such as Richeldis creating a shrine, with no clear 'role' other than 'imitating Mary' to guide her. Others such as Hildegard and Mechtilde are guided by the roles of the convent. But even there, Hildegard's correspondence with the Pope and political figures does not come from her religious vocation's expectations. And women such as Margery Kempe can be seen inhabiting the new-found freedoms that the rise of the bourgeoisie allowed in late medieval East Anglia, but, again, she chooses a combination of religious and mother, not merely a trade represented in one of the new guilds. All of these women both exemplify aspects of women's positions or roles in the middle ages, but they also transgress them in subtle and not-so-subtle ways.

One of the true joys of working on the middle ages for any student or scholar, no matter what the academic discipline, is the sheer spaciousness of area left to be investigated. Lining these women up next to one another helps to show the varieties of ways that their works have been approached. It shows varieties within their messages, texts, lives and legacies. But for the student or scholar it shows something perhaps more important: the relative gaps in our current and previous studies of these women and the vast areas yet to be explored regarding many aspects of medieval thought.

Writing about women's writings as if women inhabited a different sphere from men has created a subspecies of certain topics that are taken to be women's topics: discussions of marriage, clothing, domestic tasks, parental obligations, child-rearing, and so forth. And yet these categories prove how difficult it is to capture a 'Platonic form' of women's spirituality; the writer who mentions Jesus as mother could be female (such as Julian of Norwich) or male (such as Anselm of Canterbury). Furthermore, women from different vocational backgrounds had different experiences (mother, nun, anchoress).

And yet, although there is no crystallized 'women's spirituality', there are three themes that have appeared repeatedly throughout the women we have examined. The first theme is love. The second theme concerns pilgrimage, place and movement. The third theme is authority. What we see in the writings by and about these female thinkers in the middle ages is that around each of these themes some of the women in this collection circle, each offering a slightly different perspective on each of the issues.

In many of the women, love was a central concept in their writings, and came either from literary traditions that focused on love or from theological traditions that identified love with the divine essence. At its heart, love is the bond either between two people in the courtly love tradition, or between the Persons of the Trinity in Christian theology. It derivatively comes to be the bond between the human and God or between God and the church. Love in both of these traditions serves as a promise and convention of connection, strengthened through the mutual desires of the two (or three) parties and finalized in some way in an everlasting union (marriage as an unbreakable bond; love as the force that connects the inseparable, unchangeable God; the beatific vision as enwrapping the human in this love).

Much of the time in each chapter was spent examining the words of the women, attempting to discern whence they borrowed their words about love, and what sorts of discussions of love affected their expressions of love. In exploring where each thinker received her notions of love and what love meant, we could find a great diversity in the types of thought among these women. For instance, Hadewijch of Brabant's notions of love came from Augustine's philosophical treatise *On the Trinity* and from the courtly love tradition. Others, such as Julian, tied love in the concept of motherhood. Still others rooted their discussions of love in the courtly love traditions, gathering either the forms of their writing, or their notions of union, or the tropes of their writing styles from the courtly love poets of the twelfth and thirteenth centuries.

These multiplex discussions of love both emphasize the corporate nature of writing in the middle ages, particularly the writings by these women, and emphasize the overwhelming importance of love as a topic in a variety of different writing forms: literary, theological and philosophical. The ways in which these women discussed love are particularly illuminative of the breadth of women's learning in the middle ages, and particularly illustrative of the types of conversations to which women attempted to contribute. Their focus on love also shows a deep understanding of theology, for their discussions assume a Trinitarian theology in which love is the bond between the Persons of the Trinity; their discussions also evidence their theological anthropologies in terms of this divine association.

The second theme is that of location, pilgrimage, and women's movements and locations. When I chose the women for this book, I did so carefully in order to include women that were representative of major trends in spirituality, as well as women who would represent a wide diversity within the geography of western Europe. Yet, as we note through women such as Richeldis, Margery, Catherine, Teresa or even Julian, location was something that the women themselves were keenly aware of as well. Location often determined, or was determined by, a woman's vocation.

Location could be quite static. Richeldis probably never physically left Walsingham after she oversaw the building of the shrine to Mary; Richeldis' legacy was to be known according to a place that people could come to visit. Location could also be incredibly dynamic. Margery Kempe's adventures represent the opposite extreme; she continually wandered from shrine to holy site. Here, she was not to leave a legacy in terms of a physical location. Rather, the physical location of her house, with all the attendant duties it demanded of her, was something that she strove to avoid. In other cases, location could help to guide the actions of women by presenting certain possibilities. Angela's ability to go on a pilgrimage to Assisi puts her in close relationship with the Franciscans, for whom she goes on to become a spokeswoman. Similarly, Catherine's location in Italy made it possible for her to be involved in reconciling the Great Schism in ways that would not have been available for a woman such as Margery from the British Isles.

The third theme of authority is one that has impacted all of the women: some did not have authority (Marguerite Porete, Richeldis of Faverches), which worked to their advantage or not; others managed to claim authority through their writings of lives. (Angela of Foligno's life served as a proof of her Franciscan charism and her growing spiritual depth; Catherine of Siena's prayer life blossomed forth to an epistolary life in which she offered advice to friends, religious and others, and then into a life in which she advised Pope Gregory.)

The threat of danger was a keen motivator that inspired women to seek out authority. The fact that women sought approval of their visions, writings and lifestyles from the reigning powers in the church – powerful abbots, popes, theologians at the University of Paris – reminds us of the liminal position that many of these women held. This position put women in danger from the various powers that sought to extinguish differences in theological vision, with women's voices, lay voices and vernacular writings often being condemned as heresy. But many of these sources could also be used by women to help them claim the necessity of their writings, citing the requests of friends, family and communities that these women provide them with spiritual instruction.

Authority also came from the titles and established roles that people – men and women – held within the church. A *magistra* such as Hildegard commanded a certain respect because of her role in her monastic community. Others such as Mechtilde of Hackeborn did not hold official office, but were considered to be serious seekers of the spiritual life by virtue of their vocations, and thus had at least some respect. But many of the women discussed here – especially the beguines Hadewijch of Brabant, Mechtild of Magdeburg and Marguerite Porete – lived without the authority that church-recognized vocations afforded. Still other women such as Margery Kempe and Christina the Astonishing tried to combine aspects of multiple vocations, and found themselves being challenged by authorities who could not easily conceive of their vocations based on received traditions.

Another way in which women's writings offered contention had to do with the development of theological loci of authority. During the period covered in this book, theology saw a systemization in the form of scholasticism. The eleventh century saw the beginnings of this movement, in the form of the cathedral schools, which, developed in order to train clergy and canons, would focus around the particular teachers at each school and their theological world-views. The twelfth century saw the rise of the mendicant orders, whose teachings became centralized in the newly established universities of Paris, Oxford, Bologna and others. With scholasticism, the method of teaching through debates came to form many of the genres of writing (such as the summa) and determined what constituted an acceptable authority to rely upon. In the twelfth and thirteenth centuries, scholars discussed the use of pagan sources of learning, such as the recently rediscovered Aristotle and Plato, as well as the works of heretical writers such as Origen.

Yet these women's writings offer a serious challenge to this systemization. The scholastic tradition effectively declared that there was a canon of theological knowledge which was sanctioned, and it was to be learned only through a particular course of study, at the universities, under the control of the orders. It could only be achieved as the highest level of learning; after the study of the *trivium*, the *quadrivium*, and philosophy, only then could a man study theology. And it was limited to men, particularly men who were destined for clerical work. The language for this work was Latin. In contrast, these women show that there are several derivative challenges to this system. First, if the theology is to have an effect on the church, it is going to be preached and taught derivatively to the people, so they should be able to theologize if they have learned their lessons correctly. In the cases of all of these women, we see accurate expressions of theological ideas, even though none but Teresa and Mechtilde of Hackeborn received any official education that we know of. The rest presumably heard preachers, and learned their theology from them as the vast majority of medieval Christian Europe did. These women's writings then challenge the divide of a theology that is meant for the church, but which is officially recognized only in a small, educated, male clerical elite. Second, the women sidestep the issue of loci of authority in an ingenious way; the men looked to tradition in the form of sayings of the Church Fathers as one way to shore up authority on dogmatic issues. Obversely, the women turn to the ultimate authority – God – to shore up their own authority. Whereas a man could say his theology was correct because Augustine backed him up, we see these medical mystics repeatedly stating their visions are accurate because God or Christ granted them. Effectively, this was a stronger authority than even tradition could claim.

The writings of these women should show that the experiences of women in the middle ages were extremely varied and variable. What was accepted in one place or in one generation did not necessarily meet with the same approval in other places or generations. The fact that women strove to discover how to express their experiences of God, wrote about them, or allowed others to write about them, shows the urgency many of them felt regarding their abilities to respond to God. There is no one paradigm that explains the religious life of medieval women, any more so than there is one to describe the women of any age, such as our own. But it is precisely in this diversity of vocations, spiritualities, expressions and lives that we can see a part of the world that women inhabited in these medieval centuries.

Glossary

Anchoress: A woman contemplative who has renounced the world in favour of a life of contemplation, asceticism and fasting, enclosed as a hermit in an anchorhold.

Annunciation, the: This is the name for the revelation in which the Angel Gabriel came to Mary to announce that she would bear the child of God. The liturgical calendar celebrated this feast on 25 March, nine months before the Nativity.

Anticlericalism: Criticisms of the church, suggesting a need for reform or suggesting that the institution of the church is in error in some way.

Apophatic theology: Also known as the *via negativa* or 'Negative Theology', it is a form of theology that attempts to talk about God by describing what God is not. It holds that God is beyond all created things, and thus is ineffable – i.e., God cannot be described in language. By describing what God is not, apophatic theology attempts to dispel misconceptions about God.

Asceticism: The practice of mortifications in order to grow in virtue and purify the soul. Medieval Christians saw the human as a psychosomatic unity of body, soul and spirit; the denial of physical pleasures or indulgences – such as abstaining from sex, extravagant foods or sleep – could help bring the body, soul and spirit into obedience to God and remove mundane things that would distract it from God.

Beatification: The process whereby a dead person of exceptional holiness was given the title 'Blessed'. In the medieval church, the process for beatification and canonization often overlapped.

Beguine: A laywoman living a religious life without formal vows to a monastery or an order. Beguines often lived alone, gathering together for prayer and good works, and supporting themselves through handicrafts and labour.

Benedictines: The oldest order of the church, founded by Benedict. This order is characterized by houses of monks or nuns called monasteries (for men, women, or double houses containing both) or convents (for women exclusively). Monks and nuns in the Benedictine order follow the *Rule of Benedict* and take vows of obedience, stability (remaining in the same monastery) and conversion of life.

Canonization: The process by which a dead person of exceptional holiness is given the title 'Saint'.

Carmelites: An order of contemplative friars and nuns, founded in the Holy Land by crusaders who went to live by the well of Elijah on Mount Carmel.

Cathars: A heretical group that existed from the eleventh to thirteenth centuries, and which taught a dualistic view of the universe. They believed that matter was evil and must be transcended; because of their denigration of the physical world, they also denied the Incarnation.

Cistercians: An eleventh-century reform of the Benedictine order that emphasized a return to the 'primitive values' of the *Rule of Benedict*. Cistercian monasteries used little decoration, required manual labour, practised more stringent asceticism, and were located far away from centres of population. Although the General Chapter in 1228 forbade houses of Cistercian women to be formed anew, women's houses of other orders were allowed to adopt the Cistercian customaries, thus becoming, effectively, Cistercian houses.

Counter-Reformation, the: An institutional and popular movement from the mid-fifteenth to late-sixteenth century in which Catholicism experienced a revival of doctrine, devotions and art, and reformed and clarified a number of practices in response to the criticism of various Reformation leaders.

Divine Offices, the (or Liturgy of the Hours): The public prayer of vowed religious. These consist of various 'hours' (set times for prayer) periodically spaced throughout the day from pre-dawn to evening, in which psalms, readings and prayers are publicly recited by the religious as a group.

Dominicans (or Order of Preachers): An order founded in the thirteenth century by Dominic (1170–1221) to counteract the Albigensian heresy (the Albigensians were also known as the Cathars), in the Languedoc region in the French Pyrenees, through preaching. The emphases of the order were on preaching catholic doctrine and on evangelical poverty and learning.

Eucharist: Literally, 'Thanksgiving', this is the celebration of the Mass of the Lord's Supper, in which the priest consecrates the elements of bread and wine, turning them into the body and blood of Christ. The term 'Eucharist' can also refer specifically to these consecrated elements. In medieval theology, these elements were considered to contain the real presence of Christ's body and blood.

Extreme unction: One of the seven sacraments, also known as 'Last Rites' or *viaticum*. This sacrament offers remission of sins and reception of the Eucharist as a person is dying, in order to send him or her on towards God and allow entrance into salvation.

Fasting: The practice of bodily asceticism. In the medieval church, there were many periods, such as Lent, in which fasting was required by the church.

Franciscans (or Friars Minor): A thirteenth-century order, formed by Francis of Assisi (1181–1226), in response to the need for a return to evangelical ideals including poverty and piety.

Great Schism, the: a political (not theological) division in the Latin Church from 1378 to 1417, in which rival popes were established in both Avignon and Rome.

Hagiography: A genre of writing in which a life of a person reputed to be a saint is provided in order to encourage prayers to and devotions towards them. Often, hagiographies were written in the hope that a person would be canonized or beatified.

Holy House, the: The House of the Annunciation, or the house where Mary was when the Angel Gabriel visited her.

Liturgical calendar, the: A yearly cycle of readings, feasts and fasts that begins in Advent.

Lollardy: A heresy based upon the teachings of Jean Wyclif. The Lollards challenged a number of Catholic practices such as pilgrimage and the use of images in church architecture and worship, and Lollards denied the effectiveness of sacraments celebrated by priests who lacked 'vital piety'.

Mantellate: A group of older widows who took the habit of the Order of Preachers, but who remained living at home and engaging as a group in public prayer and works of charity.

Marian devotion: Any of several forms of devotion to Mary, the mother of Jesus. Devotions directed towards Mary often focus on her close link to Christ as his mother, or on her specially favoured status as having been chosen by God to bear the Incarnate Lord.

Mendicant friars: Literally, 'begging' friars, this refers to the Franciscans and Dominicans, who relied upon begging when they entered towns to preach and at first did not own property.

Mysticism: A process by which a person comes to know or experience God more fully. This can take many forms, including the contemplation and its fruits, reception of discernible experiences, visions or revelations, or the reception of inexpressible 'knowledge' of God.

Negative theology: See apophatic theology.

Neo-Platonism: Any of a number of philosophical and theological systems that derive from the works of Plato and his followers. Among the most common Neo-Platonic elements that appear in mysticism involve notions of the soul's exit from and return to God, and the hierarchy of the body, soul and spirit; it was transmitted through the works of theologians such as Augustine, Boethius, Denys and Eriugena.

Penance, theology of: A system whereby a person's sins were forgiven. In the medieval church, this encompassed both the confession of sins and the enactment of a penance as assigned by the confessor. The penitential act to be undertaken could be a public act, such as going on pilgrimage or a public humiliation, or it could be a private one, such as the saying of certain prayers for a set number of repetitions.

Pilgrimage: The act of travelling to a shrine or sacred place for religious reasons, such as undertaking an act of penance.

Purgatory: A 'place' in which the souls of the dead who are to eventually see God in the beatific vision go in order to be purified. Since only the pure can see God 'face to face', and all humans have sinned, a place of purgation was necessary after death before the saved would see God. Traditionally, purgatory was viewed as a place with torments that were bearable and which allowed the souls to grow in the virtues. When people died, medievals believed that, if they were to be damned, they would go to hell; if people were to be saved, they would go to purgatory for an amount of time commensurate with their sins before being received in heaven.

Bibliography

Primary works

Angela of Foligno. *Complete Works*. Translated and introduced by Paul Lachance. Mahweh, NJ: Paulist Press, 1993.

Bernard of Clairvaux. *On the Song of Songs*. Translated by Kilian Walsh, OCSO and Irene M. Edmonds. 4 vols. Kalamazoo: Cistercian Publications, 1971, 1976, 1979, 1980.

Catherine of Siena. *Dialogue*. Translated and introduced by Suzanne Noffke. Mahweh, NJ: Paulist Press, 1980.

Catherine of Siena. *The Letters of Catherine of Siena*, 3 vols. Edited and translated by Suzanne Noffke. Tempe, AZ: Arizona Center for Medieval and Renaissance Studies, 2000, 2001, 2007.

Gertrude the Great. *The Herald of God's Loving-Kindness: Books One and Two*. Translated by Alexandra Barratt. Kalamazoo: Cistercian Publications, 1991.

Gertrude the Great. *The Herald of God's Loving-Kindness: Book Three*. Translated by Alexandra Barratt. Kalamazoo: Cistercian Publications, 1999.

Gregory the Great. *Dialogues*. Translated by Odo John Zimmerman. Washington, D.C.: Catholic University Press, 2005 reprint.

Hadewijch of Brabant. *The Complete Works*. Translated and introduced by Columba Hart. Mahwah, NJ: Paulist Press, 1980.

Hildegard of Bingen. *Scivias*. Translated by Mother Columba Hart and Jane Bishop. New York: Paulist Press, 1990.

Hildegard of Bingen. *Symphonia: A Critical Edition of the Symphonia armonie celestium revelationem.* Edited and translated by Barbara Newman. Ithaca, NY: Cornell University Press, 1998.

Julian of Norwich. *A Book of Showings to the Anchoress Julian of Norwich.* Edited by Edmund Colledge and James Walsh. Toronto: PIMS, 1978.

Julian of Norwich. *Showings.* Introduction by Edmund Colledge and James Walsh. New York: Paulist Press, 1978.

King, Margot H. and David Wiljer, trans. and ed. *The Life of Christina the Astonishing by Thomas de Cantimpré.* Toronto: Peregrina Publishing, 2000.

Margery Kempe, *The Book of Margery Kempe.* Edited by Sanford Brown Meech, and Preface by Hope Emily Allen. Early English Texts Society #212. Oxford: OUP, 1982.

Margery Kempe. *The Book of Margery Kempe.* Translated and introduced by John Skinner. New York: Doubleday Image, 1998.

Marguerite Porete. *The Mirror of Simple Souls.* Edited by Ellen L. Babinsky. Mahweh, NJ: Paulist Press, 1993.

Mechtild of Hackeborn. *The booke of gostlye grace of Mechtild of Hackeborn.* Edited by Theresa A. Halligan. Tornoto: PIMS, 1979.

Mechtild of Magdeburg. *The Flowing Light of the Godhead.* Translated and introduced by Frank Tobin. Mahweh, NJ: 1998.

Raymond of Capua. *The Life of Saint Catherine of Siena.* Translated by George Lamb. London: Harvill Press, 1960.

Raymond of Capua. *Die Legenda Maior (Vita Catharinae Senensis) des Raimund von Capua.* Edited and translated by Jörg Jungmayr. Berlin: Weidler Buchverlag, 2004.

Teresa of Avila. *The Complete Works of Saint Teresa of Jesus.* Translated and edited by E. Alison Peers. London: Sheed & Ward, 1946.

Teresa of Avila. *The Complete Works of Saint Teresa of Jesus.* Translated and edited by Kieran Kavanaugh and Otilo Rodriguez. Washington: ICS Publications, 1976–85.

Thomas Aquinas, *The Summa Theologica of Saint Thomas Aquinas.* Translated and edited by the Fathers of the English Dominican Province. New York: Benzinger Bros., 1912–1925.

Thomas de Cantimpré. *Vita Beatae Christinae Mirabilis Trudonopolis in Hasbania.* Edited by J. Pinius. Paris: Th. Gauss, 1868.

Secondary works

Ahlgren, Gillian T.W. 'Ecstasy, Prophecy and Reform: Catherine of Siena as a Model for Holy Women of Sixteenth-Century Spain', in *The Mystical Gesture: Essays on Medieval and Early Modern Spiritual Culture in Honor of Mary E. Giles*, edited by Robert Boenig, 53–65. Aldershot: Ashgate, 2000.

Andersen, Elizabeth A. *The Voices of Mechthild of Magdeburg*. Oxford: Peter Lang, 2000.

Atkinson, Clarissa W. *Mystic and Pilgrim: The Book and the World of Margery Kempe*. Ithaca, NY: Cornell University Press, 1983.

Axters, Stephanus, O.P. *The Spirituality of the Low Countries*. Translated by Donald Attwater. London: Blackfriars Publications, 1954.

Bauerschmidt, Frederick Christian. 'Seeing Jesus: Julian of Norwich and the Text of Christ's Body', *Journal of Medieval and Early Modern Studies* 27:2 (Spring 1997): 189–214.

Becker, Ernest J. *A Contribution to the Comparative Study of the Medieval Visions of Heaven and Hell, With Special Reference to the Middle English Versions*. Baltimore, MD: John Murphy, 1899.

Beckman, Patricia Zimmerman. 'The Power of Books and the Practice of Mysticism in the Fourteenth Century: Heinrich of Nordlingen and Margaret Ehner on Mechthild's Flowing Light of the Godhead', *Church History* 76:1 (March 2007): 61–83.

Bell, David N. *The Image and the Likeness: The Augustinian Anthropology of William of St-Thierry*. Kalamazoo, MI: Cistercian Publications, 1994.

Bell, Raymond. *Holy Anorexia*. Chicago: University of Chicago Press, 1987.

Berrigan, Joseph. 'The Tuscan Visionary: St. Catherine of Siena,' in *Medieval Women Writers*, edited by Katharina M. Wilson, 252–55. Athens, GA: University of Georgia Press, 1984.

Blamires, Alcuin. 'Women and Preaching in Medieval Orthodoxy, Heresy, and Saints' Lives', *Viator* 26 (1995): 135–52.

Boon, Jessica. 'Trinitarian Love Mysticism: Ruusbroes, Hadewijch, and the Gendered Experience of the Divine', *Church History* 72:3 (September 2003): 484–503.

Bowie, Fiona and Oliver Davies, *Hildegard of Bingen: An Anthology*. London: SPCK, 1990.

Bradley, Ritamarie. 'Perceptions of Self in Julian of Norwich's Showings', *Downside Review* 105 (1986): 227–39.

Brown, Peter. *The Cult of the Saints: Its Rise and Function in Latin Christianity*. Chicago: University of Chicago Press, 1981.

Bryant, Gwendolyn. 'The French Heretic Beguine: Marguerite Porete', in *Medieval Women Writers*, edited by Katharina M. Wilson, 204–26. Athens, GA: University of Georgia Press, 1984.

Burr, David. *The Spiritual Franciscans: From Protest to Persecution in the Century After Saint Francis.* University Park, PA: Pennsylvania State Press, 2001.

Carney, Sheila. 'Exemplarism in Hadewijch: The Quest for Full-Grownness', *Downside Review* 103:353 (October 1985): 276–95.

Caron, Ann Marie, R.S.M. 'Invitations of the Divine Heart: The Mystical Writings of Mechtild of Hackeborn', *American Benedictine Review* 45:3 (1994): 321–38.

Castagna, Valerie. 'Margery Kempe and her Becoming "Authoress"', *Textus* 19 (2006): 323–38.

Caviness, Madeline H. 'Hildegard as Designer of the Illustrations to her Works', in *Warburg Institute Colloquia #4*, edited by Charles Burnett and Peter Dronke. London: Warburg Institute, 1998.

Chenu, Marie Dominique. *Nature, Man and Society in the Twelfth Century: essays on new theological perspectives in the Latin West.* Translated by Jerome Taylor and Lester K. Little. Toronto: University of Toronto Press, 1997.

Clark, J.P.H. 'Predestination in Christ According to Julian of Norwich', *Downside Review* 340 (1982): 79–91.

Clark, J.P.H. 'Nature, Grace and the Trinity in Julian of Norwich', *Downside Review* 340 (1982): 203–20.

Coakley, John W. *Women, Men and Spiritual Power: Female Saints and Their Male Collaborators.* New York: Columbia University Press, 2006.

Coakley, Sarah. *Powers and Submissions: Spirituality, Philosophy and Gender.* Oxford: Blackwell, 2002.

Colón, Susan E. '"Gostly Labowrys": Vocation and Profession in *The Book of Margery Kempe*', *English Studies* 86:4 (August 2005): 283–97.

Cooper, Christine F. 'Miraculous Translation in *The Book of Margery Kempe*', *Studies in Philology* (2004): 270–98.

Datsko Barker, Paula S. 'The Motherhood of God in Julian of Norwich's Theory', *Downside Review* 341 (1982): 290–304.

Davies, Oliver. *Meister Eckhart: Mystical Theologian.* London: SPCK, 1991.

de Paepe, Norbert. *Hadewijch, Strofische Gedichten. Een studie van de mine in het kader der 12e en 13e eeuwse mystiek en profane minnelyriek.* Ghent, 1967.

Dickinson, John Compton. *The Shrine of Our Lady of Walsingham.* Cambridge: Cambridge University Press, 1956.

Dieker, Alberta. 'Mechtilde of Hackeborn: Song of Love', in *Medieval Women Monastics: Wisdom's Wellsprings*, edited by Miriam Schmitt and Linda Kulser, 231–44. Collegeville, MN: Liturgical Press, 1996.

Dronke, Peter. 'Hildegard of Bingen as Poetess and Dramatist', in *Poetic Individuality in the Middle Ages: New Departures in Poetry 1000–1151.* Oxford: Oxford University Press, 1970.

Dronke, Peter. 'Problemata Hildegardiana', *Mittellateinisches Jahrbuch* 16 (1981): 97–131.

Dronke, Peter. *Women Writers of the Middle Ages: A Critical Study of Texts from Perpetua (+203) to Marguerite Porete (+1310).* Cambridge: Cambridge University Press, 1984.

Dronke, Peter. 'The Allegorical World-Picture of Hildegard of Bingen: Revaluations and New Problems', in *Hildegard of Bingen: The Context of her Thought and Art*, edited by Charles Burnett and Peter Dronke, 1–16. London: Warburg Institute, 1998.

English, Leona M. 'An Analysis of Power in the Writing of Mechtild of Magdeburg', *Feminist Theology* 14:2 (2006): 189–204.

Farrell, Thomas J., ed. *Bakhtin and Medieval Voices.* Gainesville, FL: University Press of Florida, 1995.

Finnegan, Mary Jeremy. 'St Mechtilde of Hackeborn: *Nemo Communior*', in *Medieval Religious Women*, edited by Lillian Thomas Shank and John A. Nichols, v. 2, 213–21. Kalamazoo, MI: Cistercian Publications, 1987.

Finnegan, Mary Jeremy. *The Women of Helfta: Scholars and Mystics.* Athens, GA: University of Georgia Press, 1991.

Foster, Kenelm. 'St. Catherine's Teaching on Christ,' *Life of the Spirit* 16 (1962): 310–23.

Gallyon, Margaret. *Margery Kempe of Lynn and Medieval England.* Norwich: The Canterbury Press, 1995.

Gambero, Luigi. *Mary in the Middle Ages: The Blessed Virgin Mary in the Thought of Medieval Latin Theologians.* San Francisco: Ignatius Press, 2005.

Gardiner, Helen. *Visions of Heaven and Hell Before Dante.* New York: Italica Press, 1989.

Gardner, Catherine V. *Women Philosophers: Genre and the Boundaries of Philosophy.* Boulder, CO: Westview Press, 2003.

Gillett, H.M. *Walsingham and its Shrine.* London: Burns Oates and Washbourne, 1934.

Graef, Hilda. *Mary: A History of Doctrine and Devotion.* Westminster, MD: Christian Classics, 1985.

Grundman, Herbert. 'Die Frauen und die Literatur im Mittelalter: Ein Beitrag zur Frage nach der Entstehung des Schriftums in der Volksprache', *Archiv für Kulturgeschichte* 26 (1936): 129–61.

Guest, Tanis. 'Hadewijch and Minne', in *European Context: Studies in the History and Literature of the Netherlands Presented to Theodoor Weevers*, edited by P.K. King and P.F. Vincent, 14–29. Cambridge: Modern Humanities Research Association, 1971.

Guest, Tanis. *Some Aspects of Hadewijch's Poetic Form in the 'Strofische Gedichten'*. Martinus Nijhoff, The Hague, 1975.

Harper-Bill, Christopher. 'The Foundation and Later History of the Medieval Shrine', in *Walsingham: Pilgrimage and History*, 63–79. Walsingham: R.C. National Shrine, 1999.

Higley, Sarah L. *Hildegard of Bingen's Unknown Language: An Edition, Translation, and Discussion*. Basingstoke: Palgrave Macmillan, 2002.

Hinderer, Drew. 'On Rehabilitating Margery Kempe', *Studia Mystica* 5 (1982): 27–43.

Hollywood, Amy. *The Soul as Virgin Wife: Mechtilde of Magdeburg, Marguerite Porete, and Meister Eckhart*. London: University of Notre Dame Press, 1995.

Jantzen, Grace. *Power, Gender and Christian Mysticism*. Cambridge: Cambridge University Press, 1995.

Jantzen, Grace. *Julian of Norwich: Mystic and Theologian*. New York: Paulist Press, 2000.

Jones, Catherine. 'The English Mystic: Julian of Norwich', in *Medieval Women Writers*, edited by Katharina M. Wilson, 269–96. Athens, GA: University of Georgia Press, 1984.

Kavanaugh, Kieran. 'Introduction' in *Teresa of Avila: The Interior Castle*, New York: Paulist Press, 1979.

Kerby-Fulton, Kathryn and Dyan Elliott. 'Self Image and the Visionary Role in Two Letters from the Correspondence of Elizabeth of Schonau and Hildegard of Bingen', in *On Pilgrimage: The Best of Ten Years of Vox Benedictina*, edited by Margot King. Toronto: Peregrina Press, 1994.

Kieckhefer, Richard. *Unquiet Souls: Fourteenth-Century Saints and their Religious Milieu*. Chicago, IL: University of Chicago Press, 1987.

Kieckhefer, Richard. 'Convention and Conversion: Patterns in Late Medieval Piety', *Church History* 67:1 (March 1998): 32–51.

King, Margot H. 'The Sacramental Witness of Christina *Mirabilis*: The Mystic Growth of a Fool for Christ's Sake', in *Medieval Religious Women: Peacemakers*, vol. 2, edited by Lillian Thomas Shank and John A. Nichols, 145–64. Kalamazoo, MI: Cistercian Publications, 1987.

Kraft, Kent. 'The German Visionary: Hildegard of Bingen', in *Medieval Women Writers*, edited by Katharina M. Wilson, 109–30. Athens, GA: University of Georgia Press, 1984.

Lachance, Paul. *The Mystical Journey of Angela of Foligno*, Peregrina Papers #2. Toronto: Peregrina Publishing, 1990.

Lambert, M.D. *Medieval Heresy: Popular Movements from Bogomil to Hus.* London: Edward Arnold, 1977.

Landale, Scilla. 'A Pilgrim's Progress to Walsingham', in *Walsingham: Pilgrimage and History*, 13–37. Walsingham: R.C. National Shrine, 1999.

Lea, Henry Charles. *A History of the Inquisition of the Middle Ages*, vol. 1. London, 1888.

Le Goff, Jacques. *The Birth of Purgatory.* Chicago, IL: University of Chicago Press, 1984.

Liebeschütz, Hans. *Das allegorische Weltbild der heiligen Hildegard von Bingen.* Leipzig–Berlin, 1930.

Lochrie, Karma. *Margery Kempe and Translations of the Flesh.* Philadelphia, PA: Penn Press, 1991.

Lucas, Elona. 'The Enigmatic, Threatening Margery Kempe', *Downside Review* 105/361 (1987): 294–306.

Marzac-Holland, Nicole. *Three Norfolk Mystics.* Norfolk: C.J. & M. Isaacson, 1983.

Mazzoni, Christina, ed., and John Cirignano, trans., *Angela of Foligno's* Memorial. Cambridge: D.S. Brewer, 1999.

McGinn, Bernard. 'The Changing Shape of Late Medieval Mysticism', American Society of Church History Presidential Address, 6 January 1996.

McGinn, Bernard. *The Presence of God: A History of Western Christian Mysticism*, 6 vols. New York: Crossroad, 1991, 1996, 1998, 2005 and forthcoming.

McNamara, J. 'The Need to Give: Suffering and Female Sanctity in the Middle Ages', in *Images of Sainthood*, edited by R. Blumenfeld-Kosinski and T. Szell, 199–221. Ithaca, NY: Cornell University Press, 1991.

Mews, Constant J. 'Hildegard and the Schools', in *Warburg Institute Colloquia #4*, edited by Charles Burnett and Peter Dronke, 89–110. London: Warburg Institute, 1998.

Morrou, Henri Irénée. *Les Troubadours.* Paris: Éditions de Seuill, c. 1971.

Murk-Jansen, Saskia. *The Measure of Mystic Thought: A Study of Hadewijch's Meneldichten.* Göppingen: Kümmerle Verlag, 1991.

Murk-Jansen, Saskia. 'The Mystic Theology of the Thirteenth Century Mystic, Hadewijch, and its Literary Expression', in *The Medieval Mystical Tradition in England*, edited by Marion Glasscoe, 117–27. Cambridge: D.S. Brewer, 1992.

Murk-Jansen, Saskia. 'The Use of Gender and Gender-Related Imagery in Hadewijch', in *Gender and Text in the Later Middle Ages*, edited by Jane Chance, 52–68. Gainesville, FL: University Press of Florida, 1996.

Murk-Jansen, Saskia. *Brides in the Desert: The Spirituality of the Beguines.* London: Darton, Longman & Todd Ltd, 1998.

Newman, Barbara. *From Virile Woman to WomanChrist: Studies in Modern Religion and Literature.* Philadelphia, PA: University of Pennsylvania Press, 1995.

Newman, Barbara. *Sister of Wisdom: St Hildegard's Theology of the Feminine.* Berkeley, CA: University of California Press, 1997.

Newman, Barbara. 'Possessed by the Spirit: Devout Women, Demoniacs, and the Apostolic Life in the Thirteenth Century', *Speculum* 73 (1998): 733–70.

Newman, Barbara. 'Three-Part Invention: The *Vita S. Hildegardis* and Mystical Hagiography', in *Hildegard of Bingen: The Context of her Thought and Art*, edited by Charles Burnett and Peter Dronke, 189–210. London: The Warburg Institute, 1998.

Noffke, Suzanne. *Catherine of Siena: Vision Through a Distant Eye.* Collegeville, MN: Liturgical Press, 1996.

Noffke, Suzanne. 'Catherine of Siena: Justly Doctor of the Church?' *Theology Today* 60 (2005): 49–62.

O'Dell, M. Colman. 'Elizabeth of Schonau and Hildegard of Bingen: Prophets of the Lord', in *Medieval Religious Women: Peaceweavers*, edited by Lillian Thomas Shank and John A. Nichols, 85–102. Kalamazoo, MI: Cistercian Publications, 1987.

Panicelli, Debra Scott. 'Finding God in the Memory: Julian of Norwich and the Loss of Visions', *Downside Review* 357 (1986): 299–317.

Patten, A. Hope. *England's National Shrine of Our Lady Past and Present.* Cambridge: R.I. Severs, 1944/5.

Petroff, Elizabeth A. *Medieval Women's Visionary Literature.* Oxford: Oxford University Press, 1986.

Petroff, Elizabeth Alvida. *Body and Soul: Essays on Medieval Women and Mysticism.* New York: Oxford University Press, 1994.

Provost, William. 'The English Religious Enthusiast, Margery Kempe', in *Medieval Women Writers*, edited by Katharina M. Wilson, 297–302. Athens, GA: University of Georgia Press, 1984.

Rawcliffe, Carol and Richard Wilson. *Medieval Norwich.* New York: Hambledon & London, 2004.

R.C. National Shrine, Walsingham. *Walsingham: Pilgrimage and History. Papers Presented at the Centenary Historical Conference 23rd–27th March 1998.* Fakenham, Norfolk: Lanceni Press, 1999.

Reynaert, J. 'Hadewijch: Mystic Poetry and Courtly Love', in *Medieval Dutch Literature in its European Context*, edited by Erik Cooper, 208–25. Cambridge: Cambridge University Press, 1994.

Rex, Richard. *The Lollards.* New York: Palgrave, 2002.

Roisin, Simone. 'La Méthod hagiographique de Thomas de Cantimpré', in *Miscellanea Historica in Honorem Alberti de Meyer.* I. Louvain: Bibliothèque de l'Université, 1946.

Rorem, Paul. 'The Company of Medieval Women Theologians', *Theology Today* 60 (2003): 82–93.

Rudy, Gordon. *Mystical Language of Sensation in the Later Middle Ages.* London: Routledge, 2002.

Schroeder-Sheker, Therese. 'The Use of Plucked-string Instruments in Medieval Christian Mysticism', *Mystics Quarterly* 15 (September 1989): 133–9.

Schroeder-Sheker, Therese. 'The Alchemical Harp of Mechtild of Hackeborn', in *On Pilgrimage: The Best Ten Years of Vox Benedictina*, edited by Margot King, 41–55. Toronto: Peregrina Press, 1994.

Sells, Michael A. *Mystical Languages of Unsaying.* London: University of Chicago Press, 1994.

Singer, Charles. *From Magic to Science: Essays on the Scientific Twilight.* London: 1928.

Spearing, A.C. 'The Book of Margery Kempe; Or, *The Diary of a Nobody*', *Southern Review* 38 (2002): 625–35.

Stephenson, Colin. *Walsingham Way.* London: Darton, Longman and Todd, 1970.

Stevens, John. 'The Musical Individuality of Hildegard's Songs: A Liturgical Shadowland', in *Warburg Institute Colloquia #4*, edited by Charles Burnett and Peter Dronke, 163–88. London: Warburg Institute, 1998.

Stone, Robert Karl. *Middle English Prose Style: Margery Kempe and Julian of Norwich.* The Hague: Mouton, 1970.

Sumption, Johnathan. *Pilgrimage: An Image of Medieval Religion.* London: Faber & Faber, 2002.

Suydam, Mary. 'The Touch of Satisfaction: Visions and the Religious Experience According to Hadewijch of Antwerp', *Journal of Feminist Studies in Religion* 12:2 (Fall 1996): 5–27.

Sweetman, Robert S. 'Christine of Saint-Trond's Preaching Apostolate: Thomas of Cantimpré's Hagiographical Method Revisited', in *On Pilgrimage: The Best of Ten Years of Vox Benedictina*, compiled by Elizabeth Druries and Dewey Kramer, edited by Margot H. King, 410–32. Toronto: Peregrina Publishing, 1994.

Thurston, Herbert. *Surprising Mystics.* London: Burns & Oates, 1955.

Tobin, Frank. *Mechthild von Magdeburg: A Medieval Mystic in Modern Eyes.* Columbia, SC: Camden House, 1995.

Tugwell, Simon. *Ways of Imperfection: an exploration of Christian Spirituality.* London: Darton, Longman and Todd, 1984.

Turner, Edith and Victor Turner. *Image and Pilgrimage in Christian Culture: Anthropological Perspectives.* New York: Columbia University Press, 1978.

Vanderauwera, Ria. 'The Brabant Mystic: Hadewijch', in *Medieval Women Writers*, edited by Katharina M. Wilson, 186–203. Athens, GA: University of Georgia Press, 1984.

van Mierlo, J. *Hadewijch, strophische Gedichten.* Antwerp–Brussels–Ghent–Leuven, 1942.

van Mierlo, J. *Hadewijch: Visionen.* 2 vols. Louvain: Vlaamsch Boekenhalle, 1924–1925.

Vauchez, André. 'La Sainteté feminine dans le mouvement franciscain', *Les laics au moyen âge*, 189–202. Paris: Éditions de Cerf, 1987.

Voaden, Rosalynn. *God's Words, Women's Voices: The Discernment of Spirits in the Writing of Late-medieval Women Visionaries.* Suffolk: York Medieval Press, 1999.

von Balthasar, Hans Urs. *Mechthilds kirchlicher Auftrafe.* Einsiedeln, 1955.

Walker Bynum, Caroline. *Jesus as Mother: Studies in the Spirituality of the High Middle Ages.* Berkeley, CA: University of California Press, 1982.

Walker Bynum, Caroline. *Holy Feast and Holy Fast.* Berkeley, CA: University of California Press, 1988.

Walker Bynum, Caroline. *Fragmentation and Redemption: Essays on Gender and the Human Body in Medieval Religion.* New York: Zone Books, 1991.

Ward, B. *Miracles and the Medieval Mind: Theory, Record and Event, 1000–1215.* Philadelphia, PA: University of Pennsylvania Press, 1982.

Watson, Nicholas. 'Conceptions of the Word: The Mother Tongue and the Incarnation of God', *New Medieval Literature* I (1997): 85–124.

Webb, Diana. *Medieval European Pilgrimage.* London: I.B.Tauris, 2002.

Weevers, Theodoor. *Poetry of the Netherlands in its European context: 1170–1930.* London: Athlone Press, 1960.

Weinstein, D. and R. Bell, *Saints and Society: The Two Worlds of Western Christendom, 1000–1700.* Chicago: University of Chicago Press, 1982.

Wilson, Katharina M., ed. *Medieval Women Writers.* Athens, GA: University of Georgia Press, 1984.

Yoshikawa, Naoë Kukita. 'The Jerusalem Pilgrimage: The Center of the Structure of the *Book of Margery Kempe*', *English Studies* 86:3 (June 2005): 193–205.

Zum Brunn, Emily and Georgette Epiney-Burgard. *Women Mystics in Medieval Europe.* St Paul, MN: Paragon, 1989.

Endnotes

Introduction

1   Mechtild of Magdeburg, *The Flowing Light of the Godhead*, 3.17.

2   Bernard McGinn, 'The Changing Shape of Late Medieval Mysticism', American Society of Church History Presidential Address, 6 January 1996.

3   This also implies a structuring of disciplines, in which literature is not as lofty as theology, perhaps a holdover from the medieval notion of theology as the queen of the sciences, a notion that still persists in some of the theology of the twenty-first century, as, for instance, in Radical Orthodoxy.

4   Discussions concerning the relationships between mysticism and visionary literature, prophecy and the apocalyptic can and have filled entire books. A good starting place for the study of mysticism is Bernard McGinn's six-volume series, *The Presence of God: A History of Western Christian Mysticism* (New York: Crossroad, 1991, 1996, 1998, 2005 and forthcoming).

5   The first to popularize this argument was Herbert Grundman, 'Die Frauen und die Literatur im Mittelalter: Ein Beitrag zur Frage nach der Entstehung des Schrifttums in der Volksprache', *Archiv für Kulturgeschichte* 26 (1936): 129–61.

6   See Edmund Colledge and James Walsh, *A book of showings to the anchoress Julian of Norwich* (Toronto: PIMS, 1978).

7   Catherine Jones, 'The English Mystic: Julian of Norwich', in Katharina M. Wilson, ed., *Medieval Women Writers* (Athens, GA: University of Georgia Press, 1984), 273.

8   Nicholas Watson. 'Conceptions of the Word: The Mother Tongue and the Incarnation of God', *New Medieval Literature* I (1997): 85–124.

9   Jessica Boon, 'Trinitarian Love Mysticism: Ruusbroeck, Hadewijch, and the Gendered Experience of the Divine', *Church History* 72:3 (September 2003), 493.

10   Raymond Bell, *Holy Anorexia* (Chicago: University of Chicago Press, 1987). A more comprehensive look at this phenomenon is found in Caroline Walker Bynum, *Holy Feast and Holy Fast* (Berkeley, CA: University of California Press, 1988); see also K. Lochrie, *Margery Kempe and Translations of the Flesh* (Philadelphia, PA: Penn Press, 1991); D. Weinstein and R. Bell, *Saints and Society: The Two Worlds of Western Christendom, 1000–1700* (Chicago: University of Chicago Press, 1982); Caroline Walker Bynum, *Fragmentation and Redemption: Essays on Gender and the Human Body in Medieval Religion* (New York: Zone Books, 1991); J. McNamara, 'The Need to Give: Suffering and Female Sanctity in the Middle Ages', in *Images of Sainthood*, edited by R. Blumenfeld-Kosinski and T. Szell, 199–221 (Ithaca, NY: Cornell University Press, 1991).

11   If not entirely female, at least part of a 'lay' devotional trend.

12   See, for instance, Grace Jantzen, *Power, Gender and Christian Mysticism* (Cambridge: Cambridge University Press, 1995); Sarah Coakley, *Powers and Submissions: Spirituality, Philosophy and Gender* (Oxford: Blackwell, 2002); Rosalynn Voaden, *God's Words, Women's Voices : The Discernment of Spirits in the Writing of Late-medieval Women Visionaries* (Suffolk: York Medieval Press, 1999).

13   Bynum, *Holy Feast and Holy Fast*, 233.

14   John Coakley, *Women, Men, and Spiritual Power: Female Saints and their Male Collaborators* (New York: Columbia University Press, 2006).

15   Elizabeth Alvida Petroff, *Body and Soul: Essays on Medieval Women and Mysticism* (New York: Oxford University Press, 1994), 139–40.

16   Paul Rorem, 'The Company of Medieval Women Theologians', *Theology Today*, 60 (2003): 82–93.

1. Mary's Handmaid: Richeldis of Faverches

1   Nicole Marzac-Holland, *Three Norfolk Mystics* (Norfolk: C.J. & M. Isaacson, 1983). See notes to Richeldis chapter, p. 38.

2   See stanza 17, ll. 110–16.

3   Pynson ballad, reprinted in John Compton Dickinson, *The Shrine of Our*

Lady of Walsingham (Cambridge: Cambridge University Press, 1956). Appendix I. Stanza 3, ll. 12–15. Along with the ballad's dating, one book of hours in the University Library at Cambridge mentions the 1061 date as well. See Edith Turner and Victor Turner, *Image and Pilgrimage in Christian Culture: Anthropological Perspectives* (New York: Columbia University Press, 1978), 177.

4   Pynson ballad, Stanza I, ll. 1–4.

5   Luke 1.26–38.

6   Pynson ballad, ll. 33–4.

7   Pynson ballad, stanza 2, ll. 7–9; stanza 4, ll. 19–25.

8   Pynson ballad, stanza 6, ll. 37–9.

9   Judges 6.36–40; Pynson ballad, stanza 8, ll. 49–53. The founding legend concerning Santa Maria Maggiore in Rome mentions a similar sort of marking of the site.

10 Pynson ballad, stanza 7, ll. 40–6.

11 Pynson ballad, stanza 11, l. 68; stanza 9, l. 75.

12 Pynson ballad, stanza 12, l. 77.

13 Pynson ballad, stanza 20, ll. 131–7.

14 Christopher Harper-Bill, 'The Foundation and Later History of the Medieval Shrine', in R.C. National Shrine, Walsingham. *Walsingham: Pilgrimage and History. Papers Presented at the Centenary Historical Conference 23rd–27th March 1998* (Fakenham, Norfolk: Lanceni, 1999), 77.

15 Hilda Graef, *Mary: A History of Doctrine and Devotion* (Westminster, MD: Christian Classics, 1985), 208 n. 2.

16 Luigi Gambero, *Mary in the Middle Ages: The Blessed Virgin Mary in the Thought of Medieval Latin Theologians* (San Francisco: Ignatius Press, 2005), 88–9.

17 Gambero, *Mary*, 88.

18 Interestingly, Bury St Edmunds had a connection with the Lords of Clare, the Faverches being tenants of the Lords of Clare in Walsingham Parva, and were thus connected with one of the families associated with the shrine.

19 Peter Brown, *The Cult of the Saints: Its Rise and Function in Latin Christianity* (Chicago: University of Chicago Press, 1981).

20 Johnathan Sumption, *Pilgrimage: An Image of Medieval Religion* (London: Faber & Faber, 2002), 156. Unfortunately, he seems to have not had to fill his contractual obligations, although he seems to have stopped bothering those gathered to study.

21 Scilla Landale, 'A Pilgrim's Progress to Walsingham', in R.C. National Shrine, *Walsingham*, 13. See also Turner and Turner, *Image and Pilgrimage*, 163ff.

22 Diana Webb, *Pilgrims and Pilgrimage in the Medieval West* (London: I.B.Tauris, 2002), 54–5.

23 Sumption, *The Age of Pilgrimage*, 8.

24 H.M. Gillett, *Walsingham and its Shrine* (London: Burns, Oates & Washbourne Ltd, 1934), 40–1.

25 Pynson ballad, stanza 21, l. 144.

26 A. Hope Patten, *England's National Shrine of Our Lady Past and Present* (Cambridge: R.I. Severs, 1944/5), 6–7.

27 Jerusalem had been one of the five patriarchs in the early church. Canterbury was one of the archbishoprics in England; the pilgrimage routes to Santiago received support from the Cluniac empire and the shrine was at the cathedral; Rome was the head of the Latin church.

28 The tomb of Beckett in Canterbury shows that the saint was much more popular than the trappings of apostlehood (Santiago), the foundation of the church (Rome), or the foundings of vast orders – for English pilgrims, at least.

29 Patten, *England's National Shrine*, 7–8.

30 Turner, *Image and Pilgrimage*, 179.

31 Gillett, *Walsingham and its Shrine*, 3. The first attestations to the Loreto shrine, however, do not occur until 1472. No papal records indicate the existence of the Loreto shrine until after 1507, and these early mentions of the shrine are quite guarded in tone.

32 Landale, 'Pilgrim's Progress', in R.C. National Shrine, *Walsingham*, 15. Quotation from Walsingham Charter-Cotton MS Nero E. VII/Dugdale, *Monasticon Anglicanum*.

2. Sybil of the Rhine: Hildegard of Bingen

1 *Scivias*, Vision 1. Quotations from the Scivias are taken from Hildegard of Bingen, *Scivias*, translated by Mother Columba Hart and Jane Bishop (New York: Paulist Press, 1990).

2 For a complete assessment of the composite nature of this work (and how it includes Hildegard's own material as well as the writings of two male redactors), see John W. Coakley, *Women, Men and Spiritual Power: Female Saints and Their Male Collaborators* (New York: Columbia University Press, 2006), esp. 49–52.

3 Her visions have been explained a number of different ways. One such was the attempt by Charles Singer to say that they were migraines: Charles Singer,

'The Visions of Hildegard of Bingen', in *From Magic to Science: Essays on the Scientific Twilight* (London: 1928), 199–239, pls. I, XI–XIV, 95, 97–9, 106–8. See also Barbara Newman, *Symphonia: A Critical Edition of the Symphonia armonie celestium revelationem* (Ithaca: Cornell University Press, 1998), 2 n. 3.

4   Newman, *Symphonia*, 3. For more on the uniqueness of Hildegard's call to preach, see Newman, 'Three-Part Invention: The *Vita S. Hildegardis* and Mystical Hagiography', in Charles Burnett and Peter Dronke, eds, *Hildegard of Bingen: The Context of her Thought and Art* (London: The Warburg Institute, 1998), 189–210, esp. 204–10. And Alcuin Blamires, 'Women and Preaching in Medieval Orthodoxy, Heresy, and Saints' Lives', *Viator* 26 (1995) 135–52.

5   Newman, *Symphonia*, 5.

6   Emily Zum Brunn and Georgette Epiney-Burgard, *Women Mystics in Medieval Europe* (St Paul, MN: Paragon, 1989), 4.

7   See Ep. 24 for Hildegard's description of the situation surrounding the interdict, and Ep. 24r for Archbishop Christian of Mainz' reply.

8   Kent Kraft, 'The German Visionary: Hildegard of Bingen', in Katharina M. Wilson, *Medieval Women Writers* (Athens GA: University of Georgia Press, 1984), 116.

9   *Visio S. Hildegardnsis ad Guibertum missa*. 26.432.

10   Peter Dronke, 'Hildegard of Bingen as Poetess and Dramatist', in *Poetic Individuality in the Middle Ages: New Departures in Poetry 1000–1151* (Oxford: Oxford University Press, 1970), 152. Newman disagrees, arguing that although she takes the cyclic form for inspiration, her compositions bear little resemblance to Notker's classical sequence. Newman, *Sister of Wisdom*, 25. For another view of the nature of the development of the final version of the *Symphoniae* that takes away from Hildegard's conscious shaping, see John Stevens, 'The Musical Individuality of Hildegard's Songs: A Liturgical Shadowland', *Warburg Institute Colloquia #4*, edited by Charles Burnett and Peter Dronke (London: Warburg Institute, 1998), 163–88.

11   Dronke, 'Poetess', 151.

12   Other works, such as the *Symphoniae*, also include some of these words in their text. For an introduction to this artificial language, and a list with translations of the words, see Sarah L. Higley, *Hildegard of Bingen's Unknown Language: An Edition, Translation, and Discussion* (Basingstoke: Palgrave Macmillan, 2002).

13   At the time of the preparation of this manuscript, a work of Hildegard's *Opera minor* (*Minor Works*) is being prepared by H. Feiss, C. Evans, B.M.

Kienzle, C. Muessig, B. Newman and P. Dronke (eds) as part of the Corpus Christianourm Continuatio Medievalis series, to be published in late 2007; it will include the gospel expositions as well as her commentaries on the Athanasian Creed, the *Rule of Benedict* and sermons.

14 Madeline H. Caviness, 'Hildegard as Designer of the Illustrations to her Works', in *Warburg Institute Colloquia #4*, edited by Charles Burnett and Peter Dronke (London: Warburg Institute, 1998), 30. Part of Caviness' argument assumes the argument of Charles Singer that they were migraines, and explains that the aura-like mandalas of some of her drawings are reminiscent of migraine auras: 31, 33.

15 Caviness, 'Hildegard as Designer', 31.

16 There were others, such as Joachim of Fiore, who identified themselves as prophets, preachers and mystics, and who wrote as well as illustrated their works. The big difference between Joachim and Hildegard is that Joachim's visions became suspect, whereas Hildegard's received official approval.

17 Cologne, see Ep. 48; Mainz, see Ep. 10, *Analecta*, 348–51.

18 Kraft, 'German Visionary', 109.

19 Dronke, 'Poetess', 178–9.

20 *Symphonia* '22. O quam preciosa'.

21 Newman, *Symphonia*, 14.

22 *Scivias*, III.13.12.

23 Barbara Newman, *Sister of Wisdom: St Hildegard's Theology of the Feminine* (Berkeley, CA: University of California Press, 1997), 29.

24 M. Colman O'Dell, 'Elizabeth of Schonau and Hildegard of Bingen: Prophets of the Lord', in *Medieval Religious Women, 2: Peaceweavers*, edited by Lillian Thomas Shank and John A. Nichols (Kalamazoo, MI: Cistercian Publications, 1987), 85.

25 O'Dell, 'Prophets'.

26 Constant J. Mews, 'Hildegard and the Schools', in *Warburg Institute Colloquia #4*, edited by Charles Burnett and Peter Dronke (London: Warburg Institute, 1998), 49.

27 *Vita* 2.3.25. LVM: *Analecta*, p. 244.

28 Kathryn Kerby-Fulton and Dyan Elliott, 'Self Image and the Visionary Role in Two Letters from the Correspondence of Elizabeth of Schonau and Hildegard of Bingen', in *On Pilgrimage: The Best of Ten Years of Vox Benedictina*, edited by Margot King (Toronto: Peregrina Press, 1994), 537; 546 n. 7.

29 Peter Dronke, *Women Writers of the Middle Ages: A Critical Study of Texts from Perpetua (+203) to Marguerite Porete (+1310)* (Cambridge: Cambridge University Press, 1984), 146.

30   Kraft, 'German Visionary', 119.

31   Barbara Newman, *Sister of Wisdom: St Hildegard's Theology of the Feminine* (Berkeley, CA: University of California Press, 1997), 34–5.

32   Kraft, 'German Visionary', 115.

33   Marie Dominique Chenu, *Nature, Man and Society in the Twelfth Century: essays on new theological perspectives in the Latin West*, translated by Jerome Taylor and Lester K. Little (Toronto: University of Toronto Press, 1997), 30–7.

34   Zum Brunn, *Women Mystics*, 8 n. 24, referencing Peter Dronke, 'Problemata Hildegardiana', *Mittellateinisches Jahrbuch* 16 (1981): 107–17; and Elizabeth A. Petroff, *Medieval Women's Visionary Literature* (Oxford: Oxford University Press, 1986), 139.

35   For a good discussion on the uses Hildegard makes of allegory and the way they are tied in to her microcosmic–macrocosmic vision, see Peter Dronke, 'The Allegorical World-Picture of Hildegard of Bingen: Revaluations and New Problems', in *Hildegard of Bingen: The Context of her Thought and Art*, edited by Charles Burnett and Peter Dronke (London: Warburg Institute, 1998), which comments upon the seminal work dealing with Hildegard's uses of allegory: Hans Liebeschütz, *Das allegorische Weltbild der heiligen Hildegard von Bingen* (Leipzig–Berlin, 1930).

36   Brunn, *Medieval Women*, 11.

37   Brunn, *Medieval Women*, 11–12.

38   Hildegard, *Book of Divine Works*, vision 4.11. Translation from Fiona Bowie and Oliver Davies, *Hildegard of Bingen: An Anthology* (London: SPCK, 1990).

39   Hildegard, *Book of Divine Works*, vision 4.

40   Mews, 'Hildegard and the Schools', 50.

41   Kraft, 'German Visionary', 109.

42   Newman, *Sister of Wisdom*, 77ff.

43   Newman, *Sister of Wisdom*, 92.

44   Newman, *Sister of Wisdom*, 158.

45   For a good summary of Hildegard and the politics of her not admitting her contemporary theological sources, see Mews, 'Hildegard and the Schools', esp. 99–100.

46   Hildegard, *Book of Divine Works*, vision 8.2.

3. Penitential Demoniac: Christina of St Trond/Christina Mirabilis

1   Thomas de Cantimpré, *Vita Beatae Christinae Mirabilis Trudonopolis in Hasbania*, edited by J. Pinius AASS Jul t.5 (Paris: Th. Gauss, 1868), 637–60.

2   Margot H. King and David Wiljer, trans. and ed., *The Life of Christina the Astonishing by Thomas de Cantimpré* (Toronto: Peregrina Publishing, 2000), 7. Quotations from *The Life of Christina the Astonishing* will be from this translation.

3   *Life of Christina*, 1.4.

4   *Life of Christina*, 1.7.

5   *Life of Christina*, 1.8.

6   Caroline Walker Bynum, *Holy Feast and Holy Fast* (Berkeley, CA: University of California Press, 1987), 24; Margot H. King, 'The Sacramental Witness of Christina *Mirabilis*: The Mystic Growth of a Fool for Christ's Sake', in *Medieval Religious Women: Peacemakers*, vol. 2, edited by Lillian Thomas Shank and John A. Nichols (Kalamazoo, MI: Cistercian Publications, 1987), 145.

7   For more on authenticating miracles, see B. Ward, *Miracles and the Medieval Mind: Theory, Record and Event, 1000–1215* (Philadelphia, PA: University of Pennsylvania Press, 1982), esp. 192–200.

8   *Life of Christina*, 5.55.

9   For more on the insights between men's hagiographic writings and women's writings, see Amy Hollywood, *The Soul as Virgin Wife: Mechtild of Magdeburg, Marguerite Porete, and Meister Eckhart* (London: University of Notre Dame Press, 1995).

10   King, 'Sacramental Witness', 147.

11   King and Wiljer, *Life*, introduction, 5.

12   Simone Roisin, 'La Méthod hagiographique de Thomas de Cantimpré', in *Miscellanea Historica in Honorem Alberti de Meyer* I. (Louvain: Bibliothèque de l'Université, 1946), 546–7; Herbert Thurston, 'Christine of Saint Trond', in *Surprising Mystics* (London: Burns & Oates, 1955), 149.

13   *Life of Christina*, 1.4.

14   King and Wiljer, *Life*, introduction, 7. For longer descriptions of this literary trend, see Helen Gardiner, *Visions of Heaven and Hell Before Dante* (New York: Italica Press, 1989); somewhat dated, but still containing some good insights is Ernest J. Becker, *A Contribution to the Comparative Study of the Medieval Visions of Heaven and Hell, With Special Reference to the Middle English Versions* (Baltimore, MD: John Murphy, 1899; see also Jacques Le Goff, *The Birth of Purgatory* (Chicago: University of Chicago Press, 1984).

15   King, 'Sacramental Witness', 150.

16   Each of William's main spiritual writings provides a slightly different ascent. Arguably, his most famous is the one found in his Roman commentary. Here,

King collapses the three-stage ascents found in William's *Nature and Dignity of Love* and his commentary on the *Song of Songs* into the ascent she describes (see King, 'Sacramental Witness', 149–54). Although the three stages fit the text of Christina's *Life* well, it seems perhaps an artificial reading of the Cistercian tradition. One thing that remains unclear in King's account is why one of William's multitudinous ladders of ascent should have become an unnamed echo in a later document by a writer who does not appear to rely on William for anything else.

17   *Life of Christina*, 1.9.

18   King, 'Sacramental Witness', 147, 151, 162 n. 45. See also Saskia Murk-Jansen, *Brides in the Desert: The Spirituality of the Beguines* (London: Darton, Longman & Todd Ltd, 1998), 102–12 for a full discussion of the trope of the desert as it appears in the beguine tradition in the Low Countries.

19   See de Vitry, *Life of Marie d'Oignies.*

20   For scripture on his time in the desert before his public ministry, see: Mark 1.12–13; Matthew 4.1–11; Luke 4.1–13.

21   *Life of Christina*, 1.9.

22   *Life of Christina*, 1.9.

23   *Life of Christina*, 2.20.

24   *Life of Christina*, 2.16.

25   Barbara Newman, 'Possessed by the Spirit: Devout Women, Demoniacs, and the Apostolic Life in the Thirteenth Century', *Speculum* 73 (1998), 766.

26   *Life of Christina*, 1.7.

27   *Life of Christina*, 1.8.

28   Robert S. Sweetman, 'Christine of Saint-Trond's Preaching Apostolate: Thomas of Cantimpré's Hagiographical Method Revisited', in *On Pilgrimage: The Best of Ten Years of Vox Benedictina*, compiled by Elizabeth Druries and Dewey Kramer, edited by Margot H. King (Toronto: Peregrina Publishing, 1994), 415 and 415 n. 18.

29   *Life of Christina*, 5.56. The Latin here is worth quoting: 'Et quid aliud in omni vita sua Christina clamavit, nisi penitentiam agree, et paratos esse hominess omni hora? Hoc verbis multis, hoc fletibus, hoc ejulatibus, hoc clamoribus infinitis, hoc exemplo vitae plus docuit, plus clamavit, quam de aliquo praecedentium vel subsequentium scripto vel relatione percepimus, in laudem et gloriam Christi, qui cum Patre et Spiritu sancto vivit et regnat Deus, per omnia saecula saeculorum. Amen.'

30   *Life of Christina*, 4.40; Sweetman, 'Preaching Apostolate', 416.

31   *Life of Christina*, 1.11.

32   *Life of Christina*, 1.12.

33 Here I take a different approach from Hollywood, *The Soul as Virgin Wife*, 46, where she says the *Life* shows a 'profound ambivalence of medieval attitudes toward the body and, in particular, women's bodies'.

34 LeGoff, *The Birth of Purgatory*, esp. chapter 9; Newman, 'Possessed by the Spirit', 746 n. 52.

35 *Life of Christina*, 2.22.

36 Bynum, *Holy Feast and Holy Fast*, 193.

37 *Life of Christina*, 1.9.

38 *Life of Christina*, 2.19.

39 Bynum, *Holy Feast and Holy Fast*, 122–3.

40 Caroline Walker Bynum, *Jesus as Mother: Studies in the Spirituality of the High Middle Ages* (Berkeley, CA: University of California Press, 1982), 256.

41 *Life of Christina*, 3.27.

42 *Life of Christina*, 4.44.

43 Bynum, *Holy Feast and Holy Fast*, 117.

44 Newman, 'Possessed by the Spirit', 768.

45 *Life of Christina*, 1.5.

46 *Life of Christina*, 1.10.

47 *Life of Christina*, 2.21.

48 *Life of Christina*, 1.9.

49 *Life of Christina*, 3.33.

4. Jouster for Love: Hadewijch of Brabant

1 See Theodoor Weevers, *Poetry of the Netherlands in its European context: 1170–1930* (London: Athlone Press, 1960).

2 Hadewijch, *Letter* 25. All quotations from Hadewijch are taken from *The Complete Works*, translated and introduced by Columba Hart (Mahweh, NJ: Paulist Press, 1980).

3 Emily Zum Brunn and Georgette Epiney-Burgard, *Women Mystics in Medieval Europe* (New York: Paragon, 1989), 98.

4 There is debate as to whether these additional poems in couplets are Hadewijch's or whether they were written by another beguine who emulated her. Zum Brunn and Epiney-Burgard, *Women Mystics*, 97, says 4 mss. On the poems: Ria Vanderauwera, 'The Brabant Mystic: Hadewijch', in *Medieval Women Writers*, edited by Katharina M. Wilson (Athens, GA: University of Georgia Press, 1984), 186. Critical edition: J. van Mierlo, *Hadewijch: Visionen*.

2 vols. (Louvain: Vlaamsch Boekenhalle, 1924–1925). The main argument is the poems might be written by another beguine of her 'group', which would seem unusual, as Hadewijch complains that she has been exiled from her group of beguines.

5   Vanderauwera, 'Brabant Mystic', 190.

6   Mary Suydam, 'The Touch of Satisfaction: Visions and the Religious Experience According to Hadewijch of Antwerp', *Journal of Feminist Studies in Religion* 12:2 (Fall 1996): 5–27.

7   For a wonderful description of the poetic form of her poems, see Tanis Guest, *Some Aspects of Hadewijch's Poetic Form in the 'Strophische Gedichten'* (The Hague: Martinus Nijhoff, 1975).

8   Vanderauwera, 'Brabant Mystic', 188. There is still much debate about the authenticity of the latter-numbered poems in couplets. Mary A. Suydam and Saskia Murk-Janson hold that some, or perhaps all, are true to Hadewijch's style and emphasis, while the majority of scholars hold that the later poems are 'too abstract' to be Hadewijch. For more information, see Suydam, 'Touch of Satisfaction'.

9   Suydam, 'Touch of Satisfaction', 5.

10   Vanderauwera, 'Brabant Mystic', 187.

11   Norbert de Paepe, *Hadewijch, Strofische Gedichten. Een studie van de mine in het kader der 12e en 13e eeuwse mystiek en profane minnelyriek* (Ghent, 1967). See Vanderauwera, 'Brabant Mystic', 188, who thinks he goes too far.

12   J. van Mierlo, *Hadewijch, Strophische Gedichten* (Antwerp–Brussels–Ghent–Leuven, 1942). II. 121.

13   See, for instance, de Paepe, *Hadewijch, Strofische Gedichten*. For a summary of the argument that *Minne* must be both the personification as well as the experience, and also the grounding love of God that informs both, see two pieces by Tanis Guest: Tanis Guest, 'Hadewijch and Minne', in *European Context: Studies in the History and Literature of the Netherlands Presented to Theodoor Weevers*, edited by P.K. King and P.F. Vincent (Cambridge: Modern Humanities Research Association, 1971); and Tanis Guest, *Some Aspects of Hadewijch's Poetic Form in the 'Strofische Gedichten'* (The Hague: Martinus Nijhoff, 1975), 14.

14   Gordon Rudy, *Mystical Language of Sensation in the Later Middle Ages* (London: Routledge, 2002), 78.

15   Rudy, *Mystical Language*, 78.

16   *Poems in Couplets*, 12.25.

17   *Poems in Couplets*, 10.71.

18   *Vision* 11.62–8.

19 Cf. Psalms 102.5 for reference to love growing in heaven and on earth.

20 *Vision* 11.69–71.

21 *Vision* 11.75–82.

22 Much less important, really, are her family of origin's social status compared to the suggestion that by choosing the courtly love tradition she in fact chooses an audience with a particular social status. One can read her courtly images thus as reflecting either her own social milieu or that of her audience. I believe the latter holds more promise in terms of guiding what we could possibly intuit from Hadewijch's writings.

23 Petroff, *Medieval Women's Visionary Literature*, 176–7.

24 The one exception was Peter Abelard, who was a leading theologian who also wrote love lyrics. He was held up as an example, following his ill-fated affair with Heloise, of the problems the courtly love tradition could lead people into.

25 Zum Brunn and Epiney-Burgard, *Women Mystics*, 101. See Henri Irénée Morrou, *Les Troubadours* (Paris: Éditions de Seuill, c. 1971), 161–3.

26 See, for instance, 9.3 for the knight's fidelity of service to his lady.

27 See 8.4–5 for examples of service; see 13.5: for results of fidelity.

28 See Guest, *Some Aspects*, especially chapters 3 for rhyme, and chapters 7 and 8 for imagery.

29 Jessica Boon, 'Trinitarian Love Mysticism: Ruusbroes, Hadewijch, and the Gendered Experience of the Divine', *Church History* 72:3 (September 2003), 491.

30 Bynum, *Fragmentation and Redemption*, 181–238.

31 Boon, 'Trinitarian Love Mysticism', 492.

32 J. Reynaert, 'Hadewijch: mystic poetry and courtly love', in *Medieval Dutch Literature in its European Context*, edited by Erik Cooper (Cambridge: Cambridge University Press, 1994), 212.

33 de Paepe, *Hadewijch, Strofische Gedichten*, 47–9.

34 Rudy, *Mystical Language*, 79.

35 Rudy, *Mystical Language*, 81.

36 *Vision* 1, 295–306.

37 *Vision* 14.40–2.

38 *Poems in Stanza*,1.4; 36.2; 1.6, 8; 2.9; 3.2; 22.4; 24.4, 5; 6.4.

39 *Letter* 2.118; Job 4.12.

40 *Poems in Couplets*, 5.29–34.

41 Bynum, *Holy Feast*, 209.

42 Bynum, *Holy Feast*, 242.

43 *Letter* 3. A word of warning: Rudy problematically identifies Hadewijch with

the narrator, not recognizing the distance in terms of gender pronouns, and missing much of the courtly love reversals in her work. In other words, he reads her too literally.

44 *Letter* 32.57–61/ 5, 39.

45 Saskia Murk-Jansen, 'The Use of Gender and Gender-Related Imagery in Hadewijch', in *Gender and Text in the Later Middle Ages*, edited by Jane Chance (Gainesville, FL: University Press of Florida, 1996), 59. Bynum, *Holy Feast*, 39, 360–1, n. 31. Bynum holds Hadewijch's use of both male and female pronouns to be a sign that she likes to use androgynous terms to represent herself. Bynum's assessment, however, misses the point about how Hadewijch identifies herself, and the role of gender reversal as her dialogue is based upon a genre that uses male pronouns for the role she is identifying with. Hadewijch's use of gender reversal follows literary conventions, but turns these to a specific purpose in recognizing the reversal of power in the literary convention. By highlighting where a man has little power, and with her identification with Mary Magdalene, Hadewijch in fact claims power for women.

46 *Poems in Couplets*, 3.50–4.

47 Petroff, *Body and Soul,* 184.

48 Bynum, *Holy Feast*, 153.

49 Bynum, *Holy Feast*, 158.

50 *Poems in Couplets*, 6.3; 6.14.

5. Divine Lover: Mechtild of Magdeburg

1 Although Mechtild of Magdeburg ended her life in the convent of Helfta, I shall here treat her as a beguine, since that represents most accurately the majority of her time spent developing spiritually. For treatment of Mechtild specifically relating her to the spirituality of the Helfta nuns, see Bynum, *Jesus as Mother*, esp. 228–47.

2 *Flowing Light of the Godhead*, 4.2, 8–13. All quotations come from *The Flowing Light of the Godhead*, translated and introduced by Frank Tobin (Mahweh, NJ: Paulist Press, 1998).

3 Leona M. English, 'An Analysis of Power in the Writing of Mechtild of Magdeburg', *Feminist Theology*, 14:2 (2006), 189–204.

4 *Flowing Light of the Godhead*, 2.26; 4.2; 4.13.

5 *Flowing Light of the Godhead*, 2.26.

6 *Flowing Light of the Godhead*, 4.13.

7   See, for instance, in the Prologue to the work, where the Trinity is named as the author, or throughout Book I.

8   Hollywood says there is a progression in Mechtild in which she moves from a place of having no markers of cultural status as a woman and in which she writes in multiple voices to a distillation of these voices as they become fewer in number, eventually residing in an 'I' narrator upon occasion in the later books. This can occur only once as Mechtild's authority and confidence in her vocation and writing are established: *The Soul as Virgin Wife*, 61.

9   See Hollywood, *The Soul as Virgin Wife*, 57–9, for an overview of how reading the work as a *confessio* or as a diary affects the outcomes of what one is to make of the text.

10 Elizabeth A. Andersen, *The Voices of Mechthild of Magdeburg* (Oxford: Peter Lang, 2000). Also, Thomas J. Farrell, ed., *Bakhtin and Medieval Voices* (Gainesville, FL: University Press of Florida, 1995).

11 *Flowing Light of the Godhead*, 4.2; Hollywood, *The Soul as Virgin Wife*, 59.

12 Andersen, *The Voices of Mechthild of Magdeburg*, 147.

13 Catherine V. Gardner, *Women Philosophers: Genre and the Boundaries of Philosophy* (Boulder, CO: Westview Press, 2003), 152.

14 *Flowing Light of the Godhead*, 2.26.

15 Thomas Aquinas, *The Summa Theologica of Saint Thomas Aquinas*, ed. and trans. by the Fathers of the English Dominican Province (New York: Benzinger Bros., 1912–1925), I.1.

16 Zum Brunn and Epiney-Burgard, *Women Mystics*, 43. The title for this section comes from Barbara Newman, *From Virile Woman to Woman Christ: Studies in Medieval Religion and Literature* (Philadephia, PA: Penn Press, 1995).

17 Zum Brunn and Epiney-Burgard, *Women Mystics*, 44, mentions the Greek fathers, a common mistake not seeing the erotic in Augustine, a more proximate source.

18 *Flowing Light of the Godhead*, 2.7; 2.24; 3.3.

19 *Flowing Light of the Godhead*, 3.15.

20 *Flowing Light of the Godhead*, 3.15.

21 *Flowing Light of the Godhead*, 1.19.

22 *Flowing Light of the Godhead*, 5.30.

23 *Flowing Light of the Godhead*, 3.15.

24 *Flowing Light of the Godhead*, 3.13.

25 *Flowing Light of the Godhead*, 2.12.

26 *Flowing Light of the Godhead*, 2.9.

27 *Flowing Light of the Godhead*, 7.1.

28 *Flowing Light of the Godhead*, 1.4; 4.17; 3.1.

29 *Flowing Light of the Godhead*, 1.22.

30 *Flowing Light of the Godhead*, 1.3.

31 *Flowing Light of the Godhead*, 1.44.

32 *Flowing Light of the Godhead*, 3.9.

33 *Flowing Light of the Godhead*, 4.2; 5.35.

34 *Flowing Light of the Godhead*, 1.44.

35 *Flowing Light of the Godhead*, 1.44.

36 *Flowing Light of the Godhead*, 5.4; Hollywood, *The Soul as Virgin Wife*, 79.

37 *Flowing Light of the Godhead*, 5.4. Adjectives come from the poem at the end of the section.

38 *Flowing Light of the Godhead*, 5.4.

39 Mechtild's view of Christ's humanity is thus based on the virtues, not on the whole human being. Certainly this view is not based on being physically embodied, as not all virtues require a body.

40 Hollywood, *The Soul as Virgin Wife*, 183.

41 *Flowing Light of the Godhead*, 5.4.

42 She explains that pain is a necessary part of reconciliation to God because of human sinfulness; the human is not able to withstand the presence of God and union with God until sin has been purified by love and suffering, which are a pair in her thought. If Hollywood's understanding on how to read the development of the *Flowing Light of the Godhead* is correct, then Hadewijch's dislike for the body gradually grows into a sadism that allows the body to suffer because she sees the purpose in suffering.

43 *Flowing Light of the Godhead*, 2.26.

44 *Flowing Light of the Godhead*, 2.26.

45 *Flowing Light of the Godhead*, 2.23.8–9; 2.23.14–16.

46 *Flowing Light of the Godhead*, 5.34; 6.3; 6.36.

47 *Flowing Light of the Godhead*, Just some of her visions of purgatory include: 2.8; 3.15; 3.17; 3.21; 5.5; 5.14; 5.15; 6.8; 6.10; 7.2; *Flowing Light of the Godhead*, 7.41; 7.49.

48 Gardner, *Women Philosophers*.

49 *Flowing Light of the Godhead*, 3.10, 21; 5.8.

50 Bynum, *Jesus as Mother*, 232–4.

51 Hans Urs von Balthasar, *Mechthilds kirchlicher Auftrafe* (Einsiedeln, 1955).

52 This began with Oliver Davies, *Meister Eckhart: Mystical Theologian* (London: SPCK, 1991).

6. Community Visionary: Mechtild of Hackeborn

1 Mechtilde, *Book of Ghostly Grace*, 1. prol. All references to Mechtilde's book will be to the more readily-accessible Middle English version edited by Teresa Halligan and available in microform by PIMS. I have modernised the language for readability.

2 My quotations will be modernized renditions based on the Middle English version, which has only five books rather than all seven. The reason for choosing this version is that it is readily accessible to students of medieval history and literature in Teresa Halligan's critical edition, whereas the Latin or modern French translation of the Latin are much less readily accessible.

3 Petroff, *Medieval Women's Visionary Literature*, 208.

4 Mechtilde, *Book of Ghostly Grace*, prol.; see also Ann Marie Caron, R.S.M., 'Invitations of the Divine Heart: The Mystical Writings of Mechtild of Hackeborn', *American Benedictine Review* 45:3 (1994), 323, 324.

5 See Bynum, *Jesus as Mother*, 256.

6 For reinforcing the notion that the community is part of the mystical body of Christ, see, for instance, 1.77.

7 Gregory the Great, *Dialogues*, trans. Odo John Zimmerman (Washington, D.C.: Catholic University Press, 2005 reprint), II.37.

8 Alberta Dieker, 'Mechtilde of Hackeborn: Song of Love', in *Medieval Women Monastics: Wisdom's Wellsprings*, edited by Miriam Schmitt and Linda Kulser (Collegeville, MN: Liturgical Press, 1996), 241.

9 Mechtilde, *Book of Ghostly Grace*, 1.19.

10 Mechtilde, *Book of Ghostly Grace*, 2.2; Galatians 5.22 is the passage she is referring to.

11 Mechtilde, *Book of Ghostly Grace*, 5.12.

12 Mechtilde, *Book of Ghostly Grace*, 1.84.

13 Mechtilde, *Book of Ghostly Grace*, 2.43.

14 Mechtilde, *Book of Ghostly Grace,* 1.30.

15 Bynum, *Jesus as Mother*, 256.

16 Bynum, *Jesus as Mother*, 22.

17 Mechtilde, *Book of Ghostly Grace*, 1.60.

18 Mechtilde, *Book of Ghostly Grace*, 4.37.

19 Mechtilde, *Book of Ghostly Grace*, 4.37.

20 Mechtilde, *Book of Ghostly Grace*, 5.3.

21 Mechtilde, *Book of Ghostly Grace*, 1.5.

22 Mechtilde, *Book of Ghostly Grace*, 1.63.

23 Mechtilde, *Book of Ghostly Grace*, 2.18.

24 Mechtilde, *Book of Ghostly Grace*, 1.85.
25 For a discussion of this in one of the leading Cistercian theologians a generation before Mechtild, see David N. Bell, *The Image and the Likeness: The Augustinian Anthropology of William of St-Thierry* (Kalamazoo, MI: Cistercian Publications, 1994).
26 The doctrine of the Immaculate Conception, whose feast was established in 1476 by Pope Sixtus IV, stated that Mary was born without sin in order to be an appropriate container for nurturing the Incarnate Word. In the middle ages it was not yet defined as a doctrine.
27 Mechtilde, *Book of Ghostly Grace*, 1.84.
28 Mechtilde, *Book of Ghostly Grace*, 1.86.
29 Mechtilde, *Book of Ghostly Grace*, 1.64.
30 Mechtilde, *Book of Ghostly Grace*, 1.84.
31 Mechtilde, *Book of Ghostly Grace*, 1.5.
32 Mechtilde, *Book of Ghostly Grace*, 1.63.
33 Mechtilde, *Book of Ghostly Grace*, 1.11.
34 Mechtilde, *Book of Ghostly Grace*, 1.63.
35 Mechtilde, *Book of Ghostly Grace*, 1.81.
36 Mechtilde, *Book of Ghostly Grace*, 1.61.
37 Mechtilde, *Book of Ghostly Grace*, 1.58.
38 Mechtilde, *Book of Ghostly Grace*, 1.57.
39 Mechtilde, *Book of Ghostly Grace*, 1.5.
40 Mechtilde, *Book of Ghostly Grace*, 1.83.
41 Mechtilde, *Book of Ghostly Grace*, 1.78.
42 Theresa Schroeder-Sheker, 'The Use of Plucked-string Instruments in Medieval Christian Mysticism', *Mystics Quarterly* 15 (September 1989), 136. See also her other article on Mechtild and music, which has a similar passage: 'The Alchemical Harp of Mechtild of Hackeborn', in *On Pilgrimage: The Best Ten Years of Vox Benedictina*, edited by Margot King, 41–55 (Toronto: Peregrina Press, 1994).
43 Dieker, *Song of Love*, 236; *Lib. spir.* 1.53; 1.62 and many others.
44 Mechtilde, *Book of Ghostly Grace*, 1.85.
45 Mechtilde, *Book of Ghostly Grace*, 1.12.
46 Mechtilde, *Book of Ghostly Grace*, 1.9; the sweetness of Christ is a common motif in Cistercian spirituality – see Franz Posset, 'Christi Dulcedo: "The Sweetness of Christ" in Western Christian Thought', *Cistercian Studies Quarterly* 30:3 (1995): 245–65.
47 Mary Jeremy Finnegan, 'St Mechtilde of Hackeborn: *Nemo Communior*', in *Medieval Religious Women: Peacemakers*, vol. 2, edited by Lillian Thomas

Shank and John A. Nichols (Kalamazoo, MI: Cistercian Publications, 1987), 213.

48 Mechtilde, *Book of Ghostly Grace*, 1.54.

49 Mechtilde, *Book of Ghostly Grace*, 2.16.

50 Mechtilde, *Book of Ghostly Grace*, 2.16.

51 Mechtilde, *Book of Ghostly Grace*, 3.34.

52 The motif of the kiss probably comes from the *Song of Songs*, through Bernard, who makes it a major theme of his sermons on that passage. The kiss, an intimate gesture of love, also comes to point to the nearness of Christ and bodiliness of the Son as well as focus on his mouth, from which he, as God's word, speaks further words of the Trinity.

53 Mechtilde, *Book of Ghostly Grace*, 1.9.

54 Bernard of Clairvaux, *On the Song of Songs*, Kilian Walsh, OCSO and Irene M. Edmonds, trans. 4 vols. (Kalamazoo: Cistercian Publications, 1971, 1976, 1979, 1980). See *Sermons* 1-3 in particular.

55 We have no clear sense of the real order she received the visions. We only know that they were organized according to the liturgical calendar when they were compiled into one work.

56 Although she revealed her visions eventually to her community, she still showed doubts about revealing her visions outside her own community: 2.53; 4.7; 5.22–4, 31.

57 Mechtilde, *Book of Ghostly Grace*, 4.22–38.

58 Bynum, *Jesus as Mother*, 220.

7. Franciscan Penitent: Angela Foligno

1 *Memorial*, IX. All references to her works are to the following edition: Angela of Foligno, *Complete Works*, translated and introduced by Paul Lachance (New York: Paulist Press, 1993).

2 Although his work does not discuss Angela of Foligno, Richard Kieckhefer's *Unquiet Souls: Fourteenth-century Saints and their Religious Milieu* (Chicago: University of Chicago Press, 1984) explores this arena of thought. See especially pp. 2–3 for his reading of how others have 'read' the fourteenth century and the significance of saints' lives.

3 For a brief summary of her use by Bataille, see Amy Hollywood, '"Beautiful as a wasp:" Angela of Foligno and Georges Bataille', *Harvard Theological Review* 92:2 (1999): 219–36. For a summary of her use by Kristeva and Bataille, see Cristina Mazzoni, 'Feminism, Abjection, Transgression:

Angela of Foligno and the Twentieth Century', *Mystics Quarterly* 17 (1991), 61–70.

4   *Memorial*, 1.87–95 (138).

5   See Anna Benvenuti Papi, 'Mendicant Friars and Female Pinzochere in Tuscany', in *Women and Religion in Medieval and Renaissance Italy*, edited by Daniel Bornstein and Roberto Rusconi, translated by Margery J. Schneider, 84–103 (Chicago: University of Chicago Press, 1996).

6   Petroff, *Medieval Women's Visionary Literature*, 231.

7   Petroff, *Medieval Women's Visionary Literature*, 231–2.

8   Petroff, *Medieval Women's Visionary Literature*, 232.

9   Lachance, *Introduction* to Paulist Press translation of Angela's *Complete Works*, 44.

10   The Poor Clares were names after a female, Saint Clare of Assisi, a fellow evangelist with Francis.

11   Petroff, *Medieval Women's Visionary Literature*, 232.

12   *Memorial*, ch. 3.

13   See, for instance, John Coakley, 'Hagiography and Theology in the Memorial of Angela of Foligno', in *Women, Men, and Spiritual Power: Female Saints and their Collaborators*, 111–29, 274–5 (New York: Columbia University Press, 2006); and Catherine Mooney, 'The Authorial Role of Brother A. in the Composition of Angela of Foligno's Revelations', in *Creative Women in Medieval and Early Modern Italy: A Religious and Artistic Renaissance*, edited by E. Ann Matter and John Coakley, 34–63 (Philadelphia, PA: University of Pennsylvania Press, 1994).

14   *Memorial*, 2.

15   *Memorial*, 2.

16   *Memorial*, 2.

17   Coakley, 'Hagiography and Theology', 113.

18   Coakley, 'Hagiography and Theology', 122.

19   Coakley, 'Hagiography and Theology', 120.

20   The editors of the Latin edition posit two redactions of the text – one before the approbation and one after it gained approval of the ecclesiastic authorities. There are several different 'schools of thought' on the order of these redactions. For the argument that the minor redaction is actually excerpts from the major redaction, see Coakley, 'Hagiography and Theology', n. 1, 276–77.

21   See also David Burr, *The Spiritual Franciscans: From Protest to Persecution in the Century After Saint Francis* (University Park, PA: Pennsylvania State Press, 2001).

22 Dronke, *Women Writers*, 217.

23 Dronke, *Women Writers*, 215.

24 Angela, *Memorial*, 1, where she mentions this as part of step 9; Dronke, *Women Writers*, 215.

25 Lachance, *Introduction*, 39. See also Vauchez, André, 'La Sainteté feminine dans le mouvement franciscain', *Les laics au moyen âge*, 189–202 (Paris: Éditions de Cerf, 1987).

26 *Memorial*, 1.

27 For an excellent article on iconography and its relation to women's piety in late medieval Italy, see Chiara Frugoni, 'Female Mystics, Visions, and Iconography', in *Women and Religion in Medieval and Renaissance Italy*, edited by Daniel Bornstein and Roberto Rusconi, translated by Margery J. Schneider, 130–64 (Chicago: University of Chicago Press, 1996).

28 *Memorial*, 6.

29 *Memorial*, 1.

30 *Memorial*, 7.

31 *Memorial*, 1.

32 *Instructions*, 34.

33 Matthew, new testament, 25.40.

34 *Instructions*, 2.

35 Petroff, *Medieval Women's Visionary Literature*, 231.

36 *Instructions*, 2.

37 *Instructions*, 34.

38 *Instructions*, 34.

39 Mooney, 'The Authorial Role of Brother A.', 48.

40 *Instructions*, 2.

41 Coakley, 'Hagiography and Theology', 126.

8. Annihilated Soul: Marguerite Porete

1 *Mirror*, 68. Quotations from *The Mirror of Simple Souls* are from Marguerite Porete, *The Mirror of Simple Souls*, edited by Ellen L. Babinsky (New York: Paulist Press, 1993).

2 *Mirror*, 1, 122.

3 Murk-Jansen, *Brides in the Desert*, 77.

4 *Mirror*, 61, 118.

5 Yet Porete identifies the soul as her own (chapter 11) when the soul talks about composing a book.

6   *Mirror*, 27.
7   *Mirror*, 12, 92.
8   Stage 4, *Mirror*, 6 and 8.
9   *Mirror*, 8.
10 *Mirror*, 8.
11 Michael A. Sells, *Mystical Languages of Unsaying* (London: University of Chicago Press, 1994), 132.
12 *Mirror*, 21.
13 *Mirror*, 81, 89, 91, 111, 134.
14 *Mirror*, 119.
15 *Mirror*, 121.
16 *Mirror*, 122.
17 *Mirror*, 19, 101.
18 Dronke, *Women Writers of the Middle Ages*, 217.
19 See, for instance, Beckman, 'The Power of Books and the Practice of Mysticism in the Fourteenth Century: Heinrich of Nordlingen and Margaret Ehner on Mechthild's Flowing Light of the Godhead', *Church History* 76:1 (March 2007), 67.
20 M.D. Lambert, *Medieval Heresy: Popular Movements from Bogomil to Hus*, 175–6 (London: Edward Arnold, 1977). This is a bad inference on the parts of clerics, though, considering how elitist some of the beguine theology tended to be. Rather than being democratic, it tended to focus on a small circle of spiritually advanced people as its audience.
21 Zum Brunn and Epiney-Burgard, *Women Mystics*, 144–5.
22 Zum Brunn and Epiney-Burgard, *Women Mystics*, 146. We might see similar millenarianism in Marguerite's comments on Holy Church the Less (institutional church) and Holy Church the Greater (freed souls).
23 Zum Brunn and Epiney-Burgard, *Women Mystics*, 146.
24 Henry Charles Lea, *A History of the Inquisition of the Middle Ages*, vol. 1 (London, 1888), 123.
25 Gwendolyn Bryant, 'The French Heretic Beguine: Marguerite Porete', in *Medieval Women Writers*, edited by Katharina M. Wilson (Athens, GA: University of Georgia Press, 1984), 207.
26 Petroff, *Medieval Women's Visionary Literature*, 282; Grace Jantzen, *Power, Gender and Christian Mysticism*, 263.
27 Lambert, *Medieval Heresy*, 178.
28 Lambert, *Medieval Heresy*, 179.
29 Lambert, *Medieval Heresy*, 179.
30 Lambert, *Medieval Heresy*, 178.

31 Lambert, *Medieval Heresy*, 177.

32 *Mirror*, 119.

33 Sells, *Mystical Languages*, 118.

9. Bodily Mystic: Julian of Norwich

1   Best known of these, from England, is the *Ancrene Rewle*.

2   Julian of Norwich, *Showings*, LT, chapter 2. All Julian quotations come from the Classics of Western Spirituality printing. Quotations from the Short Text are identified with an 'ST' and quotations from the Long Text are preceded by an 'LT'.

3   Edmund Colledge and James Walsh, eds, *A Book of Showings to the Anchoress Julian of Norwich* (Toronto: PIMS, 1978), 22.

4   Mary J. Carruthers, *The Book of Memory: A Study of Memory in Medieval Culture* (New York: Cambridge University Press, 1990).

5   See Colledge and Walsh, *Book of Showings*, Appendix, 735–48, where the editors enumerate and define each of the devices, using examples from Julian, the Vulgate and Chaucer's *Boethius*.

6   Jones, 'English Mystic', 273.

7   Jones, 'English Mystic', 273.

8   Jones, 'English Mystic', 269; see also Colledge and Walsh, *Book of Showings*, part 2, 421–2.

9   Jones, 'English Mystic', 269.

10 Jones, 'English Mystic', 269; see also Wolfgang Riehle, *The Middle English Mystics* (Boston: Routledge & Kegan Paul, 1981).

11 Frederick Christian Bauerschmidt, 'Seeing Jesus: Julian of Norwich and the Text of Christ's Body', *Journal of Medieval and Early Modern Studies* 27:2 (Spring 1997), 192.

12 Jones, 'English Mystic', 272.

13 Jones, 'English Mystic', 272–3.

14 Julian of Norwich, *Showings*, LT 18.

15 Julian of Norwich, *Showings*, LT 10.

16 Julian of Norwich, *Showings*, LT 22.

17 Julian of Norwich, *Showings*, LT 15.

18 J.P.H. Clark, 'Nature Grace and the Trinity in Julian of Norwich', *Downside Review* 340 (1982), 203.

19 Bauerschmidt, 'Seeing Jesus', 194.

20 Bauerschmidt, 'Seeing Jesus', 190 ff.

21 Julian of Norwich, *Showings*, LT 9.
22 Julian of Norwich, *Showings*, LT 7.
23 Jones, 'English Mystic', 274.
24 Paula S. Datsko Barker, 'The Motherhood of God in Julian's Theory', *Downside Review* 341 (1982), 293.
25 Datsko Barker, 'Motherhood', 295.
26 Julian of Norwich, *Showings*, LT 27.
27 Julian of Norwich, *Showings*, LT 27.
28 Julian of Norwich, *Showings*, LT 27.
29 Julian of Norwich, *Showings*, LT 39.
30 For a complete list of those who used this image, see Bynum, *Jesus as Mother*, 140.
31 Debra Scott Panicelli, 'Finding God in the Memory: Julian of Norwich and the Loss of Visions', *Downside Review* 357 (1986), 312 ff.
32 Julian of Norwich, *Showings*, LT 52.
33 Julian of Norwich, *Showings*, LT 60.
34 Datsko Barker, 'Motherhood'.
35 Julian of Norwich, *Showings*, LT 60.
36 Julian of Norwich, *Showings*, LT 60.
37 Colledge and Walsh, *Book of Showings*, 159; Jones, 'English Mystic', 275.
38 Julian of Norwich, *Showings*, LT 58.
39 Julian of Norwich, *Showings*, LT 61.
40 Julian of Norwich, *Showings*, LT 6.
41 Julian of Norwich, *Showings*, LT 4.
42 Bauerschmit, 'Seeing Jesus', 199.
43 Bauerschmidt, 'Seeing Jesus', 190.
44 Simon Tugwell, *Ways of Imperfection: an exploration of Christian Spirituality* (London: Darton, Longman and Todd, 1984), 187.

10. Papal Advisor: Catherine of Siena

1 Catherine of Siena, *Letter* T136. All references to the letters are to the English translation, *The Letters of Catherine of Siena*, 3 vols. Edited and tranlsated by Suzanne Noffke (Tempe, AZ: Arizona Center for Medieval and Renaissance Studies, 2000, 2001, 2007).
2 Bell, *Holy Anorexia*. A more comprehensive look at this phenomenon is found in Bynum, *Holy Feast*.
3 Raymond of Capua, *Die Legenda Maior (Vita Catharinae Senensis) des*

Raimund von Capua. Edited and translated by Jörg Jungmayr (Berlin: Weidler Buchverlag, 2004), 1.3.39.

4   Raymond of Capua, *Legenda*, 1.12.

5   Raymond of Capua, *Legenda*, 1.2.31, 1.3.38.

6   Raymond of Capua, *Legenda*, 1.12.115–16.

7   Raymond of Capua, *Legenda*, 2.1.122.

8   Kenelm Foster, 'St. Catherine's Teaching on Christ', *Life of the Spirit*, 16 (1962), 310–23.

9   Suzanne Noffke, *Catherine of Siena: Vision Through a Distant Eye* (Collegeville, MN: Liturgical Press, 1996), 15.

10   Catherine of Siena, *Dialogue*, 1.26; for further descriptions of this vision, see *Letter* T272.

11   Noffke, *Vision*, 15.

12   Richard Kieckhefer, *Unquiet Souls: Fourteenth-century Saints and their Religious Milieu* (Chicago: University of Chicago Press, 1987), 10.

13   Raymond of Capua, *Legenda*, 3.1.

14   Clarissa W. Atkinson, *Mystic and Pilgrim: The Book and the World of Margery Kempe* (Ithaca, NY: Cornell University Press, 1983), 121–2 and before.

15   Joseph Berrigan, 'The Tuscan Visionary: St. Catherine of Siena', in *Medieval Women Writers*, edited by Katharina M. Wilson (Athens, GA: University of Georgia Press, 1984), 252–55.

16   Catherine of Siena, *Letter* T69.

17   Catherine of Siena, *Dialogue*, 26.

18   Foster, 'St. Catherine's Teaching', 320–21.

19   Catherine of Siena, *Dialogue*, 27.

20   Catherine of Siena, *Dialogue*, 27.

21   Catherine of Siena, *Dialogue*, 27.

22   Catherine of Siena, *Letter* T34. Catherine's image here parallels her example of stairs in *Dialogue* 26, where she discusses Christ as the bridge.

23   Catherine of Siena, *Letter* T86 to abbess of Santa Maria degli Scalzi, from Noffke, *Vision*, 29.

24   Catherine of Siena, *Letter* T73.

25   Catherine of Siena, *Dialogue*, 1.2.33–4.

26   Bell, *Holy Anorexia*, 23–4.

27   Bynum, *Holy Feast*, 165. Bell sees Catherine as becoming a model for two following centuries of holy anorexics (p. 25) and tries to develop a psychological portrait based on a Freudian-like reading of her life and things that were influential upon her. The problem is that we cannot read back into Catherine what her psychological states were, not only because we have a

selective account about her, but because it was written by another person. And the *Legenda* was not written in order to construct an accurate psychology of Catherine; its purpose was to help her canonization process. Bell's lapse here points to a temptation that is all too common when reading medieval mystics, namely to read them within modern categories as if they had the same struggles for power that modern women have. To read Catherine's eating struggles as anorexia is to place it within a specific psychological nexus; to say that she was anorexic because her twin died at birth and she felt guilt takes Catherine out of the medieval context in which she lived, and in which half of all children died; her twin's unfortunate death was on the whole a pretty average event. Undoubtedly the medieval women who were mystics had struggles for power and voice; the question remains whether they had similar let alone identical struggles and expressions of insolence.

28 Bynum, *Holy Feast*, 169; Catherine of Siena, *Letter* 64 to hermit William Flete.
29 Bynum, *Holy Feast*, 166; Raymond of Capua, *Legenda*, 1.3.64; 2.5.173; 2.6.183–4.
30 Raymond of Capua, *Legenda*, 2.4.163.
31 Raymond of Capua, *Legenda*, 2.8.212–18.
32 Bynum, *Holy Feast*, 178.
33 Bynum, *Holy Feast*, 171–2; Catherine of Siena, *Dialogue*, 14, 96, 141, 511; *Letter* 1, 86, 260, 2.
34 Bynum, *Holy Feast*, 177.
35 Bynum, *Holy Feast*, 173.
36 Bynum, *Holy Feast*, 177.
37 Suzanne Noffke, 'Catherine of Siena: Justly Doctor of the Church?' *Theology Today* 60 (2005), 49–62.

11. Contemplative Pilgrim: Margery Kempe

1 *Book of Margery Kempe*, 1.28. Quotations from Margery Kempe come from *The Book of Margery Kempe*, translated and introduced by John Skinner (New York: Doubleday Image, 1998).
2 Herbert Thurston, *Surprising Mystics* (London: Burns & Oates, 1955), 33.
3 Susan E. Colón, '"Gostly Labowrys": Vocation and Profession in *The Book of Margery Kempe*', *English Studies* 86:4 (August 2005), 284.
4 *Book of Margery Kempe*, 1.1.

5   William Provost, 'The English Religious Enthusiast, Margery Kempe', in *Medieval Women Writers*, edited by Katharina M. Wilson, 297–302 (Athens, GA: University of Georgia Press, 1984).

6   Petroff, *Medieval Women's Visionary Literature*, 301.

7   Another similar contemporary example of religious autobiography was Ruhlman Merswin's writings on his conversion. This one-time leader of the Friends of God in Germany was not as widely known, however, as Suso.

8   Valerie Castagna, 'Margery Kempe and her Becoming "Authoress"', *Textus* 19 (2006), 330. A.C. Spearing, 'The Book of Margery Kempe; Or, *The Diary of a Nobody*', *Southern Review* 38 (2002): 625–35.

9   *Book of Margery Kempe*, 1.6–7.

10   *Book of Margery Kempe*, 1.28–9.

11   *Book of Margery Kempe*, 1.78–81.

12   *Book of Margery Kempe*, 1.82.

13   This structure is described much more fully in Naoë Kukita Yoshikawa's book *Margery Kempe's Meditations* (Cardiff: University of Wales Press, 2007).

14   Atkinson, *Mystic and Pilgrim*, 114 n.13.

15   *Book of Margery Kempe*, 1.58.

16   The Book of Margery Kempe, ed. Sanford Brown Meech. Pref. by Hope Emily Allen. EETS #212 (Oxford: OUP, 1982).

17   Provost, 'English Religious Enthusiast', 297. See Robert Karl Stone, *Middle English Prose Style: Margery Kempe and Julian of Norwich* (The Hague: Mouton, 1970).

18   For this and other examples of 'miraculous translation', see Christine F. Cooper, 'Miraculous Translation in *The Book of Margery Kempe*', *Studies in Philology* (2004), 274.

19   Atkinson, *Mystic and Pilgrim*, 126.

20   *Book of Margery Kempe*, 1.3.

21   Kieckhefer notes that her unconventional behaviour was already conventional on the continent by this time, although perhaps not yet so in England. Richard Kieckhefer, 'Convention and Conversion: Patterns in Late Medieval Piety', *Church History*, 67:1 (March 1998), 40–1.

22   Elona Lucas, 'The Enigmatic, Threatening Margery Kempe', *Downside Review* 105/361 (1987), 294–306.

23   *Book of Margery Kempe*, 1.4; 1.14; 1.22; 1.28; 1.30; 1.46; 1.60; 1.79–81.

24   In fact, in chapter 35, the text says that she marries God the Father, although in chapter 36, she then consummates the relationship with Christ the Son.

25   *Book of Margery Kempe*, 1.13.

26 *Book of Margery Kempe*, 1.26.

27 Petroff, *Medieval Women's Visionary Literature*, 302.

28 *Book of Margery Kempe*, 1.62.

29 Jesus wept – John 11.35.

30 Thurston, *Surprising Mystics*, 32

31 Romans 8.26.

32 Atkinson, *Pilgrim and Mystic*, 59–66.

33 *Book of Margery Kempe*, 1.28.

34 *Book of Margery Kempe*, 1.18.

35 Psalm 22.1; Mt 27.46.

36 Naoë Kukita Yoshikawa, 'The Jerusalem Pilgrimage: The Center of the Structure of *The Book of Margery Kempe*', *English Studies* 86:3 (June 2005): 193–205.

37 Yoshikawa, 'Jerusalem Pilgrimage', 193–4.

38 Yoshikawa, 'Jerusalem Pilgrimage', 202.

39 Assisi: *The Book of Margery Kempe*, 1.31; Rome: 1.31–3; St Brigit's House: 1.39; Compostela: 1.44; Leicester, 1.46; Lincoln and Ely: 1.55.

40 *Book of Margery Kempe*, 1.18.

41 *Book of Margery Kempe*, 1.23; 1.19.

42 Lollards, however, did not believe in the spiritual usefulness of pilgrimage, nor did they think that images were useful in devotion, so the balance of aspects of her spirituality which could be considered Lollard is indeed small.

43 *Book of Margery Kempe*, 53.

44 *Book of Margery Kempe*, 1.10. With reference to Jeremiah 14.20.

45 *Book of Margery Kempe*, 1.22.

46 *Book of Margery Kempe*, 1.22.

47 *Book of Margery Kempe*, 1.13; 1.16.

48 Kieckhefer, *Unquiet Saints*, 196. Drew Hinderer 'On Rehabilitating Margery Kempe', *Studia Mystica* 5 (1982), 35.

12. Carmelite Reformer: Teresa of Avila

1 Teresa of Avila, Poem 19, stanzas 3 and 4. The translations used for Teresa's works are from the three-volume series published by the Institute of Carmelite Studies: Teresa of Avila, *The Collected Works of St. Teresa of Avila*, 3 vols. trans. Kieran Kavanaugh and Otilio Rodriguez (Washington, D.C.: ICS Publications, 1976–1985).

2   For good discussions of the social setting of Teresa and her family, see Rowan Williams, *Teresa of Avila* (London: Continuum, 1991); and Jodi Bilinkoff, *The Avila of Saint Teresa: Religious Reform in a Sixteenth-century City* (London: Cornell University Press, 1989).

3   Teresa of Avila, *Life*, 23.

4   Bilinkoff, *Avila of Saint Teresa*, 118–19.

5   Teresa of Avila, *Life*, 32.11.

6   Alison Weber, *Teresa of Avila and the Rhetoric of Femininity* (Princeton, NJ: Princeton University Press, 2000), 125.

7   Kieran Kavanaugh, 'Introduction' in *Teresa of Avila: The Interior Castle* (New York: Paulist Press, 1979), 4.

8   Weber, *Teresa of Avila*, 126.

9   Also included were Luis de Granada, Francisco de Osuna, Bernardino de Laredo, Alonso de Madrid, Barnabé de Palma, and the Dominicans Pedro Ibáñez, Domingo Báñez, and St Peter of Alcántara.

10   Teresa of Avila, *Life*, 26.5.

11   Weber, *Teresa of Avila*, 29ff.

12   Kavanaugh, 'Introduction', 11.

13   Teresa of Avila, *Spiritual Testimonies*, 15.

14   Teresa of Avila, *Spiritual Testimonies*, 20.

15   Teresa of Avila, *Life*, 8.5.

16   Kavanaugh, 'Introduction', 14.

17   Teresa of Avila, *Spiritual Testimonies*, 21.

18   Teresa of Avila, *Spiritual Testimonies*, 42.

19   Teresa of Avila, *Interior Castle*, 1.1.1. For an introduction to this text, see Julienne McLean, *Towards Mystical Understanding: A Modern Commentary on the Mystical Text 'The Interior Castle' by St Teresa of Avila* (London, St Paul's, 2003).

20   Teresa of Avila, *Interior Castle*, 1.2.8.

21   Teresa of Avila, *Interior Castle*, 1.1.7.

22   Teresa of Avila, *Interior Castle*, 1.2.9.

23   Teresa of Avila, *Interior Castle*, 1.1.

24   Teresa of Avila, *Interior Castle*, 1.2.10.

25   Teresa of Avila, *Interior Castle*, 1.1.8; 1.2.15–16.

26   Teresa of Avila, *Interior Castle*, 2.2.

27   Teresa of Avila, *Interior Castle*, 2.1.3.

28   Teresa of Avila, *Interior Castle*, 2.1.2.

29   Teresa of Avila, *Interior Castle*, 3.1.5.

30   Teresa of Avila, *Interior Castle*, 5.1.2.

31   Teresa of Avila, *Interior Castle*, 5.1.6.
32   Teresa of Avila, *Interior Castle*, 5.1.7.
33   Teresa of Avila, *Interior Castle*, 5.1.8.
34   Teresa of Avila, *Interior Castle*, 5.2.12.
35   Teresa of Avila, *Interior Castle*, 5.2.5.
36   Teresa of Avila, *Interior Castle*, 5.2.3.
37   Teresa of Avila, *Interior Castle*, 6.1.5–6.
38   Teresa of Avila, *Interior Castle*, 6.3.
39   Teresa of Avila, *Interior Castle*, 6.4.3.
40   Teresa of Avila, *Interior Castle*, 7.2.
41   Teresa of Avila, *Interior Castle*, 7.3.2.
42   Kavanaugh, 'Introduction', 6.
43   Kavanaugh, 'Introduction', 7.

Index

Index